Oxford Revise

AQA GCSE

RELIGIOUS STUDIES
Christianity and Buddhism

COMPLETE REVISION AND PRACTICE

T0347349

Series Editor: Dawn Cox

Dawn Cox

Steven Humphrys

OXFORD
UNIVERSITY PRESS

Great Clarendon Street, Oxford, OX2 6DP, United Kingdom

Oxford University Press is a department of the University of Oxford. It furthers the University's objective of excellence in research, scholarship, and education by publishing worldwide. Oxford is a registered trade mark of Oxford University Press in the UK and in certain other countries.

© Oxford University Press 2023

Written by Dawn Cox and Steven Humphrys

Series Editor: Dawn Cox

The moral rights of the authors have been asserted

First published in 2023

All rights reserved. No part of this publication may be reproduced, stored in a retrieval system, or transmitted, in any form or by any means, without the prior permission in writing of Oxford University Press, or as expressly permitted by law, by licence or under terms agreed with the appropriate reprographics rights organization. Enquiries concerning reproduction outside the scope of the above should be sent to the Rights Department, Oxford University Press, at the address above.

You must not circulate this work in any other form and you must impose this same condition on any acquirer

British Library Cataloguing in Publication Data
Data available

978-1-382-04037-2

10 9 8 7 6 5 4 3

The manufacturing process conforms to the environmental regulations of the country of origin.

Printed in the UK by Bell and Bain Ltd, Glasgow

Acknowledgements
The publisher and authors would like to thank the following for permission to use photographs and other copyright material:

Text: Scripture quotations taken from the **Holy Bible, New International Version Anglicised** Copyright © 1979, 1984, 2011 Biblica. Used by permission of Hodder & Stoughton Ltd, an Hachette UK company. All rights reserved. 'NIV' is a registered trademark of Biblica UK trademark number 1448790; **p50:** Extract from "Bodhi Sutta: Awakening (1)" (Ud 1.1), translated from the Pali by Thanissaro Bhikkhu. Access to Insight (BCBS Edition), 1 December 2012; **p60:** Extract from "Mula Sutta: Roots" (AN 3.69), translated from the Pali by Thanissaro Bhikkhu. Access to Insight (BCBS Edition), 3 July 2010; **p66:** Extract from "The Threefold Refuge: tisarana", edited by Access to Insight. Access to Insight (BCBS Edition), 30 November 2013; **p78:** Extract from "Maha-parinibbana Sutta: Last Days of the Buddha" (DN 16), translated from the Pali by Sister Vajira & Francis Story. Access to Insight (BCBS Edition), 30 November 2013; **p82:** Extracts from "Yamakavagga: Pairs" (Dhp I), translated from the Pali by Thanissaro Bhikkhu. Access to Insight (BCBS Edition), 30 November 2013; **p83:** Extracts from "Abhisanda Sutta: Rewards" (AN 8.39), translated from the Pali by Thanissaro Bhikkhu. Access to Insight (BCBS Edition), 30 November 2013.

Artworks: Newgen Publishing.

Photos: p8: Damon Ace / Shutterstock; **p11(l):** rudall30/Shutterstock; **p11(r):** rudall30/Shutterstock; **p12(l):** rudall30/Shutterstock; **p12(r):** AndryDj/Shutterstock; **p13(l):** AndryDj/Shutterstock; **p13(r):** rudall30/Shutterstock; **p16(l):** AndryDj/Shutterstock; **p16(r):** fizkes / Shutterstock; **p30:** Godong / Alamy Stock Photo; **p31:** Ken Jack / Demotix / Corbis; **p36(t):** Doidam 10 / Shutterstock; **p36(b):** Elena Rostunova / Shutterstock; **p40:** Corry Meela; **p41(t):** CAFOD; **p41(m):** Christian Aid; **p41(b):** Mark Boulton / Alamy Stock Photo; **p77(l):** Myimagefiles / Alamy Stock Photo; **p77(r):** Newscom / Alamy Stock Photo; **p82:** Dorit Bar-Zakay / Getty Images; **p84(tl):** Ground Picture / Shutterstock; **p84(tr):** Aerial Mike / Shutterstock; **p84(ml):** zhukovvvlad / Shutterstock; **p84(mr):** Min C. Chiu / Shutterstock; **p84(bl):** Zdenka Darula / Shutterstock; **p84(br):** FocusStocker / Shutterstock; **p105:** Bisual Studio / Shutterstock; **p109:** Aphelleon/ Shutterstock; **p110:** Sogno Lucido/Shutterstock; **p130(t):** Tooykrub/ Shutterstock; **p130(m):** photoJS/Shutterstock; **p130(b):** Wirestock Creators / Shutterstock; **p142:** Mario Segovia Guzman/Shutterstock; **p155:** GRANGER - Historical Picture Archive / Alamy Stock Photo; **p160:** Plum Village Community of Engaged Buddhism (PVCEB); **p161(t):** Christian Aid; **p161(b):** Tzu Chi UK; **p164:** Universal History Archive / Contributor / Getty Images; **p177:** fongbeerredhot / Shutterstock; **p179:** Pressmaster / Shutterstock; **p195:** Salvacampillo/ Shutterstock; **p199:** Rawpixel.com / Shutterstock; **p201(t):** © Copyright 2015 the General of The Salvation Army; **p201(b):** ricochet64 / Shutterstock; **p204:** Dragana Gordic / Shutterstock; **p205(t):** Yupa Watchanakit / Shutterstock; **p205(b):** Christian Aid.

Although we have made every effort to trace and contact all copyright holders before publication this has not been possible in all cases. If notified, the publisher will rectify any errors or omissions at the earliest opportunity.

Links to third party websites are provided by Oxford in good faith and for information only. Oxford disclaims any responsibility for the materials contained in any third party website referenced in this work.

The manufacturer's authorised representative in the EU for product safety is Oxford University Press España S.A. of el Parque Empresarial San Fernando de Henares, Avenida de Castilla, 2 – 28830 Madrid (www.oup.es/en).

Contents

 Shade in each level of the circle as you feel more confident and ready for your exam.

Key

✝ Christianity   ☸ Buddhism

Contents

Contents

 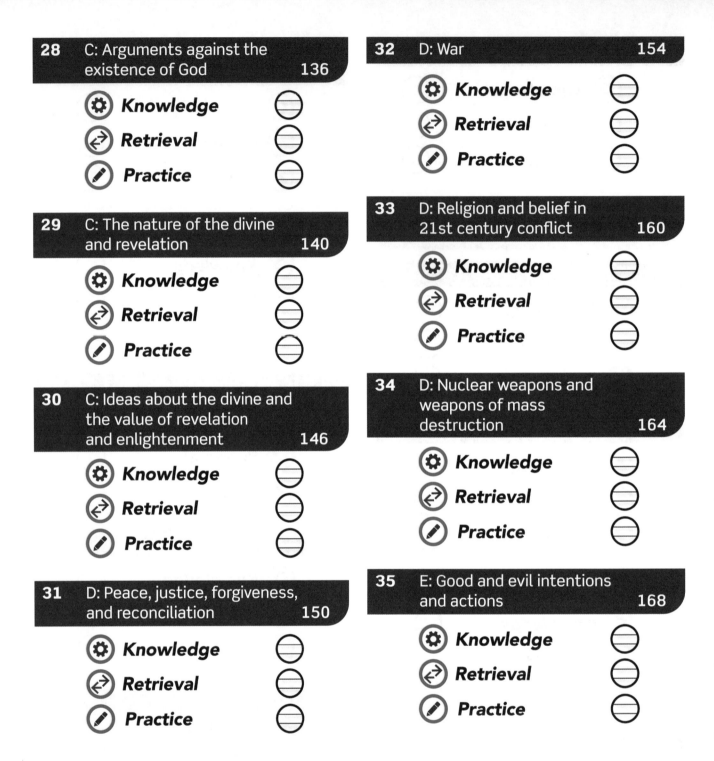

How to use this book

This book uses a three-step approach to revision: **Knowledge**, **Retrieval**, and **Practice**.
It is important that you do all three; they work together to make your revision effective.

Knowledge comes first. Each chapter starts with a **Knowledge Organiser**. These are clear easy-to-understand, concise summaries of the content that you need to know for your exam. The information is organised to show how one idea flows into the next so you can learn how everything is tied together, rather than lots of disconnected facts.

Answers and Glossary

You can scan the QR code at any time to access sample answers, mark schemes for all the exam-style questions, a glossary containing definitions of the key terms, as well as further revision support go.oup.com/OR/GCSE/AA/RS/ChristianityBuddhism

Key terms — Make sure you can write a definition for these key terms

The **Key terms** box highlights the key words and phrases that you need to know, remember and be able to use confidently.

REVISION TIP

Revision tips offer you helpful advice and guidance to aid your revision and help you to understand key concepts and remember them.

Retrieval

The **Retrieval questions** help you learn and quickly recall the information you've acquired. These are short questions and answers about the content in the Knowledge Organiser you have just reviewed. Cover up the answers with some paper and write down as many answers as you can from memory. Check back to the Knowledge Organiser for any you got wrong, then cover the answers and attempt all the questions again until you can answer *all* the questions correctly.

Make sure you revisit the Retrieval questions on different days to help them stick in your memory. You need to write down the answers each time, or say them out loud, otherwise it won't work.

Previous questions

Each chapter also has some **Retrieval questions** from **previous chapters**. Answer these to see if you can remember the content from the earlier chapters. If you get the answers wrong, go back and do the Retrieval questions for the earlier chapters again.

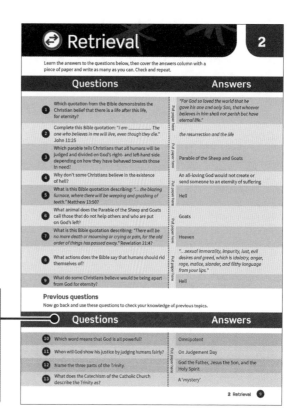

Practice

Once you think you know the Knowledge Organiser and Retrieval answers really well, you can move on to the final stage: **Practice**.

Each chapter has **Exam-style Questions**, including some questions from previous chapters, to help you apply all the knowledge you have learnt and can retrieve.

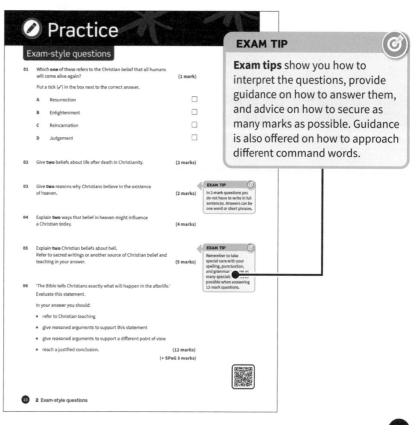

⚙ Knowledge

1 ✝ Beliefs and teachings: The nature of God and beliefs about creation

The nature of God

Christians believe that God has certain characteristics that make him unique. They find these characteristics in the Bible.

Belief	Meaning	Example in the Bible
Omnipotent	God is all powerful.	God created the universe and everything in it: ❝ *In the beginning God created the heavens and the earth.* ❞ (Genesis 1:1)
Benevolent (loving)	God loves his **creation** including all humans.	God sacrificed Jesus to enable humans to achieve salvation: ❝ *For God so loved the world that he gave his one and only Son, that whoever believes in him shall not perish but have eternal life.* ❞ (John 3:16)
Just	God is fair and treats humans fairly.	God will judge people fairly on Judgement Day, as described in the Bible: ❝ *For he has set a day when he will judge the world with justice by the man he has appointed. He has given proof of this to everyone by raising him from the dead.* ❞ (Acts 17:31)

↓

The problem of evil and suffering

Atheists believe there is no God. One of the reasons they give for this is because there is so much evil and suffering in the world, for example, floods, diseases, and war. They argue that if God exists then he is not omnipotent, loving, or all-knowing (**omniscient**).

Theists believe that God exists, but evil and suffering present them with a problem because if God exists, and if they believe he is omnipotent, loving, just, and all-knowing, then why is there still evil and suffering in the world? This is known as the problem of evil and suffering.

An atheist might say...	A Christian might say...
• If God is omnipotent, he would be powerful enough to stop the evil and suffering.	• Evil and suffering (e.g., war) is caused by humans and not God, and God won't interfere with our free will.
• If he is loving, he would not want humans to suffer so he would stop it.	• Suffering can be a test, and we should follow the teachings of Christianity to pass the test. • The way humans respond to suffering can allow them to develop in moral character, for example, showing compassion to others, and therefore grow closer to the likeness of God.
• If he is just, he wouldn't allow innocent people to suffer. • If he is all-knowing, he would know that the suffering is happening and want to stop it.	• We don't know why God allows evil and suffering. We should help those who suffer, and we will find out God's purpose of suffering at the end of time.

The oneness of God and the Trinity: Father, Son, and Holy Spirit

Christians believe that God is one. However he is three 'persons': God the Father, Jesus who is 'God the Son', and the Holy Spirit.

The **Trinity** describes all three at once:

- There is only one God.
- Each person of the Trinity is fully God.
- The persons of the Trinity are experienced in different ways.
- God the Father is the omnipotent creator, who is **omnipresent** (everywhere), omniscient (knows everything), and benevolent (loving).
- Jesus the Son, is the human incarnation of God sent to Earth to save humans from their sins. He is fully God and fully human.
- The Holy Spirit is God being present on Earth today, who guides and supports Christians.

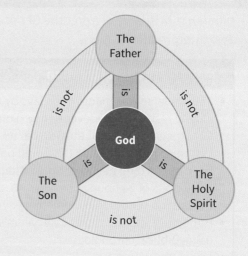

The Bible doesn't ever refer to the 'Trinity' – however, all three are present at the baptism of Jesus.

The Trinity is a complex belief to try to understand – the Catholic Catechism calls the Trinity a 'mystery'.

Creation: Genesis 1:1–3

The book of Genesis in the Old Testament of the Bible describes seven days of creation.

 REVISION TIP

This Bible reference is in the specification which means you can be asked about it in an exam question. Make sure you know what it says.

Day 1: light and darkness

Day 2: the sky

Day 3: land, sea, and plants

Day 4: the sun, moon, and stars

Day 5: fish and sea creatures, and birds

Day 6: animals and humans

Day 7: God was pleased and rested

> *In the beginning God created the heavens and the earth.* (Genesis 1:1)

→ This tells Christians that God is omnipotent (to be able to create the heavens and the earth).

> *Now the earth was formless and empty, darkness was over the surface of the deep, and the Spirit of God was hovering over the waters.* (Genesis 1:2)

→ This tells Christians that there was 'nothing', except for God, before creation, and the (Holy) Spirit of God was present.

> *And God said, 'Let there be light,' and there was light.* (Genesis 1:3)

→ This tells Christians that there was a moment that 'light' came into the world which shows God's omnipotence and omniscience. God can create simply by 'saying', and he knows what light is before it is created.

⚙ Knowledge

1 ✝ Beliefs and teachings: The nature of God and beliefs about creation

Different Christian beliefs about creation

Different Christians interpret the Genesis creation account in different ways. Two interpretations are:

Literal creation	Theistic evolution
• The universe was made in six days by God, and he rested on the seventh day (Some Christians believe that the original text for 'day' also means 'age' so this could have been over a long period of time rather than six periods of 24 hours). • On each day God created something different. • Happened approximately 6000 years ago using Biblical chronology.	• Creation started with a 'Big Bang'. • Uses evidence from the Bible and science. • The universe was formed over a long period of time. • God the omnipotent creator started it. • Happened approximately 13.8 billion years ago.

REVISION TIP

'Literal' creation means the belief that the story in Genesis 1 of the Bible is literally true. Read Genesis 1 to make sure you are familiar with what it says.

Creation: John 1:1–3

John 1:1–3 in the New Testament says:

> ❝ In the beginning was the Word, and the Word was with God, and the Word was God. He was with God in the beginning. Through him all things were made; without him nothing was made that has been made. ❞   (John 1:1–3)

The Word in this passage means Jesus the Son. This tells Christians that Jesus was present in the beginning of time, and they read it alongside Genesis 1. This means that God, Jesus, and the (Holy) Spirit (the Trinity) were present at the beginning of time.

 Key terms Make sure you can write a definition for these key terms

omnipotent   creation   just   atheist
omniscient   theist
Trinity   omnipresent   the Word

Learn the answers to the questions below, then cover the answers column with a piece of paper and write as many as you can. Check and repeat.

Questions | Answers

#	Questions	Answers
1	Which word means that God is all powerful?	Omnipotent
2	When will God show his justice by judging humans fairly?	On Judgement Day
3	Approximately how many years ago did the Big Bang happen?	13.8 billion
4	Name the three parts of the Trinity.	God the Father, Jesus the Son, and the Holy Spirit
5	Which part of the Trinity is present on Earth today, guiding and supporting humans?	The Holy Spirit
6	What does the Catechism of the Catholic Church describe the Trinity as?	A 'mystery'
7	Which part of the Trinity is the human incarnation of God?	Jesus the Son
8	Complete the Bible quotation: " _____ created the heavens and the earth." Genesis 1:1	*In the beginning God*
9	How many days does Genesis say that it took God to complete creation?	Six (he rested on the seventh)
10	What did God create in Genesis 1:3?	Light
11	The theory of theistic evolution uses which sources?	The Bible and science
12	What might 'day' be used to mean in the seven days of creation?	Twenty-four hours, or an 'age' or long period of time
13	According to theistic evolution, what caused the Big Bang?	God
14	Who do Genesis 1:1–3 and John 1:1–3 say was present at the beginning of time?	God, Jesus (the Word), and the (Holy) Spirit
15	What does 'the Word' mean in John 1?	Jesus

Put paper here

Practice

Exam-style questions

01 Which **one** of the following describes the meaning of the word 'benevolent'?

Put a tick (✓) in the box next to the correct answer.　　　　**(1 mark)**

A　Loving ☐

B　Powerful ☐

C　Just ☐

D　Creator ☐

02 Which **one** of these is the key term which means that God is fair and treats humans fairly?　　　　**(1 mark)**

Put a tick (✓) in the box next to the correct answer.

A　Just ☐

B　Loving ☐

C　Omnipotent ☐

D　Omniscient ☐

03 Name **two** of the Trinity.　　　　**(2 marks)**

04 Give **two** examples of suffering in the world.　　　　**(2 marks)**

05 Explain **two** ways that belief in the Trinity may influence Christians today.　　　　**(4 marks)**

06 Explain **two** Christian beliefs about the nature of God.

Refer to sacred writings or another source of Christian belief and teaching in your answer.　　　　**(5 marks)**

> **EXAM TIP**
>
> Remember, you don't have to state the exact verse but you must name a sacred writing or source of authority in your answer, for example 'The Bible says…'.

07 'The world was created exactly as described in the book of Genesis in the Bible.'

Evaluate this statement.

In your answer you should:

- refer to Christian teaching
- give reasoned arguments to support this statement
- give reasoned arguments to support a different point of view
- reach a justified conclusion.　　　　**(12 marks)**

　　　　(+ SPaG 3 marks)

> **EXAM TIP**
>
> Use the bullet points to help ensure that you include everything needed in a 12-mark question.

2 ✝ Beliefs and teachings: Different Christian beliefs about the afterlife

The Bible has many references to death and the **afterlife**, and this helps Christians to consider what happens after death. However, there are different interpretations of the Bible which lead to different views on the afterlife.

Resurrection and life after death

Christians think that if people believe in God and his son Jesus, they will have a life after this life, for **eternity**:

> 66 *For God so loved the world that he gave his one and only Son, that whoever believes in him shall not perish but have eternal life.* 99   (John 3:16)

This shows that humans will be resurrected from death and then will have a life after death. Some Christians believe that it will be a full-body **resurrection**.

Others believe that it will be just our souls that will live on:

> 66 *Jesus said to her, 'I am the resurrection and the life. The one who believes in me will live, even though they die.'* 99   (John 11:25)

↓

Judgement

The **Parable** of the Sheep and Goats (Matthew 25:31–46) is a story told by Jesus. Some Christians interpret it to mean people will all be judged on how they treated other people, for example how they dealt with those who are hungry or ill, etc.

> If we haven't helped others, then we will be on God's left-hand side (goats) and will 'go away to eternal punishment'.

> If we have helped other people as though we were helping Jesus, we will be on God's right-hand side (sheep) and will have a right to eternal life.

This could be interpreted as hell.   This could be interpreted as heaven.

REVISION TIP

This parable is useful when answering exam questions about life after death, but also in some of the Theme topics on how humans should behave. Find it in the Bible and read the parable, so you can use it in your answers.

Knowledge

2 ✝ Beliefs and teachings: Different Christian beliefs about the afterlife

Heaven and hell

Some Christians believe that certain actions will lead us to be apart from God after we die.

> 66 *Put to death, therefore, whatever belongs to your earthly nature: sexual immorality, impurity, lust, evil desires and greed, which is idolatry. Because of these, the wrath of God is coming. You used to walk in these ways, in the life you once lived. But now you must also rid yourselves of all such things as these: anger, rage, malice, slander, and filthy language from your lips.* 99
>
> (Colossians 3:5–8)

Some interpret this to mean that if you commit these sins, then you will go to **hell**. Others believe that this is just a warning to ensure that humans behave as God wants them to.

Heaven	Hell
In **heaven** there will be no sadness or unhappiness. Most Christians believe that heaven is being with God for eternity and not a literal place: 66 *He will wipe every tear from their eyes. There will be no more death or mourning or crying or pain, for the old order of things has passed away.* 99 (Revelation 21:4)	66 *…and throw them into the blazing furnace, where there will be weeping and gnashing of teeth.* 99 (Matthew 13:50) Some think this is a literal description of hell. It will be a painful and unhappy time. Some believe that a loving God would not create such a place or send anyone there, so it is a **symbolic** description of being 'without God', not a place called hell.

The importance of Christian beliefs about the afterlife

These beliefs will have an impact on Christians' beliefs about the value of human life as it tells them that there is a life after this life.

It emphasises that we should think carefully about how we behave in this life because we will be judged on it, and this will influence what happens to us in the afterlife.

Christians believe that after they die God will judge them on their behaviour and actions, and their faith. So it's important for Christians to follow Jesus' teachings rather than to choose sin, because it won't only have an impact on this life but also on the eternal life that Christians believe will come after death.

 Key terms Make sure you can write a definition for these key terms

afterlife eternity resurrection parable
hell heaven symbolic

Learn the answers to the questions below, then cover the answers column with a piece of paper and write as many as you can. Check and repeat.

Questions   Answers

#	Question		Answer
1	Which quotation from the Bible demonstrates the Christian belief that there is a life after this life, for eternity?	Put paper here	"For God so loved the world that he gave his one and only Son, that whoever believes in him shall not perish but have eternal life."
2	Complete this Bible quotation: "*I am _____. The one who believes in me will live, even though they die.*" John 11:25		the resurrection and the life
3	Which parable tells Christians that all humans will be judged and divided on God's right- and left-hand side depending on how they have behaved towards those in need?	Put paper here	Parable of the Sheep and Goats
4	Why don't some Christians believe in the existence of hell?		An all-loving God would not create or send someone to an eternity of suffering
5	What is this Bible quotation describing: "*… the blazing furnace, where there will be weeping and gnashing of teeth.*" Matthew 13:50?	Put paper here	Hell
6	What animal does the Parable of the Sheep and Goats call those that do not help others and who are put on God's left?		Goats
7	What is this Bible quotation describing: "*There will be no more death or mourning or crying or pain, for the old order of things has passed away.*" Revelation 21:4?	Put paper here	Heaven
8	What actions does the Bible say that humans should rid themselves of?	Put paper here	"*…sexual immorality, impurity, lust, evil desires and greed, which is idolatry, anger, rage, malice, slander, and filthy language from your lips.*"
9	What do some Christians believe would be being apart from God for eternity?		Hell

Previous questions

Now go back and use these questions to check your knowledge of previous topics.

Questions   Answers

#	Question		Answer
10	Which word means that God is all powerful?	Put paper here	Omnipotent
11	When will God show his justice by judging humans fairly?		On Judgement Day
12	Name the three parts of the Trinity.		God the Father, Jesus the Son, and the Holy Spirit
13	What does the Catechism of the Catholic Church describe the Trinity as?		A 'mystery'

Practice

Exam-style questions

01 Which **one** of these refers to the Christian belief that all humans will come alive again? **(1 mark)**

Put a tick (✓) in the box next to the correct answer.

A	Resurrection	☐
B	Enlightenment	☐
C	Reincarnation	☐
D	Judgement	☐

02 Give **two** beliefs about life after death in Christianity. **(2 marks)**

03 Give **two** reasons why Christians believe in the existence of heaven. **(2 marks)**

> **EXAM TIP**
> In 2-mark questions you do not have to write in full sentences. Answers can be one word or short phrases.

04 Explain **two** ways that belief in heaven might influence a Christian today. **(4 marks)**

05 Explain **two** Christian beliefs about hell.
Refer to sacred writings or another source of Christian belief and teaching in your answer. **(5 marks)**

> **EXAM TIP**
> Remember to take special care with your spelling, punctuation, and grammar and use as many specialist terms as possible when answering 12-mark questions.

06 'The Bible tells Christians exactly what will happen in the afterlife.'
Evaluate this statement.

In your answer you should:

- refer to Christian teaching

- give reasoned arguments to support this statement

- give reasoned arguments to support a different point of view

- reach a justified conclusion. **(12 marks)**
(+ SPaG 3 marks)

⚙ Knowledge

3 ✝ Beliefs and teachings: The incarnation, crucifixion, resurrection, and ascension of Jesus

Christians believe that God sent his son Jesus to Earth over 2000 years ago. The story of his life is narrated in the Gospels of Matthew, Mark, Luke, and John in the New Testament of the Bible.

Incarnation – Jesus is born

Jesus was born to his mother, the Virgin Mary, whilst his parents were visiting Bethlehem. The nativity story is described in the books of Matthew and Luke.

> **❝** *His mother Mary was pledged to be married to Joseph, but before they came together, she was found to be pregnant through the Holy Spirit.* **❞** (Matthew 1:18)

John 1:14 shows that Jesus was incarnate. This means that God took on human form and was on Earth.

> **❝** *The Word became flesh and made his dwelling among us.* **❞** (John 1:14)

REVISION TIP

You don't need to know the whole nativity story – focus on how the incarnation is important to Christians.

Why it is important to Christians

This proves the Old Testament prophet's prophecies to be true. It shows that Jesus is part of the Trinity.

The baptism of Jesus

Approximately 30 years later, Jesus was baptised by his cousin John in the River Jordan. When Jesus was baptised, a voice from Heaven said:

> **❝** *You are my Son* **❞** (Mark 1:11)

REVISION TIP

Knowing the key events in the life of Jesus will help you answer many different questions. Go through the Christianity practices section and try to match the practices with the events in Jesus's life.

Why it is important to Christians

This shows Christians that Jesus is the **Son of God**, and although he was without sin, provides an example of what they should do to remove sin.

⚙ Knowledge

3 ✝ Beliefs and teachings: The incarnation, crucifixion, resurrection, and ascension of Jesus

Miracles and parables

- During his life Jesus performed many miracles including bringing people back to life and healing people.
- Jesus told stories with meanings, called parables. The Parable of the Good Samaritan and the Parable of the Sheep and Goats tell Christians how they should behave towards others.

Why it is important to Christians

- Jesus's miracles prove the incarnation – that he is God.
- Jesus's parables and teachings show what they should believe in and how they should live as good Christians.

Why it is important to Christians

- The Last Supper is now remembered and re-enacted at the **Eucharist**, reminding Christians of God's sacrifice.
- The crucifixion shows that God was prepared to sacrifice his son for the sins of humans. It enabled humans to achieve salvation.

Holy Week – the final week of Jesus's lif

Palm Sunday

Jesus enters Jerusalem on a donkey.

Maundy Thursday – The Last Supper

- Jesus has the **Last Supper** with his disciples. He tells them to remember his body with bread, and his blood with wine.
- He is arrested in the Garden of Gethsemane.

Good Friday – the crucifixion

- Jesus is sentenced to death by **crucifixion**.
- He is killed on the cross, outside the city of Jerusalem, alongside two criminals.

> ❝ They crucified him there, along with the criminals … Jesus said, 'Father, forgive them, for they do not know what they are doing ❞
> (Luke 23:33–34)

> ❝ …darkness came over the whole land … And the curtain of the temple was torn in two. Jesus called out with a loud voice, 'Father, into your hands I commit my spirit.' When he had said this, he breathed his last. ❞
> (Luke 23: 44–46)

Easter Sunday – the resurrection

On the third day after the crucifixion, Jesus rose from the dead.

> ❝ *They [the women] found the stone rolled away from the tomb, but when they entered, they did not find the body of the Lord Jesus.* ❞
>
> (Luke 24:1–3)

Why it is important to Christians

- The resurrection proves that Jesus was the son of God.
- It also shows Christians that there is life after death and they will also be resurrected.

Key terms — Make sure you can write a definition for these key terms

Son of God   Eucharist
Last Supper   crucifixion   ascension

The Great Commission and the ascension

Forty days after his resurrection Jesus spoke with the disciples for the final time and told them at the Great Commission:

REVISION TIP

The Great Commission links to mission and evangelism in Christianity practices so is a useful Bible story to remember.

> ❝ *…go and make disciples of all nations, baptising them in the name of the Father and of the Son and of the Holy Spirit, and teaching them to obey everything I have commanded you…* ❞   (Matthew 28: 19–20)

He then ascended to heaven to be with God, known as the **ascension**. Christians are waiting for him to return to Earth at the end of time.

Why it is important to Christians

- The Great Commission gave the disciples clear instructions on how to spread the 'good news' (the Gospel) and this has continued today. There are now over 2 billion Christians in the world.
- The ascension tells Christians that Jesus was fully God and returned to God in Heaven. There is no body or grave of Jesus left on Earth as he is alive in Heaven, waiting to return one day.

Retrieval

Learn the answers to the questions below, then cover the answers column with a piece of paper and write as many as you can. Check and repeat.

Questions / Answers

#	Questions	Answers
1	In which event in the life of Jesus did God 'become' flesh?	The incarnation
2	In which Gospels is the life of Jesus described?	Matthew, Mark, Luke, and John
3	On which day was Jesus crucified?	Good Friday
4	Who baptised Jesus?	His cousin, John
5	What word is given to the stories with meanings told by Jesus?	Parables
6	Who was crucified alongside Jesus?	Two criminals
7	Why is the resurrection of Jesus important to Christians?	It proves that Jesus was the son of God and it shows Christians that there is life after death and they will also be resurrected
8	What happened at the ascension?	Jesus ascended to heaven
9	What did Jesus tell the disciples to do at the Great Commission?	Make disciples of all nations, baptise them in the name of the Father and of the Son and of the Holy Spirit, teach them to obey everything Jesus commanded

Put paper here

Previous questions

Now go back and use these questions to check your knowledge of previous topics.

Questions / Answers

#	Questions	Answers
10	How many days does Genesis say that it took God to complete creation?	Six (he rested on the seventh)
11	What did God create in Genesis 1:3?	Light
12	Complete this Bible quotation: "I am _____. The one who believes in me will live, even though they die." John 11:25	the resurrection and the life
13	What is this Bible quotation describing: "…the blazing furnace, where there will be weeping and gnashing of teeth." Matthew 13:50?	Hell

Put paper here

Exam-style questions

01 Which **one** of these is the event in the life of Jesus when he came back to life after dying on a cross?

Put a tick (✔) in the box next to the correct answer. **(1 mark)**

A Ascension ☐

B Incarnation ☐

C Resurrection ☐

D Crucifixion ☐

02 Which **one** of these is the belief that 'God became flesh'?

Put a tick (✔) in the box next to the correct answer. **(1 mark)**

A Ascension ☐

B Incarnation ☐

C Resurrection ☐

D Crucifixion ☐

> **EXAM TIP**
>
> As these questions are only worth 1 mark, don't spend a long time on them. However, do read the question and answer options carefully so you don't make a silly mistake.

03 Give **two** reasons why the ascension is important to Christians. **(2 marks)**

04 Give **two** reasons why the resurrection is important to Christians. **(2 marks)**

05 Explain **two** ways that the incarnation may influence the life of a Christian today. **(4 marks)**

06 Explain **two** ways that the crucifixion of Jesus may influence the life of a Christian today. **(4 marks)**

> **EXAM TIP**
>
> When a question asks about 'influence', think about what difference the belief makes to the person's life – what might they do differently because of the belief?

07 Explain **two** Christian beliefs about the incarnation.

Refer to sacred writings or another source of Christian belief and teaching in your answer. **(5 marks)**

08 'The incarnation is more important than the crucifixion of Jesus.'

Evaluate this statement.

In your answer you should:

- refer to Christian teaching
- give reasoned arguments to support this statement
- give reasoned arguments to support a different point of view
- reach a justified conclusion. **(12 marks)**

(+ SPaG 3 marks)

⚙ Knowledge

4 ✝ Beliefs and teachings: Sin and salvation

Sin

- **Sin** means deliberately going against what God wants.
- Christians believe that people sin because God has given humans free will. However, they know what God wants them to do because the Bible tells them.

There are many rules in the Old Testament, including the Ten Commandments. For example, it is wrong to murder, steal, and worship other gods. However, many Christians believe that Jesus summarised the Old Testament rules into two commandments found in the New Testament:

REVISION TIP

Matthew 22:36–40 is useful as it can help when comparing the Old Testament with the New Testament.

> ❝ *'Teacher, which is the greatest commandment in the Law?' Jesus replied: 'Love the Lord your God with all your heart and with all your soul and with all your mind.' This is the first and greatest commandment. And the second is like it: 'Love your neighbour as yourself.' All the Law and the Prophets hang on these two commandments.* ❞
>
> (Matthew 22:36–40)

Original sin and personal sin

Original sin	Personal sin
• Adam and Eve failed to follow God's instruction not to eat the fruit in the Garden of Eden. God punished Adam and Eve and the punishment was to ensure suffering in life. This is known as the Fall. • Some Christians believe that due to the Fall, we have all been born with the inclination to sin. This is called original sin. • Some Christians believe that baptism washes away original sin. 	• This is when humans use their free will to behave in a way that goes against God's wishes. 

Christians believe that due to sin, humans have moved apart from their relationship with God and whilst they have sin, they cannot be with God in Heaven. **Salvation** means being saved from sin and restoring their relationship with God.

REVISION TIP

Remember that as the Fall is a story from the Bible you can use it in an answer to a 5-mark question that requires you to refer to sacred writings or another source of religious belief and teaching.

Getting rid of sin

Different Christians have different beliefs about what can be done to get rid of sin.

How to get rid of sin	Christian belief
Prayer and repentance	Christians believe that humans can pray to God to ask for forgiveness. As he is all-loving, this act of **repentance** means he will forgive them.
Confession	The sacrament of reconciliation – Catholic Christians believe that they can confess their sins to a priest and that God will forgive them through the actions of the priest.

REVISION TIP

Where there are different opinions or beliefs these are useful for 12-mark questions which require different views.

Means of salvation

The means of salvation are the ways that God helps humans to achieve salvation.

Salvation by law

- Also known as salvation by works.
- Shown in the Old Testament:

> *For I command you today to love the Lord your God, to walk in obedience to him, and to keep his commands, decrees and laws; then you will live and increase, and the Lord your God will bless you in the land you are entering to possess.* (Deuteronomy 30:16)

- From the Old Testament text, the Pharisees (religious leaders) put together a list of 613 laws that need to be kept to gain salvation.

> *If only you had paid attention to my commands, your peace would have been like a river, your well-being like the waves of the sea.* (Isaiah 48:18)

Salvation by grace

- Christians believe that because God is all-loving and all-merciful, humans can achieve salvation even if they have sinned.
- This is possible as Jesus died on a cross to forgive all sins.
- Grace means that if someone believes in Jesus and asks for forgiveness of their sins, their faith will save them.

> *For it is by grace you have been saved, through faith – and this is not from yourselves, it is the gift of God – not by works, so that no one can boast.* (Ephesians 2:8–9)

- Grace does not mean Christians don't have to obey the law and do good works. James 2:26 says, "faith without deeds is dead."
- However, the Christian doctrine of Grace states that Christians do good works because they have salvation and not to earn salvation.

Salvation by Spirit

- Some Christians believe that the Holy Spirit is present around humans today, helping them to achieve salvation.
- The Spirit guides people in day-to-day life, through their conscience, to make the right decisions about how to behave.
- It can help Christians to understand God, including when they are reading the Bible:

> *... the Holy Spirit, whom the Father will send in my name, will teach you all things and will remind you of everything I have said to you.* (John 14:26)

4 ✝ Beliefs and teachings: Sin and salvation

The role of Christ in salvation and the idea of atonement

Christians believe that due to the Fall, humans have become separated from God. However, the Bible says that:

> 66 *For God so loved the world that he gave his one and only Son.* 99
>
> (John 3:16)

This shows that God sent Jesus to Earth for humans' sins to be forgiven.

REVISION TIP

Remember these beliefs link to the celebration of Easter in the Christianity practices section. Look at how Christians may celebrate Easter and try to identify which beliefs link to each practice.

Christians believe that Jesus's crucifixion means that his life was sacrificed for all humanity.

This means they can be reconciled (have a restored relationship) with God:

> 66 *For if, while we were God's enemies, we were reconciled to him through the death of his Son, how much more, having been reconciled, shall we be saved through his life!* 99
>
> (Romans 5:10)

This is due to **atonement**, restoring the relationship between people and God through the life, death, and resurrection of Jesus. This ensures that all humans can access Heaven and be with God. The Bible says:

> 66 *... if anybody does sin, we have an advocate with the Father – Jesus Christ, the Righteous One. He is the atoning sacrifice for our sins, and not only for ours but also for the sins of the whole world.* 99 (1 John 2:1–2)

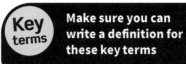 **Key terms** — Make sure you can write a definition for these key terms

sin   salvation   repentance   atonement

Retrieval

Learn the answers to the questions below, then cover the answers column with a piece of paper and write as many as you can. Check and repeat.

Questions / Answers

#	Questions	Answers
1	What word means humans choosing how they behave?	Free will
2	What type of sin has come from Adam and Eve sinning at the Fall?	Original sin
3	Which means of salvation is following the way of living that God has shown through the Bible?	Salvation by law/salvation by works
4	Which means of salvation is being saved due to God's love by having faith in him?	Salvation by grace
5	Which means of salvation is following the guidance of the Holy Spirit on Earth today?	Salvation by Spirit
6	Give one way that Christians may believe humans can get rid of sin.	One from: prayer / repentance / confession
7	Complete this Bible quotation which shows that God sent Jesus to Earth for humans' sins to be forgiven: "*For God _____.*" John 3:16	*so loved the world that he gave his one and only Son*
8	What is the word for the Christian belief that humans can be saved from their sins?	Salvation
9	Which type of sin comes from when humans use their free will to behave in a way that goes against God's wishes?	Personal sin

Put paper here

Previous questions

Now go back and use these questions to check your knowledge of previous topics.

Questions / Answers

#	Questions	Answers
10	What might 'day' be used to mean in the seven days of creation?	Twenty-four hours, or an 'age' or long period of time
11	According to theistic evolution, what caused the Big Bang?	God
12	What does 'the Word' mean in John 1?	Jesus
13	In which event in the life of Jesus did God 'become' flesh?	The incarnation/birth
14	In which Gospels is the life of Jesus described?	Matthew, Mark, Luke, and John
15	On which day was Jesus crucified?	Good Friday

Put paper here

Practice

Exam-style questions

01 Which **one** of these is a sin humans are born with due to the Fall?

Put a tick (✓) in the box next to the correct answer. **(1 mark)**

A   Original sin ☐

B   Personal sin ☐

C   Deadly sin ☐

D   Social sin ☐

02 Which **one** of these is classed as a sin in Christianity?

Put a tick (✓) in the box next to the correct answer. **(1 mark)**

A   Reconciliation ☐

B   Charity ☐

C   Forgiveness ☐

D   Murder ☐

03 Name **two** sins in Christianity. **(2 marks)**

04 Name **two** means of salvation. **(2 marks)**

> **EXAM TIP**
>
> A 4-mark question requires two developed points. Show the examiner you have done this by writing in two paragraphs.

05 Explain **two** ways that Christians may be influenced by salvation by law in their lives today. **(4 marks)**

06 Explain **two** ways that belief in sin may influence Christians today. **(4 marks)**

07 Explain **two** Christian beliefs about the role of Jesus in salvation. Refer to sacred writings or another source of Christian belief and teaching in your answer. **(5 marks)**

> **EXAM TIP**
>
> Remember to name a sacred writing or source of authority in your answer, for example, the Bible.

08 'You can only achieve salvation by following God's law.'

Evaluate this statement.

In your answer you should:

- refer to Christian teaching
- give reasoned arguments to support this statement
- give reasoned arguments to support a different point of view
- reach a justified conclusion. **(12 marks)**

(+ SPaG 3 marks)

5 ✝ Practices: Worship and prayer

Different forms of worship and their significance

Christians believe that they should worship God because:

- it shows how important he is to them
- they should praise him for everything that he has done for them
- they believe he is worthy of worship

- it outwardly shows their belief and trust in him
- they can ask for forgiveness
- it strengthens their belief.

There are different types of worship. Worship varies between individuals and the type of Church (**denomination**) they belong to.

Liturgical worship

Liturgical worship follows a formal set of practices that remains the same, for example, a church service may always have a Bible reading, songs/hymns, Eucharist, **prayers** and a sermon. The specific Bible reading, songs, and sermon are all planned in advance. It is mostly led by a religious leader, for example, a priest.

Most Catholic Church worship is liturgical.

> ❝ *Worship the Lord with gladness; come before him with joyful songs.* ❞
> (Psalms 100:2)

Why it is important

- It provides a consistent way of worshipping.
- It is traditional and often has been done that way for hundreds of years.
- Worship will always follow the same set pattern anywhere in the world; this gives a sense of community.
- It emphasises the importance of the church leader as part of a Christian's connection with God.

Non-liturgical/informal worship

Non-liturgical worship is informal. It can be spontaneous and unplanned. It can include key elements such as singing, prayers, Bible readings, and Eucharist but as it is **informal worship**, these may vary in length and in who leads them.

It may also include things such as the laying of hands/healing rituals, speaking in tongues, and personal testimonies.

Charismatic worship is often non-liturgical, and can involve the Holy Spirit inspiring and guiding the worship.

Quaker worship is informal as it involves people sitting in silence together, waiting to be inspired to speak by the Spirit. There is no leader and anyone can contribute.

> ❝ *When you come together, each of you has a hymn, or a word of instruction, a revelation, a tongue or an interpretation…* ❞
> (1 Corinthians 14:26)

Why it is important

- Anyone can be involved.
- It is spontaneous so may allow God to speak to or inspire worshippers through the Holy Spirit.

5 ✟ Practices: Worship and prayer

Private worship

Some Christians may worship by themselves or in a small family/friendship group.

They may read the Bible, pray or meditate to get closer to God.

Why it is important

- A person can choose how they want to worship.
- It develops their personal relationship with God.
- It can be done at any time.

Use of the Bible

The Bible is an important part of worship for Christians. Whilst views differ on how it should be interpreted, it is a central part of liturgical, non-liturgical and private worship.

In some churches they follow a set series of Bible passages throughout the year, often linking to important stories, for example, the nativity story at Christmas.

Other Christians use the Bible in a more spontaneous way and believe that the Holy Spirit guides them to a particular passage that gives a message for that time.

Why it is important

- It keeps the word of God central to worship.
- It reminds Christians of key stories, beliefs, and teachings of Christianity.
- It can inspire Christians and remind them how God wants them to behave.

Prayer and its significance

Prayer is communicating with God, either silently or speaking out loud.

Praise: worshipping God.

Thanksgiving: thanking God for everything he has done and does for humans.

Intercession: praying for others, e.g., praying for their salvation, for someone's health.

The purposes of prayer

Confession: repenting to God for sinning and asking for forgiveness.

Petition: praying for yourself, for guidance and support in living the Christian life.

Different Christians pray in different ways – some people:			
	Kneel		Hold their hands outwards or upwards.
	Put their hands together.		Use a rosary to focus on specific prayers.

Why prayer is important to Christians

- Prayer supports a personal relationship with God.
- It is what Jesus did, and he also told Christians how to pray.

- It is what the Bible says Christians should do:

> **❝** *I urge, then, first of all, that petitions, prayers, intercession and thanksgiving be made for all people.* **❞**
>
> (Timothy 2:1)

Set prayers

- **Set prayers** are prayers that have already been written.
- The benefit of using set prayers is that everybody can join in saying the prayer and the prayer can cover key beliefs.
- Examples of set prayers include the Rosary and the **Lord's prayer**.

The Lord's prayer

- Jesus gave the words of the Lord's prayer to his followers in Matthew 6:9–15. Different Christian denominations use different versions of the words.
- It can be said during communal worship or by an individual in private worship.
- It mentions key beliefs for Christians, including the belief in the existence of Heaven and the forgiveness of sins.
- It is sometimes called the 'Our Father'.

> **REVISION TIP**
>
> To help you remember the Lord's prayer try saying it out loud. Start with the first line. Then say the first two lines. Then say the first three lines. Continue doing this until you get to the end. Then try saying it again from memory. Keep going until you have it memorised.

The Lord's prayer

Our Father in heaven,
hallowed be your name,
your Kingdom come,
your will be done, on earth as in heaven.
Give us today our daily bread.
Forgive us our sins as we forgive those who sin against us.
Lead us not into temptation but deliver us from evil.
For the kingdom, the power, and the glory are yours now and for ever.

Amen

Informal prayer

Informal prayers haven't been planned. The words of the prayer are made up by the person saying the prayer. They can be more personal and relate to the situation that someone is in. For example, they may ask God to bless a specific person that they know is struggling. Informal prayers are often part of informal/non-liturgical worship.

Key terms Make sure you can write a definition for these key terms

| denomination | liturgical | prayer | non-liturgical |
| informal worship | set prayer | Lord's prayer | informal prayer |

Retrieval

Learn the answers to the questions below, then cover the answers column with a piece of paper and write as many as you can. Check and repeat.

	Questions		Answers
1	A Christian might say that worship is important because they can ask God for his _____.	Put paper here	Forgiveness
2	Which type of worship follows a formal set of practices that remains the same?		Liturgical
3	Which type of worship is informal, spontaneous, and unplanned?		Non-liturgical/informal
4	Give one thing that might happen as part of liturgical worship.	Put paper here	One from: a Bible reading / songs / hymns / the Eucharist / prayers / a sermon
5	Which Christian denomination involves people sitting in silence together, waiting to be inspired to speak by the Spirit?		Quakers
6	What is it called when Christians choose to worship by themselves or as part of a small family/friendship group?	Put paper here	Private worship
7	The Bible is an important part of which types of worship?		Liturgical, non-liturgical, and private worship
8	Name five purposes of prayer.	Put paper here	Praise, thanksgiving, intercession, confession, petition
9	Which prayer did Jesus teach the disciples?		The Lord's prayer or Our Father
10	What is another name for the Lord's prayer?		Our Father
11	In which part of the Lord's prayer do Christians ask God to help them avoid sin?	Put paper here	*Lead us not into temptation but deliver us from evil.*
12	Name two examples of set prayer.		The Lord's prayer, the Rosary
13	For what type of prayers have the words already been written?	Put paper here	Set prayers
14	What type of prayers are those which are spontaneous and haven't been planned?		Informal prayers

Exam-style questions

01 Which of these describes a form of worship which follows a formal set of practices that remain the same?

Put a tick (✓) in the box next to the correct answer. **(1 mark)**

A   Non-liturgical worship   ☐

B   Liturgical worship   ☐

C   Private worship   ☐

D   Informal prayer   ☐

02 Which **one** of these prayers is spontaneous and has not been planned?

Put a tick (✓) in the box next to the correct answer. **(1 mark)**

A   Informal   ☐

B   Formal   ☐

C   Set   ☐

D   The Lord's prayer   ☐

03 Give **two** reasons why prayer is important to Christians. **(2 marks)**

> **EXAM TIP**
> Answers to 2-mark questions can be written as one-word answers, short phrases, or short sentences, depending on the question. Try to keep it short.

04 Give **two** purposes of Christian prayer. **(2 marks)**

05 Explain **two** contrasting ways that Christians may use the Bible in worship. **(4 marks)**

06 Explain **two** ways that Christians pray.
Refer to sacred writings or another source of Christian belief and teaching in your answer. **(5 marks)**

> **EXAM TIP**
> Remember you must name a sacred writing or source of authority in your answer, for example the Bible. If you use quotes, you don't have to state the exact chapter or verse – you can just write: 'The Bible states…'.

07 'The Lord's prayer is the most important prayer.'
Evaluate this statement.

In your answer you should:

- refer to Christian teaching
- give reasoned arguments to support this statement
- give reasoned arguments to support a different point of view
- reach a justified conclusion. **(12 marks)**

(+ SPaG 3 marks)

⚙ Knowledge

6 ✝ Practices: The role and meaning of the sacraments

The meaning of sacrament

Sacrament comes from the Latin word meaning 'sacred' and the Greek meaning 'mystery'. It is often described as an outer expression of an inner grace. This means it is something that a Christian does to show their belief in God in a spiritual and often symbolic way.

Some Christians don't perform any sacraments at all, for example Quakers. They may argue that every day should be an outer expression of their faith and that these sacraments should not be limited to one day, for example a Sunday. These Christians are also often openly involved in helping the community in different ways, for example, the Salvation Army.

- Catholic Christians have seven sacraments (**baptism**, **confirmation**, Eucharist, **reconciliation**, the anointing of the sick, holy orders, and marriage).

- Other Christian denominations have two main sacraments (baptism and Eucharist).

Baptism and its significance for Christians

Baptism is an initiation rite in which people join the Christian family. Some Christians believe it is a sacrament; for others baptism is just an important ceremony. Some Christian Churches such as Quakers and members of the Salvation Army do not baptise at all.

Reasons for baptism:

- To remember and follow the example of the baptism of Jesus in the River Jordan by his cousin John.

- To follow Jesus's wishes – at the Great Commission, Jesus told the disciples to baptise people.

- As a symbolic demonstration of the washing away of sins.

- To welcome people into the community of the Christian Church.

The baptism of Jesus

❝ *When Jesus was baptised, a voice from Heaven said 'You are my Son.'* ❞ (Mark 1:11)

The Great Commission

❝ *Therefore go and make disciples of all nations, baptising them in the name of the Father and of the Son and of the Holy Spirit.* ❞ (Matthew 28:19)

Infant and believer's baptism

Some denominations, including Anglicans and Catholics, baptise babies, others tend to baptise adults only, referring to this as 'believer's baptism'.

Reasons for infant baptism	Reasons for believer's baptism
Symbolises the washing away of original sin.	Symbolises the washing away of personal sin.
Welcomes a baby to the Church community.	Welcomes someone to the Church community.
Part of being brought up in a Christian family.	An individual's decision.

Symbols of baptism

Baptismal rites vary but they usually include common symbols with important beliefs associated with them.

 Water symbolises a washing away of sins and a new life with Jesus Christ.

 Those being baptised often wear white clothing to represent purity and the removal of sin.

 A candle is sometimes used to represent going from 'darkness' (without Jesus Christ/God) to 'light' (with Jesus Christ/God).

Holy Communion/Eucharist

The night before Jesus was crucified, he had a meal with his disciples – this is known as the Last Supper. It is an event that many Christians remember during worship, and they re-enact the meal during a sacrament known as **Holy Communion**/Eucharist.

> **❝** *And he took bread, gave thanks and broke it, and gave it to them, saying, 'This is my body given for you; do this in remembrance of me.'*
>
> *In the same way, after the supper he took the cup, saying, 'This cup is the new covenant in my blood, which is poured out for you.* **❞** (Luke 22:17–20)

Christians use bread and wine during the Holy Communion/ Eucharist sacrament as Jesus spoke about them.

 Bread – Some Christians use unleavened bread (as Jesus would have); others use leavened bread and others use wafers.

 Wine – Some Christians use red wine; others prefer not to use alcohol and use red grape juice instead.

The significance of the Eucharist and different interpretations of its meaning

Christians interpret the story of the Lord's Supper differently and enact the sacrament in different ways. Some Christians perform the sacrament every Sunday and others do it less frequently. Some Christians do not do it at all.

- Catholic Christians believe that the bread and the wine undergo a special change called transubstantiation. They believe that the bread becomes the body of Jesus, and the wine becomes the blood of Jesus.

- Some Christians take the phrase 'do this in remembrance of me' and believe that the sacrament is about remembering God's sacrifice of Jesus on the cross, leading to the forgiveness of sins.
- Other Christians believe that the bread and wine are symbolic, bringing together the community in sharing them.

 Key terms **Make sure you can write a definition for these key terms**

sacrament   baptism   confirmation   reconciliation
infant baptism   believer's baptism   Holy Communion

Retrieval

Learn the answers to the questions below, then cover the answers column with a piece of paper and write as many as you can. Check and repeat.

	Questions		Answers
1	How many sacraments do Catholic Christians have?		Seven
2	Name two different types of baptism.	*Put paper here*	Infant baptism, believer's baptism
3	What does the water symbolise in baptism?		Washing away of sins
4	Name a Christian denomination that does not use baptism.		One from: Quakers / Salvation Army
5	Why do those being baptised often wear white clothes?	*Put paper here*	To represent purity and the removal of sin
6	Which event in the life of Jesus is remembered at Holy Communion?		The Last Supper
7	Give one other name for Holy Communion.	*Put paper here*	Eucharist
8	What is the name for the Catholic Christians' belief that during the Mass the bread and the wine become the body and blood of Christ?		Transubstantiation
9	What two things do Christians use during Holy Communion to remember the death of Jesus?		Bread and wine

Previous questions

Now go back and use these questions to check your knowledge of previous topics.

	Questions		Answers
10	Which type of worship follows a formal set of practices that remains the same?		Liturgical
11	Which type of worship is informal, spontaneous, and unplanned?	*Put paper here*	Non-liturgical
12	Give one thing that might happen as part of liturgical worship.		One from: a Bible reading / songs / hymns / the Eucharist / prayers / a sermon
13	Which Christian group involves people sitting in silence together, waiting to be inspired to speak by the Spirit?	*Put paper here*	Quakers
14	Name five purposes of prayer.		Praise, thanksgiving, intercession, confession, petition

Practice

Exam-style questions

01   Which **one** of these is the event when Jesus told the disciples to 'baptise in the name of the Father, the Son and the Holy Spirit'?

Put a tick (✓) in the box next to the correct answer.   **(1 mark)**

    A   The Great Commission ☐

    B   The crucifixion ☐

    C   The incarnation ☐

    D   Pentecost ☐

02   Which **one** of these is the sacrament that remembers Jesus's Last Supper?

Put a tick (✓) in the box next to the correct answer.   **(1 mark)**

    A   Baptism ☐

    B   Reconciliation ☐

    C   Eucharist ☐

    D   Marriage ☐

> **EXAM TIP**
>
> The four options for the multiple-choice questions will include options designed to test you. Read each option carefully to select the correct answer.

03   Name **two** sacraments in Christianity.   **(2 marks)**

04   Give **two** different names for Holy Communion.   **(2 marks)**

05   Explain **two** contrasting beliefs about infant baptism.   **(4 marks)**

06   Explain **two** ways that Christians may carry out Holy Communion.

Refer to sacred writings or another source of Christian belief and teaching in your answer.   **(5 marks)**

> **EXAM TIP**
>
> Remember that you must name the source of authority when you refer to it, for example the Bible.

07   'The most important sacrament is infant baptism.'

Evaluate this statement.

In your answer you should:

- refer to Christian teaching
- give reasoned arguments to support this statement
- give reasoned arguments to support a different point of view
- reach a justified conclusion.   **(12 marks)**

    (+ SPaG 3 marks)

⚙ Knowledge

7 ✝ Practices: The role and importance of pilgrimage and celebrations

Christian pilgrimage

Christians often visit places that are important to Christianity. A **pilgrimage** is a spiritual experience in which the journey and the destination bring them closer to God.

Pilgrimages are important to Christians because:

- they can see where something important in Christianity has happened, for example, Bethlehem and Jerusalem
- it strengthens and renews their belief
- it brings together the Christian community

- it involves prayer and worship in special places
- it brings them closer to God
- they may involve receiving special blessings from God or healing **miracles**.

Lourdes, France

Why Lourdes?

- **Lourdes** is the place where in 1858, a girl called Bernadette had a vision of the Virgin Mary. Mary told Bernadette to dig into the ground and a spring of water appeared.
- Bernadette described her first vision of the Virgin Mary:

> 66 *As I raised my head to look at the grotto, I saw a Lady dressed in white, wearing a white dress, a blue girdle and a yellow rose on each foot, the same colour as the chain of her rosary; the beads of the rosary were white.* 99

▲ Sick or disabled pilgrims are accompanied by able-bodied helpers at Lourdes, a popular pilgrimage site for Catholics

FRANCE

📍 Lourdes

What happens at Lourdes?

- Each year millions of Catholic pilgrims visit the grotto where Mary appeared.
- They also drink or bathe in the spring water as they believe it has healing powers. Many will take some water home with them to share with others.

Why is Lourdes important?

- Over 67 confirmed miracles and over 6000 other cures have taken place at Lourdes.

Iona, Scotland

Why Iona?

- St Columba, (an Irish missionary) who had brought Christianity to Scotland, set up a monastery on the island of **Iona**. It is now a pilgrimage site, dedicated to the Virgin Mary.

- There is a small community on the island that runs the retreat and looks after the pilgrims.

- Due to its remote location and clear air, Iona has been described as a 'thin place' where the veil between earthly life and the spiritual, heavenly life is thinner than in other places.

- It is a place where pilgrims can become closer to God by being close to nature and his creation.

REVISION TIP

To remember information on pilgrimages, use 'Where?' 'Why?' and 'What?' *Where* is the pilgrimage to? *Why* is it an important place? *What* do pilgrims do there?

▲ *The abbey church on Iona*

What happens at Iona?

- It is a place where Christians of any denomination can visit and stay.

- Whilst there, pilgrims can take part in: daily church services; walks around the island, stopping for prayer and reflection; workshops focusing on Christian teachings; Bible reading, reflection, and prayer in the natural beauty of the island.

- If pilgrims stay in the retreat, they help with daily chores, e.g., preparing food and cleaning the centre.

Why is Iona important?

- It brings Christians together as it is a place where Christians of any denomination can visit and stay.

- It gives pilgrims time and space to reconnect with God.

- It is a place with a 'thin veil' between Earth and the spiritual realm.

- It reminds pilgrims of God's power whilst staying in a place of natural beauty.

 Key terms | **Make sure you can write a definition for these key terms** | pilgrimage   miracle   Lourdes   Iona   Christmas   Easter

⚙ Knowledge

7 ✝ Practices: The role and importance of pilgrimage and celebrations

Celebrations: Christmas

- **Christmas** is a celebration of the birth of Jesus.
- The story is told in the Gospels of Matthew and Luke. Each story gives a different perspective and Christians put them together to tell the nativity story.
- Many Christians celebrate it on 25 December. Most Orthodox Christians celebrate it on 7 January.

> ❝ *While they were there, the time came for the baby to be born, and she gave birth to her firstborn, a son. She wrapped him in cloths and placed him in a manger, because there was no guest room available for them.* ❞ (Luke 2:6–7)

REVISION TIP

Remember that this is about Christmas in Christianity not as a secular celebration. No need to mention Santa Claus or reindeer!

How is it celebrated?

Christians in Great Britain today celebrate Christmas by:
- performing nativity plays and telling the Christmas story
- giving presents to remember the gifts that Jesus received and the gift of Jesus from God
- putting up lights to represent Jesus being the light of the world
- going to church and singing songs (carols) to celebrate the birth of God's son.

Why is it important?

- It is when the incarnation occurred:

> ❝ *The Word became flesh and made his dwelling among us.* ❞ (John 1:14)

- It shows that God, in human form, was on Earth.
- The Old Testament prophecies of a messiah coming to Earth came true.

Celebrations: Easter

- **Easter** is the most important Christian festival.
- On Easter Sunday, Christians celebrate the resurrection of Jesus following his crucifixion on Good Friday.
- The story is written in the Gospels of Matthew, Mark, Luke, and John.
- Easter is celebrated on a different date each year. It is calculated from the first Sunday after the full moon that occurs on or after the spring equinox (which is always on 21 March).

> ❝ *Christ died for our sins according to the Scriptures, that he was buried, that he was raised on the third day according to the Scriptures, and that he appeared to Cephas, and then to the Twelve.* ❞
> (1 Corinthians 15:3–5)

How is it celebrated?

Christians in Great Britain today celebrate Easter by:
- going to church to celebrate the resurrection of Jesus
- singing songs/hymns to thank God for the resurrection
- celebrating new life with eggs including chocolate eggs
- eating hot cross buns (the cross symbolising the cross Jesus died on)
- sharing breakfast at early sunrise to remember his resurrection on Easter Sunday.

Why is it important?

- It proves that God has power over death, which means that all humans will also be resurrected.
- It shows God's sacrifice for humans, which enables their salvation.
- It enables humans to reconcile with God even if they have sinned.
- It enables the forgiveness of sins.
- It enables Christians to achieve atonement and access heaven to be with God.

Learn the answers to the questions below, then cover the answers column with a piece of paper and write as many as you can. Check and repeat.

Questions | Answers

#	Questions	Answers
1	In which country is Lourdes?	France
2	Who did Bernadette see in a vision at Lourdes?	The Virgin Mary
3	Why is the water at Lourdes special?	It is believed to have healing powers
4	In which country is Iona?	Scotland
5	Who founded a monastery on Iona?	St Columba
6	Why is Iona a particularly spiritual place for pilgrims?	It has a 'thin veil' between earthly life and spiritual life
7	Which event in the life of Jesus is celebrated at Christmas?	His birth
8	On which two dates is Christmas celebrated within Christianity?	25 December, 7 January
9	Which event in the life of Jesus is celebrated at Easter?	His resurrection (following his crucifixion)
10	How do Christians celebrate Easter?	Going to church, singing songs/hymns, eggs including chocolate eggs, eating hot cross buns, sharing breakfast

Put paper here

Previous questions

Now go back and use these questions to check your knowledge of previous topics.

Questions | Answers

#	Questions	Answers
11	Which prayer did Jesus teach the disciples?	The Lord's prayer
12	What is another name for the Lord's prayer?	Our Father
13	Give one other name for Holy Communion.	Eucharist
14	Name two different types of baptism.	Infant baptism, believer's baptism
15	What does the water symbolise in baptism?	Washing away of sins

Put paper here

Practice

Exam-style questions

01 Which **one** of the following is when Christians celebrate the resurrection of Jesus?

Put a tick (✓) in the box next to the correct answer. **(1 mark)**

A   Christmas ☐

B   Pilgrimage ☐

C   Spring Equinox ☐

D   Easter ☐

02 Which **one** of the following is when Christians celebrate the birth of Jesus?

Put a tick (✓) in the box next to the correct answer. **(1 mark)**

A   Christmas ☐

B   Pilgrimage ☐

C   Spring Equinox ☐

D   Easter ☐

03 Give **two** Christian beliefs about pilgrimage. **(2 marks)**

04 Give **two** ways that Christians may celebrate Christmas. **(2 marks)**

05 Explain **two** contrasting places a Christian may visit on pilgrimage. **(4 marks)**

> **EXAM TIP**
>
> Remember that a 4-mark question requires two developed points. Show the examiner you have done this by writing in two paragraphs.

06 Explain **two** reasons why Easter is an important celebration for Christians in Great Britain today.
Refer to sacred writings or another source of Christian belief and teaching in your answer. **(5 marks)**

07 'Christmas is more important than Easter for Christians today.'
Evaluate this statement.
In your answer you should:

- refer to Christian teaching
- give reasoned arguments to support this statement
- give reasoned arguments to support a different point of view
- reach a justified conclusion. **(12 marks)**

(+ SPaG 3 marks)

> **EXAM TIP**
>
> Make sure you read the question carefully and answer the exact wording in your judgement.

⚙ Knowledge

8 ✝ Practices: The church in the community, and mission, evangelism, and growth

The role of the church in the local community

Many Christians believe that the church should be at the centre of the community. They organise events and activities to help to support local people. This is an opportunity for them to show **agape** (selfless, sacrificial, unconditional love for others).

- Some events are for Christians, for example church services and prayer meetings.
- Some events are for all in the community even if they're not Christian, for example, playgroups and coffee mornings.
- These events are not always in the church building itself, for example 'outreach' work in local schools.

The community of Christians are following what the 'sheep' in the Parable of the Sheep and Goat did:

> **❝** *For I was hungry and you gave me something to eat, I was thirsty and you gave me something to drink, I was a stranger and you invited me in, I needed clothes and you clothed me, I was sick and you looked after me, I was in prison and you came to visit me.* **❞**
> (Matthew 25:34–36)

Street pastors

Some members of Christian churches volunteer as **street pastors**. Teams of street pastors go out to the local area to help people who might be in need. This is often on Friday and Saturday nights when many people go to town centres and their behaviour is affected by alcohol. The street pastors:

- check if people are OK and help if they are sick
- reunite them with friends they may have become separated from, and help to ensure they get home safely
- may try to calm down people who are upset or violent
- do not have any legal powers but often work alongside the council and local police
- don't aim to convert anyone but to show their faith through action:

> **❝** *Faith by itself, if it is not accompanied by action, is dead.* **❞** (James 2:17)

> **REVISION TIP** 📝
>
> Try to watch videos online showing what street pastors do. Seeing them in action will help you to remember what they do.

Food banks

Some churches and Christian organisations have set up **food banks** to help people in the community who don't have enough food.

- People donate food items to the food bank, and they are distributed to those who need them.
- The Trussell Trust supports over 1200 food bank centres. They base their work on Christian principles and the values of compassion, justice, community, and dignity.

⚙ Knowledge

8 ✝ Practices: The church in the community, and mission, evangelism, and growth

Mission

- Just before Jesus ascended to heaven, he told his **disciples** to:

> **"** ... go and make disciples of all nations, baptising them in the name of the Father and of the Son and of the Holy Spirit. **"** (Matthew 28:19)

- This event is called 'The Great Commission'.

- A commission is a specific task or job for an individual or group to do.

- It has the word '**mission**' in it – in Christianity this means the vocation or calling of a Christian organisation or individual to go out into the world and spread their faith.

- Many Christians feel that they have an individual mission in life called a vocation, given by God, for them to work for God in a specific way. This may link to something that they already do, for example a surgeon may volunteer to be a surgeon in a place that needs their specialism but would not normally be able to have their expertise.

- Since the Great Commission, many people, known as missionaries, travel to, and often live in, other countries to complete their mission.

- Some Christians believe that they can complete their mission closer to home and work in their local community.

REVISION TIP

Think of a 'mission' like a task or job someone needs to do. Hopefully not a 'Mission Impossible'!

Evangelism

Evangelism is an important part of mission: spreading the Christian gospel by public preaching or personal witness.

The disciples were the first people to evangelise, and St Paul travelled in many areas of the Mediterranean Sea telling communities about Jesus. This can be read in his letters in the New Testament.

Giving out leaflets to passers-by in public places.

Today, Christians evangelise in different ways

Some organisations give away copies of the Bible in the local language of the country, placing them in public spaces such as hotel rooms.

The Alpha course is an 11-week cross-denominational course to help people learn about and potentially convert to Christianity. Millions of people have taken part, in hundreds of countries and different languages.

Christ was once offered to bear the sins of many

Hebrews 9:28

Evangelism

Some Christians don't agree with some methods of evangelism:

- Some groups have used pressurising tactics or discrimination to try to get others to convert
- There are accounts of missionaries around the world not behaving in a loving way towards non-Christian communities.

REVISION TIP

Have you ever seen someone in the street talking about God and Jesus? Have you ever had someone knock at your door to try and talk about God? This will help you to remember forms of evangelism.

Church growth

| The Christian **Church** began at Pentecost, sometimes known as the birth of the Christian Church.

(Church with a capital 'C' means the community of Christians.) | → | After the ascension, the disciples waited in Jerusalem for a sign, as Jesus had told them to. | → | They then started to spread the word about God and Jesus. After this the Bible says:

"So the word of God spread. The number of disciples in Jerusalem increased rapidly, and a large number of priests became obedient to the faith."

(Acts 6:7) | → | All but one of the disciples were killed for their beliefs, but the Christian Church began to grow around Europe. |

- Today, Christianity is the largest religion in the world with an estimated 2.6 billion followers.
- Roman Catholicism is the biggest denomination.
- Christianity is declining in Europe and the Americas, but it is growing in Africa and in Asia.
- The 2011 England and Wales census reported that 59% of people selected 'Christianity'. By 2021, this figure had fallen to 46%, showing that fewer than half of the population say they are Christian.

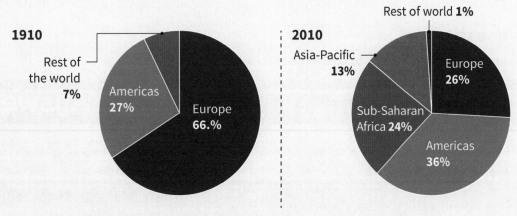

▲ *Approximate regional distribution of Christians in 1910 and 2010*

Key terms — Make sure you can write a definition for these key terms

agape   street pastors   food bank   disciples   mission
evangelism   Church

⇄ Retrieval

Learn the answers to the questions below, then cover the answers column with a piece of paper and write as many as you can. Check and repeat.

Questions | Answers

#	Questions	Answers
1	What is the word used in the Bible that describes selfless, sacrificial, unconditional love for others?	Agape
2	Name two types of event that the Christian community might organise for the whole community.	Two from: playgroup / coffee morning / outreach work in local schools
3	Which parable tells Christians to help the hungry, thirsty, and sick, and visit those in prison?	Parable of the Sheep and Goats
4	Name the values that The Trussell Trust bases its work on.	Compassion, justice, community, dignity
5	What is the name of people who volunteer to go out into their local area to help people in need, often at weekends?	Street pastors
6	What did Jesus tell the disciples to do at the Great Commission?	*"... go and make disciples of all nations, baptising them in the name of the Father and of the Son and of the Holy Spirit."*
7	Who travelled around the Mediterranean Sea evangelising to communities and writing them letters about Christianity (now in the New Testament)?	St Paul
8	What is the name of the 11-week course that aims to tell non-Christians about the basics of Christianity?	The Alpha course
9	What does the word Church (with a capital 'C') mean?	The community of Christians
10	Approximately how many Christians are there in the world today?	2.6 billion

Put paper here

Previous questions

Now go back and use these questions to check your knowledge of previous topics.

Questions | Answers

#	Questions	Answers
11	In which part of the Lord's prayer do Christians ask God to help them avoid sin?	*Lead us not into temptation but deliver us from evil.*
12	Why is Iona a particularly spiritual place for pilgrims?	It has a 'thin veil' between earthly life and spiritual life
13	Which event in the life of Jesus is remembered at Holy Communion?	The Last Supper
14	Why is the water at Lourdes special?	It is believed to have healing powers
15	Which event in the life of Jesus is celebrated at Easter?	His resurrection (following his crucifixion)

Put paper here

Exam-style questions

01 Which **one** of the following is the Christian belief in spreading the Christian gospel by public preaching or personal witness?

Put a tick (✓) in the box next to the correct answer. **(1 mark)**

A   Pentecost ☐

B   Agape ☐

C   Evangelism ☐

D   Street pastors ☐

02 Which **one** of these is the event that is known as the birth of the Christian Church?

Put a tick (✓) in the box next to the correct answer. **(1 mark)**

A   Pentecost ☐

B   The Great Commission ☐

C   The Last Supper ☐

D   The resurrection ☐

03 Give **two** Christian beliefs about The Great Commission. **(2 marks)**

> **EXAM TIP**
> Remember – in 2-mark questions answers can be one word or short phrases. You do not have to write in full sentences.

04 Give **two** ways that a Christian may evangelise. **(2 marks)**

05 Explain **two** contrasting ways that a Christian might help others in the local community. **(4 marks)**

06 Explain **two** contrasting ways that a Christian may evangelise. **(4 marks)**

> **EXAM TIP**
> 'Contrasting' just means 'different' in these questions.

07 Explain **two** reasons for Church growth.

Refer to sacred writings or another source of Christian belief and teaching in your answer. **(5 marks)**

08 'All Christians should travel to another country to evangelise.'

Evaluate this statement.

> **EXAM TIP**
> Ensure you include all the parts given in the bullet points in your answer.

In your answer you should:

- refer to Christian teaching
- give reasoned arguments to support this statement
- give reasoned arguments to support a different point of view
- reach a justified conclusion. **(12 marks)**

(+ SPaG 3 marks)

⚙ Knowledge

9 ✝ Practices: The importance of the worldwide Church

How Christian churches respond to persecution

Persecution is hostility and ill treatment, especially because of race, or political or religious beliefs. Followers of many religions, including Christianity, are persecuted by being:

- made fun of in public, including unfair or biased media coverage
- banned from meeting with others
- subjected to torture or killed
- removed from their job or not having the same opportunities for work.

The Bible tells Christians to get ready to be persecuted:

> ❝ In fact, everyone who wants to live a godly life in Christ Jesus will be persecuted. ❞ (2 Timothy 3:12)

Christians may find strength in persecution, bringing them together and strengthening their faith:

> ❝ Consider it pure joy … whenever you face trials of many kinds, because you know that the testing of your faith produces perseverance … so that you may be mature and complete … ❞ (James 1:2–4)

Working for reconciliation

- The key message of Christianity is that, due to God's sacrifice, Jesus died on the cross so humans can be reconciled with God.
- Christians around the world work for reconciliation between Christians and non-Christians, and within Christianity, to improve relationships where there has been a breakdown.
- One of the Catholic sacraments is reconciliation where followers confess their sins through a priest to ensure they renew their relationship with God after they have sinned.

- The Bible encourages reconciliation when it says:

> ❝ For if, while we were God's enemies, we were reconciled to him through the death of his Son, how much more, having been reconciled, shall we be saved through his life! ❞ (Romans 5:10)

The Corrymeela Community, Northern Ireland

The Community:

- was started in 1965 by Ray Davey
- is a place where Christians and people of other religions or none can stay and meet to work together on differences
- encourages people to learn how to have difficult conversations on sensitive, potentially divisive issues through workshops, using dialogue, experiential play, art, and storytelling.

▲ Corrymeela gives people from a variety of political and religious backgrounds the opportunity to discuss, and overcome their differences

The work of CAFOD, Christian Aid, Tearfund

There are Christian charities that aim to help people around the world who are in need. They believe that they should follow the Parable of the Good Samaritan and the commandment to 'Love your neighbour', by helping others.

REVISION TIP

You only need to know about the work of one of these charities.

CAFOD

CAFOD is part of Caritas International, one of the largest aid networks in the world. It is the official Catholic aid agency for England and Wales, working with poor communities to end poverty and injustice.

CAFOD aims to:

- reach people in greatest need, save lives, and relieve suffering
- change the conditions and behaviours that lead to poverty, inequality, injustice, and damage to the natural world
- encourage the Catholic community of England and Wales to work together for the common good.

CAF✚D
Catholic Agency for Overseas Development

REVISION TIP

Remember your charity by thinking 'N-A-R': *Name* (of the charity), *Action* (what they do), *Reason* (why they do it – the link to Christian teaching).

Christian Aid

For over 75 years **Christian Aid** has worked to eradicate poverty around the world by tackling its root causes.

Christian Aid aims to help people:

- uphold their rights and gain access to services such as healthcare and education, and fight discrimination
- deal with disasters such as drought, climate change, and hurricanes, and to develop resilience against them in the future
- improve their situation, for example, by getting a fair price for goods and products.

christian aid

Tearfund

Tearfund works with local churches in more than 50 countries to help to tackle and end poverty through sustainable development, by responding to disasters and challenging injustice.

Tearfund works to reduce poverty through:

- rapid response to disasters and conflicts
- working with local churches and organisations, encouraging communities to help themselves
- helping people to speak out against poverty and injustice.

Key terms Make sure you can write a definition for these key terms

persecution   CAFOD   Christian Aid   Tearfund

Retrieval

Learn the answers to the questions below, then cover the answers column with a piece of paper and write as many as you can. Check and repeat.

Questions | Answers

#	Question	Answer
1	What is the key message of Christianity?	Due to God's sacrifice, Jesus died on the cross so humans can be reconciled with God
2	In which sacrament do Catholics confess their sins through a priest?	Reconciliation
3	Which quotation in the Bible encourages reconciliation?	*"For if, while we were God's enemies, we were reconciled to him through the death of his Son, how much more, having been reconciled, shall we be saved through his life!"*
4	What is meant by persecution?	Persecution is hostility and ill treatment
5	Give one example of how Christians might be persecuted.	One from: being made fun of in public including unfair or biased media coverage / being banned from meeting with others / being subjected to torture or killed / being removed from their job or not having the same opportunities for work
6	Which quotation from the Bible tells Christians that they should be prepared for persecution?	*"In fact, everyone who wants to live a godly life in Christ Jesus will be persecuted."*
7	Which Catholic charity is part of one of the largest aid agencies in the world?	CAFOD
8	For how long has Christian Aid worked to eradicate poverty?	Over 75 years
9	Which charity works with local churches in more than 50 countries?	Tearfund

Put paper here

Previous questions

Now go back and use these questions to check your knowledge of previous topics.

Questions | Answers

#	Question	Answer
10	For what type of prayers have the words already been written?	Set prayers
11	What two things do Christians use during Holy Communion to remember the death of Jesus?	Bread and wine
12	Which event in the life of Jesus is celebrated at Christmas?	His birth
13	What is the word used in the Bible that describes selfless, sacrificial, unconditional love for others?	Agape

Put paper here

Exam-style questions

01 Which **one** of these means the restoring of harmony after relationships have broken down?

Put a tick (✓) in the box next to the correct answer. **(1 mark)**

A Sacrfice ☐

B Charity ☐

C Persecution ☐

D Reconciliation ☐

02 Which **one** of these means hostility and ill-treatment, especially because of race, or political, or religious beliefs?

Put a tick (✓) in the box next to the correct answer. **(1 mark)**

A Persecution ☐

B Charity ☐

C Sacrifice ☐

D Reconciliation ☐

> **EXAM TIP**
> These questions are only worth 1 mark so don't spend a long time on them. But remember to read the question and answer options carefully to avoid making a silly mistake.

03 Give **two** ways that Christians may be persecuted today. **(2 marks)**

04 Give **two** ways that a Christian charity may help those that are in poverty and are facing injustice. **(2 marks)**

05 Explain **two** contrasting ways that Christians may respond to persecution. **(4 marks)**

> **EXAM TIP**
> Contrasting doesn't have to be 'opposite' – it just means 'different'.

06 Explain **two** reasons why reconciliation is important in Christianity.

Refer to sacred writings or another source of Christian belief and teaching in your answer. **(5 marks)**

07 'Charities can reduce poverty and injustice by themselves.'

Evaluate this statement.

In your answer you should:

- refer to Christian teaching
- give reasoned arguments to support this statement
- give reasoned arguments to support a different point of view
- reach a justified conclusion. **(12 marks)**

(+ SPaG 3 marks)

⚙ Knowledge

10 ⊛ Beliefs and teachings: The Buddha's life and its significance

Who is the Buddha?

- 'The **Buddha**' is a title given to somebody who is 'awakened' or 'enlightened'. It is somebody who truly understands the nature of reality.
- Different Buddhist traditions have different beliefs about the status and role of Buddhas. Buddhists gain their understanding about Buddhas from many different sources. These include: the **Buddhacarita**, **Jataka 075**, and the **Pali Canon**. However, other traditions also have other sources too.
- Siddhartha Gautama is the Buddha who founded Buddhism. He was born in Nepal and was a prince. His life has great significance for many Buddhists today.

The Buddha's life

- The Buddha's life is split into five stages: birth, the **Four Sights**, life of luxury, asectic life, and enlightenment.
- Unlike many other founders of religions, there is not one complete source that recalls the life of the Buddha. Multiple different sources teach Buddhists about the Buddha's life.
- Elements of the Buddha's life are influential on the Buddha's later Dhamma (Dharma), the Four Noble Truths (see pp. 60–61), and the Three Marks of Existence (see pp. 48–49).

Birth

Siddhartha enters the world. Religious sources suggest the Buddha was born in Nepal, at a place called Lumbini.

The Buddhacarita teaches that:

- Siddhartha was born without causing pain to his mother, Queen Maya
- Siddhartha was born for a purpose – the welfare of the world
- Siddhartha's birth was miraculous. For example, he was able to walk straight after birth.

Life of luxury

This is Siddhartha's early life living in a palace.

The Buddhacarita teaches that:

- throughout his life, Siddhartha was showered with great gifts, for example gems, gold, silver, and animals
- Siddhartha spent all his time inside the palace being looked after by women.

Four Sights

Siddhartha witnesses the fundamental sights of life (the Four Sights) for the first time. They are:

- illness
- old age
- death
- a holy man.

Jataka 075 teaches that Siddhartha:

- met a sick person and became aware that everybody suffers due to illness
- met an elderly man and realised that everybody becomes old; youth does not last forever
- encountered a funeral and realised that physical life on Earth, in its current form, is not everlasting
- was encouraged by a holy man to leave his life of luxury and search for enlightenment.

Ascetic life

Siddhartha abandons worldly pleasures to focus on spirituality and the attaining of enlightenment.

The Pali Canon teaches that during Siddhartha's ascetic (simple and strict) life:

- he had little food and became extremely emaciated; some scripts even suggest he changed colour
- he met many teachers who taught him important practices leading to great insights
- he found that neither extreme luxury, nor extreme poverty, helped achieve spiritual goals; he abandoned the ascetic life and discovered the **Middle Way**.

Enlightenment

Siddhartha gains wisdom, which allows for clarity into the nature of reality. Religious sources suggest this happened in India, at a placed called Bodh Gaya.

The Pali Canon teaches that during his Enlightenment:

- Siddhartha undertook meditation to overcome temptation and desire, symbolised by the demon Mara
- Siddhartha gained knowledge of his rebirth, the realms of rebirth, and the destruction of ignorance.

The influence of the Buddha's life for Buddhists today

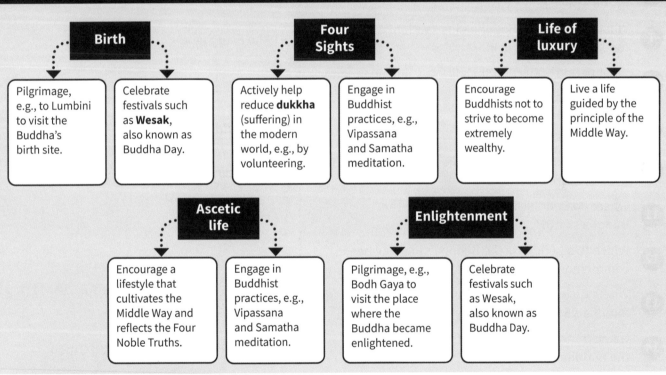

Birth

Pilgrimage, e.g., to Lumbini to visit the Buddha's birth site.

Celebrate festivals such as **Wesak**, also known as Buddha Day.

Four Sights

Actively help reduce **dukkha** (suffering) in the modern world, e.g., by volunteering.

Engage in Buddhist practices, e.g., Vipassana and Samatha meditation.

Life of luxury

Encourage Buddhists not to strive to become extremely wealthy.

Live a life guided by the principle of the Middle Way.

Ascetic life

Encourage a lifestyle that cultivates the Middle Way and reflects the Four Noble Truths.

Engage in Buddhist practices, e.g., Vipassana and Samatha meditation.

Enlightenment

Pilgrimage, e.g., Bodh Gaya to visit the place where the Buddha became enlightened.

Celebrate festivals such as Wesak, also known as Buddha Day.

 Key terms | Make sure you can write a definition for these key terms

Buddha   Buddhacarita   Jataka 075   Pali Canon   the Four Sights   the Middle Way   Wesak   dukkha

Retrieval

Learn the answers to the questions below, then cover the answers column with a piece of paper and write as many as you can. Check and repeat.

	Questions	Answers
1	What is meant by the title 'the Buddha'?	Somebody who is enlightened or awakened
2	Which Buddha founded Buddhism?	Siddhartha Gautama
3	Which period of the Buddha's life focuses on him entering the world?	Birth
4	What is the name of the Buddha's mother?	Queen Maya
5	What is the purpose of the Buddha's birth?	To ensure the welfare of the world
6	What period of the Buddha's life focuses on him living inside a palace?	Life of luxury
7	What period of the Buddha's life saw him witness four fundamental sights of life?	The Four Sights
8	What period of the Buddha's life saw him abandon worldly pleasures?	Ascetic life
9	What did the Buddha discover while abandoning worldly pleasures?	The Middle Way
10	What period of the Buddha's life saw him gain clarity on the nature of reality?	Enlightenment
11	Where do Buddhists visit to remember the Buddha's birth?	Lumbini
12	Which two periods of the Buddha's life may be commemorated by the festival Wesak?	Birth and enlightenment
13	Where do Buddhists visit to remember the Buddha's Enlightenment?	Bodh Gaya
14	Name three sources Buddhists can use to understand the Buddha's life.	Buddhacarita, Jataka 075, Pali Canon

Put paper here

Exam-style questions

01 Which **one** of the following is **not** a stage of the Buddha's life?

Put a tick (✓) in the box next to the correct answer. **(1 mark)**

A	Life of luxury	☐
B	Enlightenment	☐
C	The setting in motion of the wheel of the dharma	☐
D	Ascetic life	☐

02 Give **two** features of the Buddha's ascetic life. **(2 marks)**

03 Explain **two** ways in which the Buddha's life influences Buddhists today. **(4 marks)**

EXAM TIP

This question asks about 'influences'. This is about what Buddhists do because of their beliefs. This can include what makes them believe or the actions they carry out. Students often confuse this question and write about teachings. A useful phrase to include might be, 'Today, this means Buddhists...'.

04 Explain **two** reasons why the Buddha's life is important.

Refer to sacred writings or another source of Buddhist belief and teaching in your answer. **(5 marks)**

05 'The Buddha's witnessing of the Four Sights was the most important aspect of his life.'

Evaluate this statement.

In your answer you should:

- refer to Buddhist teaching
- give reasoned arguments to support this statement
- give reasoned arguments to support a different point of view
- reach a justified conclusion. **(12 marks)**

(+ SPaG 3 marks)

EXAM TIP

This question asks about 'importance'. This means the significance or value of the Buddha's life. Remember, each point needs to be developed, and at least one point needs to be supported with a relevant source of belief. Ensure you cite where this comes from, for example the Pali Canon.

⚙ Knowledge

11 ✸ Beliefs and teachings: The Three Marks of Existence, Dependent Arising, and Dhamma (Dharma)

What are the Three Marks of Existence?

The **Three Marks of Existence** (also known as the Universal Truths) are a series of teachings by the Buddha that characterise all things and the way they exist (ontology). They are:

- dukkha
- **anicca**
- **anatta**.

⬇

Dukkha

Dukkha broadly means suffering or dissatisfaction with life. It encourages Buddhists to:

- develop resilience, for example the Buddhist Parable of the Mustard Seed teaches that suffering is a universal condition for all
- respond to suffering, for example Buddhists may support a charity
- develop the key qualities of compassion and wisdom.

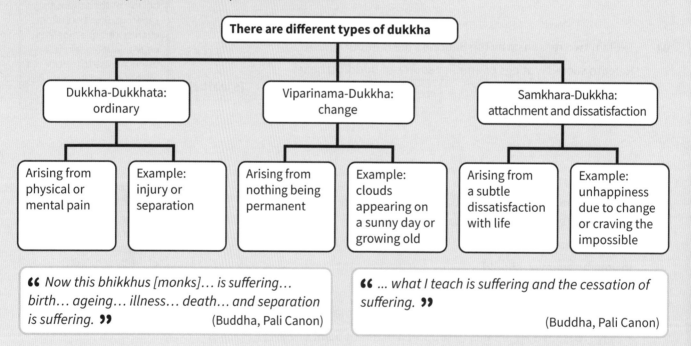

> **"** Now this bhikkhus [monks]… is suffering… birth… ageing… illness… death… and separation is suffering. **"**
> (Buddha, Pali Canon)

> **"** … what I teach is suffering and the cessation of suffering. **"**
> (Buddha, Pali Canon)

REVISION TIP

When revising quotations, consider how the quotations maybe applicable to more than one topic. For example, the Three Marks of Existence are very useful for many practices.

Anicca

Anicca means impermanence – it helps Buddhists to realise that everything is continually changing. Anicca encourages:

- Buddhists away from materialism (there is an acceptance that material goods may be necessary, but attachment to them cannot bring long-term and sustained fulfillment)
- puja practices, for example, many Buddhists use a flower to remind them of the changing nature of life.

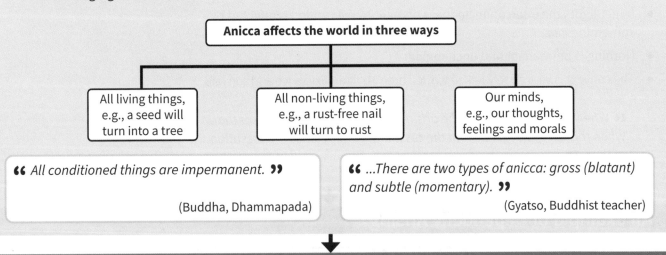

Anicca affects the world in three ways		
All living things, e.g., a seed will turn into a tree	All non-living things, e.g., a rust-free nail will turn to rust	Our minds, e.g., our thoughts, feelings and morals

> 66 *All conditioned things are impermanent.* 99
>
> (Buddha, Dhammapada)

> 66 *...There are two types of anicca: gross (blatant) and subtle (momentary).* 99
>
> (Gyatso, Buddhist teacher)

Anatta

Anatta means no fixed self or soul – there is no aspect of the human personality that remains constant or lives forever. Anatta encourages:

- eschatological beliefs and practices, for example, many Buddhists adopt a belief in rebirth, as opposed to reincarnation or resurrection
- Buddhists to perform death rites to highlight the empty nature of the material body.

> 66 *All things are not-self.* 99   (Buddha, Dhammapada)

The **Questions of King Milinda** help to explain anatta by using the chariot analogy.

- The monk Nagasena teaches that a chariot is merely a collection of parts that come together.
- There is nothing separate or independent known as a chariot, its existence is empty (**sunyata**).
- This is the same for people.

⚙ Knowledge

11 ✸ Beliefs and teachings: The Three Marks of Existence, Dependent Arising, and Dhamma (Dharma)

Dependent Arising

Dependent Arising is known as **paticcasamupada** in the Pali Canon:

- It expresses the Buddhist vision of the nature of reality.
- It can be summarised as the idea that all things exist because of other things.
- It highlights the interconnectedness of reality – everything is affected by something else.
- Nothing is permanent and unchanging.
- The concept is very closely linked to the Three Marks of Existence and sunyata.

> **❝** When this is, that is. From the arising of this comes the arising of that. When this isn't, that isn't. From the cessation of this comes the cessation of that. **❞**
>
> (Buddha, Pali Cannon)

⬇

An example of Dependent Arising

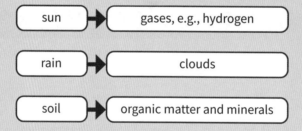

- This chain continues – each aspect has something it depends on to exist.
- Some aspects will link to another and be dependent on it for its existence too. For example, soil needs rain for nutrients.
- If the idea was drawn out, it would look like a big, messy, tangled web (Indra's Net).

⬇

Dependent Arising and its influence on Buddhist conduct

As Dependent Arising teaches that everything is interconnected, it may influence Buddhists to act in certain ways.

- Buddhists' ethical conduct towards others may be grounded in compassion (karuna) and love (metta) because they will be aware of the far-reaching consequences of a positive action, such as donating to charity.
- Buddhists may be more ecologically aware because they will consider the impact of environmental damage such as deforestation, use of nonrenewable resources, and lack of recycling on all things due to the interconnectedness of Earth.

What is Dhamma (Dharma)?

Dhamma (Dharma) is a concept found in all religions emerging from the Indian subcontinent.

It is an important concept, but it doesn't have an agreed meaning.

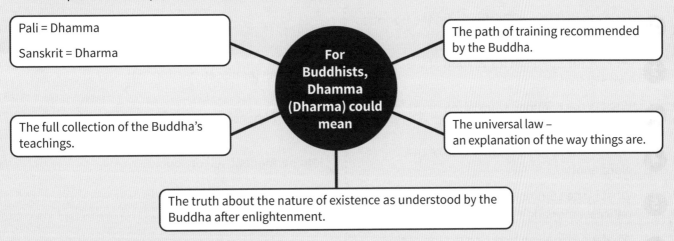

Pali = Dhamma

Sanskrit = Dharma

The full collection of the Buddha's teachings.

For Buddhists, Dhamma (Dharma) could mean

The path of training recommended by the Buddha.

The universal law – an explanation of the way things are.

The truth about the nature of existence as understood by the Buddha after enlightenment.

In Pali it is known as Dhamma, while in Sanskrit it is known as **Dharma**.

Three Refuges

- Dhamma (Dharma) is one of the **Three Refuges** (also known as Jewels or Treasures) in Buddhism.
- These are used by Buddhists to help them relieve suffering.
- They help to give life meaning, purpose, and satisfaction.
- The other two refuges are Buddha and Sangha.

Buddha	Dhamma (Dharma)	Sangha
<ul><li>The one who is awakened.</li><li>A role model – someone whose behaviour is copied.</li><li>A respected figure – someone who is shown devotion.</li></ul>	<ul><li>A collection of teachings.</li><li>A guide for living, for example, ethical conduct.</li><li>A guide for practice, for example, ritual.</li></ul>	<ul><li>A community that follows the Dhamma (Dharma).</li><li>A monastic community involved in training and learning.</li><li>A community of those who are enlightened.</li><li>Today, Sangha can refer to both lay and monastic persons in some Buddhist communities.</li></ul>

Key terms

Make sure you can write a definition for these key terms

Three Marks of Existence   anicca   anatta
Questions of King Milinda   sunyata   Dependent Arising
paticcasamupada   Dhamma (Dharma)   the Three Refuges

Retrieval

Learn the answers to the questions below, then cover the answers column with a piece of paper and write as many as you can. Check and repeat.

Questions | Answers

#	Question	Answer
1	How many Marks of Existence did the Buddha teach about?	Three
2	What is the common translation of the word dukkha?	Suffering (or dissatisfaction with life)
3	What is the common translation of the word anicca?	Impermanence
4	What is the common translation of the word anatta?	No permanent self or soul
5	What is the common translation of the word paticcasamupada?	Dependent Arising
6	What word is given to the collection of the Buddha's teachings?	Dhamma (Dharma)
7	What 'Three' is the Dhamma (Dharma) a part of?	The Three Refuges (also known as Jewels or Treasures)
8	What are two ways Dependent Arising may influence a Buddhist?	Action towards each other, action towards the earth
9	What are the three types of dukkha?	Ordinary, change, and attachment and dissatisfaction
10	Which Buddhist teacher suggests there are two types of change and what are they?	Gyatso; gross and subtle

Put paper here

Previous questions

Now go back and use these questions to check your knowledge of previous topics.

Questions | Answers

#	Question	Answer
11	What is meant by the title 'the Buddha'?	Somebody who is enlightened or awakened
12	What is the purpose of the Buddha's birth?	To ensure the welfare of the world
13	What period of the Buddha's life saw him witness four fundamental sights of life?	The Four Sights
14	Which two periods of the Buddha's life may be commemorated by the festival Wesak?	Birth and enlightenment
15	Name three sources Buddhists can use to understand the Buddha's life.	Buddhacarita, Jataka 075, Pali Canon

Put paper here

Exam-style questions

01 Which **one** of the following best describes Dependent Arising?

Put a tick (✓) in the box next to the correct answer. **(1 mark)**

A	All things cause suffering	☐
B	All things do not last	☐
C	All life is interconnected	☐
D	All things do not possess a non-changing aspect	☐

02 Give **two** understandings of Dhamma (Dharma). **(2 marks)**

> **EXAM TIP**
>
> This question is only worth two marks. Ensure you don't spend too long answering it or providing too much detail. Single words or short sentences are acceptable and encouraged.

03 Give **two** of the three Marks of Existence. **(2 marks)**

04 Explain **two** ways in which Dependent Arising may influence Buddhists today. **(4 marks)**

05 Explain **two** ways in which the Dhamma (Dharma) is important for Buddhists.

Refer to sacred writings or another source of Buddhist belief and teaching in your answer. **(5 marks)**

06 Explain **two** causes of Dukkha.

Refer to sacred writings or another source of Buddhist belief and teaching in your answer. **(5 marks)**

> **EXAM TIP**
>
> This question asks you to refer to a source of authority, for example, you can cite the Buddha, the Pali Canon, the Dhammapada, etc.

07 'Dukkha is the most important Mark of Existence for Buddhists.'

Evaluate this statement.

In your answer you should:

- refer to Buddhist teaching
- give reasoned arguments to support this statement
- give reasoned arguments to support a different point of view
- reach a justified conclusion. **(12 marks)**

(+ SPaG 3 marks)

⚙ Knowledge

12 ✸ Beliefs and teachings: The human personality and human destiny

What happened when the Buddha died?

- After the Buddha died, 500 enlightened monks formed a council to agree on the content of the Buddha's teaching and the codes that the monastic Sangha (community) should follow.

- In time, different groups interpreted the Buddha's teaching differently and how Buddhism should be practised. The councils met many times. Over time, different groups interpreted the Buddha's teaching differently and how Buddhism should be practised. Diversity in Buddhism began to grow.

Buddhist schools

- Disagreements led to different Buddhist schools being formed. These were:
  - **Theravada**
  - **Mahayana**
  - **Vajrayana**.
- The map to the right shows examples of where Buddhism is a major religion. The map shows the diversity and spread of Buddhism across different geographical regions.

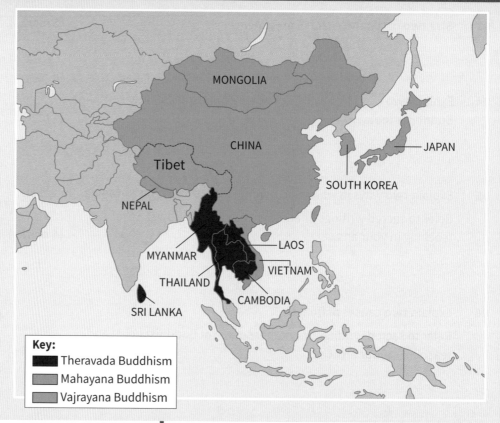

MONGOLIA

CHINA

Tibet

JAPAN

SOUTH KOREA

NEPAL

LAOS

MYANMAR

VIETNAM

THAILAND

CAMBODIA

SRI LANKA

Key:
- ⬛ Theravada Buddhism
- Mahayana Buddhism
- Vajrayana Buddhism

Overlap and divisions in Buddhist schools

- There is a lot of overlap between the schools, for example, there are many similarities between Mahayana and Vajrayana Buddhism. Some argue there is no difference between them.

- There are also divisions within each school, for example, Vajrayana Buddhism is divided – one example is Tibetan, which is also divided again.

- Mahayana Buddhism is an umbrella term, incorporating traditions such as **Pure Land**, **Zen**, and **Nichiren** Buddhism. Again, there are divisions within these traditions.

> **REVISION TIP** ☑
>
> Not all Pure Land Buddhists believe the same thing, so remember to use 'some' and 'most' when referring to them.

Key features of Theravada and Mahayana Buddhism

	Theravada	Mahayana
Views on the Buddha	A focus on a historical figure. It is no longer possible to meet or interact with him.	A divine figure. The Buddha is active and can be interacted with in the world today.
Important scriptures	Pali Canon	Lotus Sutra (and other sutras)
The human personality	**Five Aggregates (skandhas)**	Sunyata **Buddha-nature** **Buddhahood**
Human destiny	**Arhat**	**Bodhisattva**

Human personality in the Theravada and Mahayana traditions

- Human personality refers to what makes a human.
- Theravada and Mahayana Buddhists have a range of ideas about human personality. Whilst the schools do share some similar ideas about human personality, there are also some differences.
- When differences do occur, it is often because of a reinterpretation of an idea, or a particular emphasis placed on an idea within a school of Theravada and/or Mahayana Buddhism.

Theravada: the Five Aggregates

The Buddha taught that there are five aspects that interact with each other to make up a human's personality. These are known as the Five Aggregates (skandhas).

Consciousness: people's general awareness of the world around them.

Form: material/physical objects, e.g., organs, bones.

Mental formations: people's thoughts and opinions, e.g., likes, dislikes, attitudes.

Human personality

Perception: how people recognise what things are, based on their previous experience, e.g., recognising a car because they've seen one before.

Sensation: feelings that occur when someone comes into contact with things, e.g., pain when breaking a leg bone.

Mahayana: sunyata, Buddha-nature, and Buddhahood

- Mahayana Buddhism is an umbrella term, so it is not quite true to say there is a 'Mahayana teaching' about human personality. However, there is a similar belief among many Mahayana schools about what makes a human.
- For many Mahayana Buddhists, the human personality consists of: sunyata, Buddha-nature, and Buddhahood.

⚙ Knowledge

12 ☸ Beliefs and teachings: The human personality and human destiny

Mahayana: sunyata, Buddha-nature, and Buddhahood

1 Sunyata

Often translated as 'emptiness'. A Mahayana text, the Heart Sutra, says 'form is emptiness and emptiness is form'.

Sunyata teaches that nothing, including humans, has a fixed, unchanging nature or personality. Everything exists only in relation to, and because of, other things.

Example: Nagasena and the Questions of King Milinda (the chariot analogy).

2 Buddha-nature

Everybody has the seed or essence of a Buddha inside them.

Example: A Zen Buddhist Master, Huineng, stated that Buddha-nature is obscured by ignorance, like the moon by clouds.

3 Buddhahood

When somebody becomes a Buddha by achieving Enlightenment.

Theravada and Mahayana teachings about human destiny

Human destiny refers to the goal of a human's life. As with human personality, a human's destiny is a source of division between Theravada and Mahayana Buddhist schools. But again, while there is some exclusivity, there are some ideas which play a lesser role, rather than being completely rejected.

	Theravada	Mahayana
Goal	Arhat: • A perfected person or worthy one. • They have overcome the main cause of suffering and achieved enlightenment.	Bodhisattva: • Somebody who has become enlightened. • Out of compassion they choose to help others achieve enlightenment. • The Bodhisattva vow teaches: ❝ *However innumerable sentient beings are; I vow to save them.* ❞
What happens at death?	• Not reborn. • Escape the cycle of samsara. • Attain nibbana (also known as nirvana).	• Reborn • Earthly Bodhisattvas enter back into the world of samsara to help others. • Transcendent Bodhisattvas remain in a region between Earth and nibbana (nirvana). They are spiritual beings, who appear and remain active in the world to help lead others to enlightenment.
Use in other schools	Sometimes used by Mahayana Buddhists to refer to somebody far along the path of enlightenment.	Sometimes used by Theravada Buddhists to refer to somebody on the path of enlightenment.
Example	• Suddhodana – Buddha's father. • Kaundinya – one of the five earliest Buddhist monks.	• Avalokiteshvara – Bodhisattva of Compassion. • Manjushri – Bodhisattva of Wisdom.

The six perfections in the Mahayana tradition

- To become a Bodhisattva, an individual must attain six perfections in their life.
- There is a crossover between the six perfections in Mahayana Buddhism and the ten perfections found in Theravada Buddhism.

Generosity: to be charitable.

Morality: to behave ethically.

The six perfections

Patience: to be patient in all activities.

Energy: to persevere in practising the Boddhisattva vow when things get difficult.

Meditation: to develop concentration and awareness.

Wisdom: to try to understand the true nature of reality.

Buddhahood and the Pure Land

- Pure Land Buddhism is a collection of Mahayana Buddhist schools. For example, Shin and Jodo.
- Pure Land Buddhism is a school of Mahayana Buddhism.
- It began in China and spread into Japan. It is now the main type of Buddhism practised in Japan.
- It is based on faith in **Amitabha Buddha** – a king who gave up his throne and achieved enlightenment. In Pure Land Buddhism, faith in Amitabha is more important than an individual's own actions and behaviours.
- When Amitabha achieved enlightenment, he created a pure land called **Sukhavati**. The followers of Pure Land hope to be reborn there because they believe there is a greater chance of attaining Buddhahood there.
- Sukhavati is free from dukkha. In his vows, Amitabha states everybody will be the colour of gold.
- Followers of Pure Land Buddhism are encouraged to engage in five types of religious practice. It is believed these five practices help followers to be reborn into Sukhavati.
- The five practices are reciting scriptures, worshiping Amitabha, meditating on Amitabha, making praise and offerings to Amitabha, and chanting the name of Amitabha.
- For many, chanting of Amitabha's name is considered the most important practice.

The five practices
Reciting scriptures
Worshiping Amitabha
Meditating on Amitabha
Making praise and offerings to Amitabha
Chanting the name of Amitabha

 Key terms **Make sure you can write a definition for these key terms**

Theravada   Mahayana   Vajrayana   Pure Land   Zen   Nichiren
Five Aggregates (skandhas)   Buddha-nature   Buddhahood
Arhat   Bodhisattva   Amitabha Buddha   Sukhavati

Retrieval

Learn the answers to the questions below, then cover the answers column with a piece of paper and write as many as you can. Check and repeat.

Questions | Answers

	Questions		Answers
1	What are the three different schools of Buddhism?	Put paper here	Theravada, Mahayana, Vajrayana
2	Which school of Buddhism is most common in China?		Mahayana
3	Which school of Buddhism is most common in Nepal?		Vajrayana
4	Which school of Buddhism is most common in Thailand?	Put paper here	Theravada
5	Which concept states that there is the essence of a Buddha inside everybody?		Buddha-nature
6	How many Aggregates come together to make up the human personality "in Theravada Buddhism"?	Put paper here	Five
7	What is the Bodhisattva vow?		*However innumerable sentient beings are; I vow to save them*
8	What word is used to describe a perfected or worthy person in Theravada Buddhism?		Arhat
9	What is the name of the school of Buddhism that focuses on devotion to Amitabha?	Put paper here	Pure Land Buddhism
10	Which Mahayana Buddhist concept describes the emptiness of all things?		Sunyata

Previous questions

Now go back and use these questions to check your knowledge of previous topics.

Questions | Answers

	Questions		Answers
11	What word is given to the collection of the Buddha's teachings?	Put paper here	Dhamma (Dharma)
12	What did the Buddha discover while abandoning worldly pleasures?		The Middle Way
13	What is the common translation of the term anicca?		Impermanence
14	What is the common translation of the term dukkha?	Put paper here	Suffering (or dissatisfaction with life)
15	What is a common translation of the term paticcasamupada?		Dependent Arising

Exam-style questions

01 Which **one** of the following is someone who remains in the cycle of samsara out of compassion to help others achieve enlightenment? **(1 mark)**

Put a tick (✓) in the box next to the correct answer.

A	Arhat	☐
B	Buddha	☐
C	Bhikkhuni	☐
D	Bodhisattva	☐

> **EXAM TIP**
>
> You need to learn all the words stated in the specification. These can come up as answers, but they might also be used in the wording of a question. If you don't understand the question, you can't answer it.

02 Which **one** of the following is **not** one of the Five Aggregates? **(1 mark)**

Put a tick (✓) in the box next to the correct answer.

A	Form	☐
B	Dukkha	☐
C	Consciousness	☐
D	Perception	☐

03 Give **two** countries where Theravada Buddhism is dominant. **(2 marks)**

04 Give **two** of the six perfections in the Mahayana tradition. **(2 marks)**

05 Explain **two** ways that following Mahayana Buddhism may influence Buddhists today. **(4 marks)**

06 Explain **two** Buddhist teachings about human destiny.

Refer to sacred writings or another source of Buddhist belief and teaching in your answer. **(5 marks)**

> **EXAM TIP**
>
> Remember to state your source when you answer this type of question. For example, 'The Pali Canon states…' or 'The Bodhisattva vow teaches…'.

07 'It is impossible to achieve your destiny in Buddhism unless you follow Pure Land Buddhism'.

Evaluate this statement.

In your answer you should:

- refer to Buddhist teaching
- give reasoned arguments to support this statement
- give reasoned arguments to support a different point of view
- reach a justified conclusion. **(12 marks)**

(+ SPaG 3 marks)

⚙ Knowledge

13 ☸ Beliefs and teachings: The Four Noble Truths

The Four Noble Truths

- The Buddha taught about the Four Noble Truths in his first sermon, which was given to five of his earliest followers.

- This teaching is known as 'setting in motion the **Wheel of Dhamma** (Dharma)'. It is recorded in the Pali Canon (Dhammacakkappavattana Sutta).

- The Four Noble Truths focus on the issue of suffering and how it can be reduced or eliminated.

> The way to end suffering is to follow the **Eightfold Path (magga)**.
>
> ⬆
>
> There is a way to end suffering (**nirodha**).
>
> ⬆
>
> There is a cause of suffering (**samudaya**).
>
> ⬆
>
> There is suffering (dukkha).

> ❝ *The Four Noble Truths are the very foundation of Buddhist teaching, and that is why they are so important.* ❞ (The Dalai Lama)

> ❝ *But if any one goes to the Buddha, the Doctrine and the Order as a refuge, he perceives with proper knowledge the four noble truths: suffering, the arising of suffering, and the overcoming of suffering, and the noble eightfold path leading to the cessation [stopping] of suffering.* ❞
>
> (Dhammapada, 190-191)

REVISION TIP

Take extra time to ensure you can explain the Four Noble Truths, many later Buddhist teachings come from these.

⬇

The First Noble Truth

The first truth is that suffering exists.

- Dukkha is the Pali word often associated with the word suffering, although there is no exact translation.

- The Buddha taught that there are many different types of suffering.

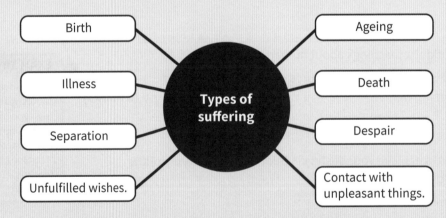

- The First Noble Truth is linked to another aspect of the Buddha's Dhamma (Dharma), the Three Marks of Existence.

The Second Noble Truth

The second truth is that there is an origin of suffering.

- The Buddha taught that one of the main origins of suffering is craving (**tanha**).

- The Buddha also taught that the Three Poisons (also known as the three fires) cause suffering.

> 66 *Greed is a root of what is unskilful, aversion is a root of what is unskilful, delusion is a root of what is unskilful.* 99 (Pali Canon)

- The poisons are to be contrasted with the three 'wholesomes': wisdom, giving, and loving kindness.

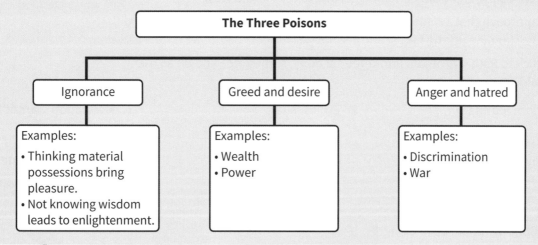

The Three Poisons

Ignorance

Examples:
- Thinking material possessions bring pleasure.
- Not knowing wisdom leads to enlightenment.

Greed and desire

Examples:
- Wealth
- Power

Anger and hatred

Examples:
- Discrimination
- War

The Third Noble Truth

The third truth is that there is an end to suffering.

- Many Buddhists believe they can end their suffering through their own actions and efforts.

- The goal of Buddhism is Enlightenment, with the end of suffering. This is sometimes referred to as nibbana (nirvana), which literally means 'extinction': the putting out of the Three Fires, also known as the Three Poisons. In other words:

  - Overcoming ignorance. There is a realisation of the nature of reality.

  - No longer feeling greed and desire. There is an inner satisfaction and appreciation.

  - No longer feeling anger and hatred. Instead you feel love (metta) and compassion (karuna) towards all beings.

Different interpretations of nibbana (nirvana)

Different Buddhist groups have different understandings of nibbana (nirvana) and the best methods to realise its truth.

Interpretation of nibbana (nirvana)	Meaning	Features
Nibbana (nirvana) with remainder.	When a Buddhist realises nibbana (nirvana) during this life.	The physical body remains. Continues to live and be conscious in this world. A different stage of consciousness is attained.
Nibbana (nirvana) without remainder (Parinibbana).	When a Buddhist realises nibbana (nirvana) after this life.	The physical body dies. The Buddhist leaves this world.

> 66 *This is the ending of craving… cessation; nibbana.* 99 (Pali Canon)

⚙ Knowledge

13 ✸ Beliefs and teachings: The Four Noble Truths

The Fourth Noble Truth

The fourth truth is the way or cure to end suffering.

- The way is eight practices that a Buddhist can undertake to overcome suffering and realise nibbana (nirvana).
- It is known as the Eightfold Path (magga) and is the Middle Way.
- It is an approach that avoids extremes in any decisions. The Buddha acquired this understanding during his ascetic period.
- The Eightfold Path is grouped into three sections, sometimes known as the **Threefold Way**:

1. Wisdom (**panna**)

- Right understanding
- Right intention

2. Ethics (**sila**)

- Right speech
- Right action
- Right livelihood

3. Meditation (**samadhi**)

- Right effort
- Right mindfulness
- Right concentration

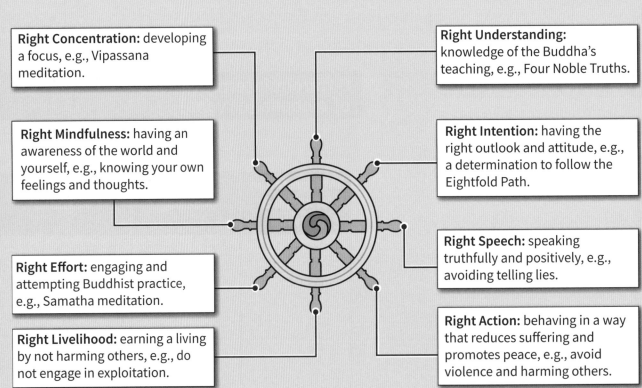

Right Concentration: developing a focus, e.g., Vipassana meditation.

Right Mindfulness: having an awareness of the world and yourself, e.g., knowing your own feelings and thoughts.

Right Effort: engaging and attempting Buddhist practice, e.g., Samatha meditation.

Right Livelihood: earning a living by not harming others, e.g., do not engage in exploitation.

Right Understanding: knowledge of the Buddha's teaching, e.g., Four Noble Truths.

Right Intention: having the right outlook and attitude, e.g., a determination to follow the Eightfold Path.

Right Speech: speaking truthfully and positively, e.g., avoiding telling lies.

Right Action: behaving in a way that reduces suffering and promotes peace, e.g., avoid violence and harming others.

 Key terms — Make sure you can write a definition for these key terms

Wheel of Dhamma (Dharma)   Eightfold Path (magga)   nirodha   samudaya   tanha   Threefold Way   panna   sila   samadhi

Learn the answers to the questions below, then cover the answers column with a piece of paper and write as many as you can. Check and repeat.

Questions

Answers

	Questions		Answers
1	How many 'Truths' did the Buddha teach?	Put paper here	Four
2	What was the name of the Buddha's first sermon?		Setting in motion the Wheel of Dhamma (Dharma)
3	What is the main topic of the Buddha's teaching in the Noble Truths?		Suffering
4	What is the Pali word for suffering?	Put paper here	Dukkha
5	What is meant by 'tanha'?		Craving
6	What are the Three Poisons?		Ignorance, greed and desire, anger and hatred
7	What is the goal for Buddhism?	Put paper here	The end of suffering, which is nibbana (nirvana)
8	What are the two different interpretations of nibbana (nirvana)?		With remainder, without remainder
9	What is the name of the Buddha's 'cure' to suffering?	Put paper here	Eightfold Path (magga), the Middle Way
10	What are the three sections of the Eightfold Path?		Wisdom (panna), Ethics (sila), Meditation (samadhi)

Previous questions

Now go back and use these questions to check your knowledge of previous topics.

Questions

Answers

	Questions		Answers
11	Where do Buddhists visit to remember the Buddha's Enlightenment?	Put paper here	Bodh Gaya
12	What is the common translation of the term anatta?		No permanent self or soul
13	What is the name of the school of Buddhism which focuses on devotion to Amitabha?		Pure Land Buddhism
14	What is the Bodhisattva vow?	Put paper here	*However innumerable sentient beings are; I vow to save them*
15	What are the three different schools of Buddhism?		Theravada, Mahayana, Vajrayana

Practice

Exam-style questions

01 Which **one** of the following is **not** one of the Four Noble Truths? **(1 mark)**

Put a tick (✓) in the box next to the correct answer.

A   Suffering exists ☐

B   Suffering is meditation ☐

C   Suffering can be overcome ☐

D   Suffering is caused by craving ☐

02 What is meant by the term dukkha? **(1 mark)**

Put a tick (✓) in the box next to the correct answer.

A   Impermanence ☐

B   Eightfold Path ☐

C   Suffering ☐

D   Perfected person ☐

03 Give **two** interpretations of nibbana (nirvana). **(2 marks)**

> **EXAM TIP**
>
> Keep your answers to two-mark questions short and summarised. If you can use one or two words, then do so.

04 Give **two** of the Four Noble Truths. **(2 marks)**

05 Explain **two** ways in which the Eightfold Path may influence Buddhists today. **(4 marks)**

06 Explain **two** of the Four Noble Truths.

Refer to sacred writings or another source of Buddhist belief and teaching in your answer. **(5 marks)**

07 'The Second Noble Truth is the most important.'

Evaluate this statement.

In your answer you should:

- refer to Buddhist teaching
- give reasoned arguments to support this statement
- give reasoned arguments to support a different point of view
- reach a justified conclusion. **(12 marks)**

(+ SPaG 3 marks)

> **EXAM TIP**
>
> Keep using the wording of the question in your answer to ensure you stay focused on the question set. This will help you to maximise your marks.

14 ☸ Practices: Places of worship

Attending a place of worship

- A place of worship is where people who share the same or similar belief systems join together to show their devotion.
- In some religions, it is extremely important to attend a place of worship.

- In Buddhism, Buddhists can worship together:
  - as a community at a place of worship and/or
  - as a family or individually at home.

Temple

A temple is a structure where devotional activity takes place

- It is not fixed. It can be large or small.

- There is a meditation hall for Buddhists to meditate. A shrine is often the focal point in this room. In Tibetan Buddhism this type of place is called a **gompa**.

- It usually includes a hall for Buddhists or other community members to gather.

- There may also be separate halls or study rooms where Buddhists study or listen to talks by Buddhist teachers.

- Some temples may have a **stupa**, a structure that contains relics of the Buddha.

Shrine

A shrine is a focal point where a Buddha or Bodhisattva statue is found

- It is not fixed. It can be large or small and can be found in a temple or home.

- For Mahayana Buddhists, it may feature the figure of a Bodhisattva e.g., Avalokiteshvara.

- It may feature a **Buddha rupa**, a statue of the Buddha.

- Buddhists may make offerings, such as a candle, flowers, or incense to thank and/or pay respect to the Buddha.

- Artefacts such as **mala beads** are used to help keep focus during chanting or recitation.

Monastery (known as a vihara in the Theravada tradition)

A **monastery** is where the ordained Buddhist community live, this includes monks and nuns

- It is not fixed. It can range from one building to a complex of buildings.

- It is often close to, or in the grounds of, a temple to allow for easy worship.

- It is often very simple, with spaces for monks or nuns to eat, sleep, and study.

- Some monasteries may have or be close to a stupa that contains relics of the Buddha.

14 ☸ Practices: Places of worship

The importance of Buddhist places of worship

Important	Not important
• Temples are important for Buddhists as they allow the Buddhist community to come together. This can help Buddhists to develop a sense of belonging, feel part of a community, and deepen their faith.	• It is not a requirement for Buddhists to gather to worship. • Buddhists can carry out many of the same worship practices individually or at home with family. • Secular spaces can be used for Buddhists to communicate and get to know one another.
• Meditation halls are important because they give Buddhists aids to help them meditate.	• Buddhists can make a shrine at home with all of the aids they need for worship, for example, a Buddha-rupa, offerings, etc.
• Monasteries are important as they enable monks or nuns to meditate and study the Dharma and teach lay people (those not ordained). • This is important as lay people can learn from monks or nuns, seek guidance and some may ask for blessings for certain life events.	• Money used for the upkeep of Buddhist places of worship (perhaps all places of worship) could be used for other projects, for example, to reduce dukkha in the world.

Buddhist sources of authority about places of worship

> ❝ This is my simple religion. There is no need for temples, no need for complicated philosophy. Our own brain, our own heart is our temple; the philosophy is kindness. ❞
>
> (Dalai Lama)

> ❝ [that which is] required to keep the shrine clean replenished [kept filled] with flowers and other offerings is considered a skilful activity to focus one's mind in the spiritual practices. ❞
>
> (Lama Rinpoche, a Tibetan monk)

> ❝ ... to the Buddha for refuge [safety] I go, to the Dhamma for refuge I go, to the Sangha for refuge I go. ❞
>
> (Tisarana chant, Dhammapada)

REVISION TIP

Try to look at images and videos of Buddhist places of worship, this will help bring them to life as they can be quite abstract. For some, you can even have virtual tours.

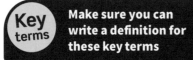

Key terms Make sure you can write a definition for these key terms

gompa   stupa   Buddha rupa   mala beads   monastery

Learn the answers to the questions below, then cover the answers column with a piece of paper and write as many as you can. Check and repeat.

Questions   Answers

#	Questions		Answers
1	Which word describes a place where Buddhists may go to undertake devotional activity?	Put paper here	Temple
2	What do Buddhists store in a stupa?	Put paper here	Relics of the Buddha
3	Which word describes a focal point where a Buddha rupa or Bodhisattva statue can be found?	Put paper here	Shrine
4	Where might Tibetan Buddhists undertake meditation?	Put paper here	Gompa
5	What might a Buddhist offer to a shrine during worship?	Put paper here	Flowers, candles, incense
6	Which place has spaces for monks or nuns to eat, sleep, and study?	Put paper here	Monastery (vihara)
7	Give three reasons why a Buddhist might attend a temple.	Put paper here	To join together with other Buddhists, to meditate, to study
8	Besides Buddha rupas, Bodhisattva statues, and offerings, what else might a Buddhist find in a shrine?	Put paper here	Artefacts, e.g., mala beads
9	What is the purpose of a meditation hall?	Put paper here	To provide a place for Buddhists to practise meditation and help them to do so
10	What are the three places of refuge in the Tisarana chant?	Put paper here	The Buddha, Dhamma (Dharma), Sangha
11	What is the purpose of mala beads?	Put paper here	To help keep focus during chanting or recitation
12	What is a Buddha rupa?	Put paper here	A statue of a Buddha
13	What might Mahayana Buddhists place in a shrine?	Put paper here	A Bodhisattva statue, e.g., Avalokiteshvara
14	How does Lama Rinpoche describe the act of attending to a temple shrine?	Put paper here	A skilful activity
15	What does the word lay people mean?	Put paper here	Those not ordained

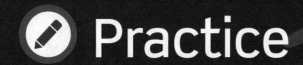

Practice

01 Which **one** of the following would you **not** find in a
Buddhist shrine? **(1 mark)**

Put a tick (✓) in the box next to the correct answer.

A A Buddha rupa ☐

B A Bodhisattva statue ☐

C Artefacts ☐

D Zazen ☐

02 Which **one** of the following would you **not** find in
a Buddhist temple? **(1 mark)**

Put a tick (✓) in the box next to the correct answer.

A A main hall ☐

B A meditation hall ☐

C A stupa ☐

D Karuna ☐

03 Give **two** features of a vihara. **(2 marks)**

04 Give **two** places of worship in Buddhism. **(2 marks)**

05 Explain **two** contrasting ways in which Buddhists can worship. **(4 marks)**

> **EXAM TIP**
> In the exam, the word 'contrasting' simply means different.

06 Explain **two** reasons why places of worship are important
for Buddhists.

Refer to sacred writings or another source of Buddhist belief and
teaching in your answer. **(5 marks)**

> **EXAM TIP**
> You can draw on any relevant material in a 12-mark question as long as it comes from the same religion and, in Paper 1, doesn't reference non-religious views. Sometimes, When answering questions on Practices it is useful to think about the beliefs you have studied.

07 'A Buddhist does not need to attend a place of worship to engage in
Buddhist practice.'

Evaluate this statement.

In your answer you should:

- refer to Buddhist teaching
- give reasoned arguments to support this statement
- give reasoned arguments to support a different point of view
- reach a justified conclusion. **(12 marks)**

(+ SPaG 3 marks)

15 ☸ Practices: Worship and meditation

Puja

Many Buddhists engage in worship, which may be referred to as **puja**.

- Buddhists can perform puja in groups in places such as temples, or in private at home, for example, at the family shrine.
- Many Buddhists perform puja to:
  - show their respect to the Buddha and Bodhisattvas
  - express their gratitude to the Buddha and Bodhisattvas for their teaching and support
  - focus on their religious tradition
  - deepen and learn more about their religious traditions by considering and reflecting upon key aspects of the Buddha's Dhamma (Dharma).

Different forms of worship

Form of worship	Why it is undertaken or used	Examples
Chanting (reciting from Buddhist scriptures)	• Traditionally a method to memorise and transmit Buddhist texts. • It helps Buddhists to remember the texts. • It can show a dedication and openness towards the Buddha's teaching. • It may help calm the mind to aid concentration.	• Tisarana Three Refuges chant • Five Moral Precepts • Bodhisattva vow • Heart sutra
Mantra recitation (the repetition of a short sequence of sacred syllables)	• For some Buddhists, mantras can transform. • They may help calm the mind to aid concentration. • They help to develop qualities of Bodhisattvas. For example, a mantra associated with Avalokiteshvara may be recited to help develop the quality of compassion.	• Om mani padme hum – a Tibetan mantra representing the sound of compassion. • Om Amideva Hrih – a Pure Land mantra representing the name of Amitabha.
Mala beads (a type of prayer bead used to count the number of recitations in a mantra)	• They help Buddhists to count the number of recitations they have made. • They may help Buddhists focus on recitation. • They may help Buddhists remember and ask for support in overcoming the **108 delusions** that impact human life.	• Mala necklace • Wrist mala

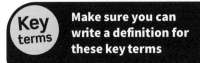

Key terms — Make sure you can write a definition for these key terms

puja 108 delusions zazen kasinas thangka

Meditation

- Another key aspect of Buddhist practice is meditation. Meditation is where the mind is calmed and focused.
- It often allows the practitioner an opportunity to reflect on the Buddha's Dhamma (Dharma).

- There are many different types of meditation, but typically Buddhists will use one of the three types depending on:
  - the tradition of Buddhism they follow
  - the aim of their meditative practice.

	Samatha (concentration and tranquility) meditation (Theravada and Mahayana)	Vipassana (insight) meditation (Theravada and Mahayana)	Visualisation (mainly Tibetan and in some Mahayana traditions)
Purpose	• Calm the mind. • Develop concentration. • Allow for tranquillity.	• Gain insight into reality.	• Visualise, develop, and emulate (copy) a Buddha or Bodhisattva and their qualities.
Practices	• Mindfulness of breathing: this allows the practitioner to become more aware and attentive to their breathing. • The aim is to help to focus the mind. • Typically, the focus is one object.	• Mindfulness of breathing: this allows the practitioner to become more aware and attentive to their breathing. • The aim is to help to focus the mind. • Typically, the focus is not confined to one object; the practitioner will focus on many. • A particular focus may be the Three Marks of Existence as this is an aspect of the Buddha's Dhamma (Dharma) that attempts to explain the true nature of reality. • Zen Buddhists undertake **zazen** – seated meditation. The practitioner will simply sit with their experiences, reflecting on reality while practising mindful breathing. • Some Buddhists may undertake Vipassana by walking.	• The practitioner imagines an object in their mind. • Once the object is visualised, the practitioner will examine its intricacies and try to hold the object in their mind for as long as possible. • Some may visualise a deity – somebody who is fully enlightened. • During this visualisation, the practitioner may focus on the qualities of the deity, in order to become more like them, e.g., Avalokiteshvara to develop compassion.
Aids used	• **Kasinas**, e.g., colours, water etc.	• Practice-dependent, e.g., kasinas, flowers, etc.	• **Thangka** and/or mandalas.
Teachings	66 *Those who have entered [on the path], meditative, will be released from Mara's fetter.* 99 (Buddha, Dhammapada)	66 *When your consciousness has become ripe… pure like clear water… realisation is possible.* 99 (Zenshin, Zen Monk)	66 *As a result of this visualisation, you slowly begin to feel an affinity with others and a deep empathy with their suffering.* 99 (Dalai Lama)

Learn the answers to the questions below, then cover the answers column with a piece of paper and write as many as you can. Check and repeat.

Questions | Answers

#	Question	Answer
1	What is the word to describe acts of worship by some Buddhists?	Puja
2	What is the word to describe reciting from Buddhist scripture?	Chanting
3	What is the word to describe a short sequence of sacred syllables?	Mantra
4	What is the name of the beads used to help count the number of mantra recitations?	Mala beads
5	What is an example of a mantra a Buddhist may perform?	Om mani padme hum, Om Amideva Hrih
6	What specific practice is used to calm the mind?	Samatha meditation
7	What specific practice is used to help gain an insight into reality?	Vipassana meditation
8	What is the word for the practice of 'seated meditation' used by many Zen Buddhists?	Zazen
9	What is the word to describe imagining or seeing an object in one's mind?	Visualisation
10	What may help a Buddhist undertake visualisation?	Thangka, Mandala

Put paper here

Previous questions

Now go back and use these questions to check your knowledge of previous topics.

Questions | Answers

#	Question	Answer
11	Which word describes a place where Buddhists may go to undertake devotional activity?	Temple
12	In which place would you find the ordained Sangha living together?	Vihara
13	Which word describes a focal point where a Buddha rupa or Bodhisattva statue can be found?	Shrine
14	What might Mahayana Buddhists place in a shrine?	A Bodhisattva statue, e.g., Avalokiteshvara
15	What is the purpose of a meditation hall?	To provide a place for Buddhists to practise meditation and help them meditate

Put paper here

✏ Practice

01 Which **one** of the following would a Buddhist **not** use during meditation? **(1 mark)**

Put a tick (✔) in the box next to the correct answer.

A A red flower ☐

B A water bowl ☐

C A mandala ☐

D A mourning ritual ☐

02 What Buddhist practice is defined as the singing or repeating of a word, prayer, or sound? **(1 mark)**

Put a tick (✔) in the box next to the correct answer.

A Mantra recitation ☐

B Chanting ☐

C Malas ☐

D Zazen ☐

> **EXAM TIP**
> Never miss out on a one-mark question. Always tick one option – there is a one in four chance you've ticked the right answer!

03 Give **two** purposes of meditation. **(2 marks)**

04 Give **two** examples of visualisation aids. **(2 marks)**

05 Explain **two** contrasting ways in which Buddhists may meditate. **(4 marks)**

06 Explain **two** reasons why Buddhists undertake puja.

Refer to sacred writings or another source of Buddhist belief and teaching in your answer. **(5 marks)**

> **EXAM TIP**
> For the fifth mark, you must provide an accurate and relevant reference to Buddhist teaching. This doesn't need to be an exact quotation, but you must state its source, for example, the Buddha, the Pali Canon, the Dalai Lama, etc.

07 'Meditation is the best expression of a Buddhist's beliefs.' **(12 marks)**

Evaluate this statement.

In your answer you should:

- refer to Buddhist teaching
- give reasoned arguments to support this statement
- give reasoned arguments to support a different point of view
- reach a justified conclusion. **(12 marks)**

(+ SPaG 3 marks)

Knowledge

16 ⊛ Practices: Buddhism and death

Ceremonies and rituals associated with death

Remembering the life of the person who has died.

Coming together as a Buddhist community to grieve and support one another.

Reflecting on the Buddha's teachings, e.g., anicca, anatta, etc.

Buddhists are helped by

Coming together as a family to grieve and support one another.

Undertaking rituals to ensure a positive rebirth for the deceased.

Gaining support from friends, teachers, nuns and or monks.

The Theravada funeral

A shrine is usually set up to display the deceased's portrait. It helps mourners to remember and reflect on the deceased's life and their memories of them.

A shrine is established with a Buddha rupa and offerings of candles, incense, and flowers. It gives mourners a focal point to remember the Buddha's Dhamma (Dharma) and to support their mourning process.

An ordained member of the Sangha (typically a monk) may attend and give a sermon. This helps mourners reflect on the life of the deceased and offer wisdom from the Buddha's Dhamma (Dharma) concerning the dukkha associated with death and mourning.

Rather than spending large sums of money on a funeral, a donation is made in memory of the deceased by their family. It is hoped that the **kammic merit** of this action will be transferred to the deceased, for example, to help them have a more favourable rebirth.

The deceased is cremated or buried. Cremation is more common.

Throughout the funeral, all present send thoughts of loving kindness to the deceased to ensure a positive rebirth.

16 ☸ Practices: Buddhism and death

Practices of a Mahayana or Vajrayana funeral

	Ceremony	Associated practices
Japan (Pure Land, Mahayana)	Funeral	• The body is covered by being placed in a coffin. • The body is placed with the head pointing to the west. This is believed to be the direction of Sukhavati, Amitabha's Pure Land. Those in attendance walk around the coffin reciting a Pure Land chant, 'Namo Amida Bu'. This chant asks for refuge in Amitabha. • Offerings are made every seven days for 49 days after death. • In Japan, funerals are influenced not only by Buddhism, but also by Shinto (the indigenous faith in Japan). Over time, funerals have adopted the practice of '**kotsuage**', where bones are removed from cremation ash using a special pair of chopsticks.
Tibet (Vajrayana)	Sky burial	• The body is left uncovered and exposed. • The body is left typically at high altitude as a gift to the vultures, who will eat the remains. This highlights the impermanence of the human body. (Note that cremation is becoming increasingly popular in some Tibetan communities.) • Prayers are made for the deceased. • Offerings of yak-butter lamps are made every seven days for 49 days after death. • Revered teachers such as **lamas** are always cremated and their remains placed in a **chorten** (stupa). The 13th Dalai Lama's chorten can be found at the Potala Palace in Tibet.

> **REVISION TIP**
>
> Buddhist teachings you can use when discussing death ceremonies and rituals include:
> - dukkha
> - anicca
> - anatta
> - **kamma** (karma).

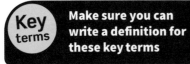

Key terms

Make sure you can write a definition for these key terms

| kammic merit | kotsuage | lamas | chorten | kamma |

Learn the answers to the questions below, then cover the answers column with a piece of paper and write as many as you can. Check and repeat.

Questions / Answers

	Questions		Answers
1	In which Buddhist tradition are funerals typically inexpensive?	Put paper here	Theravada
2	Who might attend a Buddhist funeral to give a sermon and/or a teaching reflecting on the Buddha's Dhamma (Dharma)?		A member of the Sangha or a monk
3	What is hoped to be achieved by donating on behalf of the deceased person?		Kamma merit
4	In which Buddhist tradition do funeral ceremonies involve pointing the head west?	Put paper here	Pure Land, Mahayana
5	In which Buddhist tradition do funeral ceremonies involve leaving an exposed body at high altitude?		Tibetan, Vajrayana
6	What is the name given to the ceremony where an exposed body is left at high altitude?	Put paper here	Sky burial
7	What is used to pick bones from ashes in a typical Japanese Buddhist funeral?		Special chopsticks
8	What form of worship is undertaken while walking around a coffin in a typical Japanese Buddhist funeral?		Chanting – 'Namo Amida Bu'
9	What is the purpose of leaving a body exposed in a Tibetan sky burial?	Put paper here	To allow the vultures to eat it and remind Buddhists of the impermanence of the human body
10	How many days are offerings made for after death in Japanese and Tibetan death ceremonies?		49

Previous questions

Now go back and use these questions to check your knowledge of previous topics.

Questions / Answers

	Questions		Answers
11	What is an example of a mantra a Buddhist may perform?	Put paper here	One from: Om mani padme hum / Om Amideva Hrih
12	What specific practice is used to help gain an insight into reality?		Vipassana Meditation
13	What is the word to describe acts of worship in Buddhism?		Puja
14	What is the word to describe imagining or seeing an object in one's mind?	Put paper here	Visualisation
15	What are the three places of refuge in the Tisarana chant?		The Buddha, Dhamma (Dharma), Sangha

Practice

Exam-style questions

01 Which **one** of the following is **not** a reason why Buddhists undertake ceremonies for those who have died? **(1 mark)**

Put a tick (✓) in the box next to the correct answer.

A	To reflect on the Buddha's teaching and use it as a source of support with mourning.	☐
B	To come together as a Buddhist community to remember the life of the deceased.	☐
C	To aid the deceased in their journey in the afterlife.	☐
D	To remember ethical conduct.	☐

> **EXAM TIP**
>
> Remember to read all options offered before selecting your answer. Multiple-choice questions often have incorrect 'distractors' that are similar to the correct answer.

02 Give **two** Theravada rituals performed at a funeral. **(2 marks)**

03 Give **two** Mahayana rituals performed at a funeral. **(2 marks)**

04 Give **two** Tibetan rituals performed at a funeral. **(2 marks)**

05 Explain **two** contrasting Buddhist ceremonies associated with death and mourning. **(4 marks)**

> **EXAM TIP**
>
> Remember to develop your points. Use phrases such as *because, this means that, therefore.*

06 Explain **two** reasons why death ceremony rituals are important for Buddhists.

Refer to sacred writings or another source of Buddhist belief and teaching in your answer. **(5 marks)**

07 'Buddhist death ceremonies are more for the living than the dead.' **(12 marks)**

Evaluate this statement.

In your answer you should:

- refer to Buddhist teaching
- give reasoned arguments to support this statement
- give reasoned arguments to support a different point of view
- reach a justified conclusion. **(12 marks)**

(+ SPaG 3 marks)

Festivals

A festival is a celebration for a religious reason. In Buddhism, these include:

- remembering key aspects of the Buddha's life
- getting together with other Buddhists
- engaging in a specific practice
- putting into practice an aspect of the Buddha's Dhamma (Dharma).

REVISION TIP

Use the internet to look at images and videos of Buddhist festivals. This will help to bring them to life.

Wesak and Parinirvana Day

Wesak and **Parinirvana Day** are important festivals for many Buddhists.

	Wesak	**Parinirvana Day**
Origins	• Some Buddhists celebrate Wesak as the festival of the Buddha's Enlightenment. • Some Buddhists call it Buddha Day. • Some Buddhists celebrate Wesak as the festival of the Buddha's birth, Enlightenment and passing into parinirvana. • It has officially been celebrated since 1950.	• A festival that celebrates the death of the Buddha and his attainment of, or passing into final nibbana (nirvana). • It is celebrated by Mahayana Buddhists.
Time of celebration	• On or near the date of the full moon in May.	• February
Ways of celebrating	• Lighting up home with candles. • Decorating • Giving gifts to the monastic community. • Making offerings to the Buddha. • Attending events where scriptures are being read. • Attending sermons. • Wearing traditional white dress. • In Singapore, caged animals are released as a symbol of liberation. • In Indonesia, giant lit lanterns are released into the sky.	• Taking time to reflect on an individual's own future death. • Remembering those who have passed away. • Reflecting on the Buddha's Dhamma (Dharma). • Reading scriptures (usually the Mahaparinirvana Sutra), which describes the last days of the Buddha's life. • Meditating, either at home or in the temple. • Spending the day in quiet reflection. • Undertaking pilgrimage, for example, to Kushinagar in India, where the Buddha is believed to have died.

17 ⚙ Practices: Festivals and retreats

The significance of celebrating festivals

Engage in practices carried out or suggested by the Buddha, e.g., meditation and pilgrimage. In the Pali Canon, the Buddha said:

❝ ... there are four places, Ananda, that a pious person should visit and look upon with feelings of reverence... born, became fully enlightened, set rolling the Wheel of Dhamma (Dharma) and where passed into nibbana without elements of clinging. ❞

Remember, reflect, develop, and deepen knowledge of aspects of the Buddha's life. For example:

- during Wesak, Buddhists learn about the Buddha's early life
- on Parinirvana Day, they learn about the Buddha's death.

This helps them to emulate these aspects in their own lives.

For Buddhists, festivals are an opportunity to

Meet and engage with other members of the Buddhist community (especially important for diasporic communities who live outside Buddhist-dominant nations). This helps build connections and a sense of belonging.

Remember, reflect, develop, and deepen knowledge on aspects of the Buddha's teachings, e.g., during Parinirvana Day, the concept of anicca. The Buddha taught:

❝ ... all conditioned things are impermanent... ❞   (Dhammapada)

Retreats

Retreats are a chance to temporarily leave everyday life and go to a special place to aid spiritual development.

Retreats allow Buddhists to engage in specific practices, for example:

- listening to talks about the Buddha's teachings
- meditation
- worship, or puja
- spending time with other Buddhists.

Buddhist retreats

Retreat centres in the UK include:

- Taraloka
- Amaravati
- Land of Joy
- Samye Ling
- Throssel Hole.

Some Buddhists (e.g., many Theravada monastics) undertake **Vassa**, an annual retreat. They engage in meditation and study of the Buddha's Dhamma (Dharma).

❝ ... for spirituality, pure morality, wisdom and insight to grow, we need time and space. ❞
[The Buddhist Lama Thubten Yeshe]

Key terms Make sure you can write a definition for these key terms

Parinirvana Day   Vassa

Retrieval

Learn the answers to the questions below, then cover the answers column with a piece of paper and write as many as you can. Check and repeat.

Questions | Answers

#	Questions		Answers
1	What is the word to describe a celebration for a religious reason?	Put paper here	Festival
2	Give two examples of Buddhist festivals.		Wesak, Parinirvana Day
3	What event is commonly remembered during Wesak?		The Buddha's Enlightenment
4	When is Wesak typically celebrated?	Put paper here	On or near the date of the full moon in May
5	What is another name for Wesak?		Buddha Day
6	What event is commonly remembered on Parinirvana Day?	Put paper here	The death of the Buddha and his attainment of, or passing into, final nibbana (nirvana)
7	What Sutra is usually read on Parinirvana Day?		Mahaparinirvana Sutra
8	What kind of journey might a Buddhist undertake to commemorate Parinirvana Day?	Put paper here	Pilgrimage
9	What is the word to describe where a Buddhist may temporarily leave their everyday life and go to a special place to aid their spiritual development?		Retreat
10	What is the name of the annual retreat undertaken by many Theravada monastics?		Vassa

Previous questions

Now go back and use these questions to check your knowledge of previous topics.

Questions | Answers

#	Questions		Answers
11	What form of worship is undertaken whilst walking around a coffin in a typical Japanese Buddhist funeral?	Put paper here	Chanting – 'Namo Amida Bu'
12	What is hoped to be achieved by donating on behalf of the deceased person?		Kamma merit
13	In which Buddhist tradition do funeral ceremonies involve leaving an exposed body at high altitude?		Tibetan, Vajrayana
14	What specific practice is used to calm the mind?	Put paper here	Samatha meditation
15	What is the word to describe a short sequence of sacred syllables?		Mantra

✏ Practice

01 Which **one** of these practices is associated with a Buddhist retreat? **(1 mark)**

Put a tick (✓) in the box next to the correct answer.

A Attending a large celebration ☐

B Picking bones from ashes ☐

C Undertaking a long and difficult journey ☐

D Visiting a quiet and relaxed place, where there is a focus on meditation and reflection ☐

02 Which **one** of the following is **not** associated with Parinirvana Day? **(1 mark)**

Put a tick (✓) in the box next to the correct answer.

A Ensuring there is a full moon ☐

B Reading the Mahaparinirvana Sutra ☐

C Undertaking pilgrimage to Kushinagar, where the Buddha passed into final nibbana (nirvana) ☐

D Reflecting on the impermanence of one's own life ☐

03 Give **two** reasons why a Buddhist may celebrate a festival. **(2 marks)**

04 Give **two** practices associated with retreats. **(2 marks)**

05 Give **two** features of Wesak celebrations. **(2 marks)** ◄

> **EXAM TIP** 🎯
> In two-mark questions you do not have to write in full sentences. Answers can be one word or short phrases.

06 Explain **two** contrasting ways of celebrating the Buddha. **(4 marks)**

07 Explain **two** reasons why retreats are important for Buddhists.

Refer to sacred writings or another source of Buddhist belief and teaching in your answer. **(5 marks)**

> **EXAM TIP** 🎯
> Remember to give two sides of an argument for a 12-mark question. Consider why somebody might agree and a different point of view. Try to directly counter your arguments, if you can.

08 'Parinirvana Day is the most important Buddhist festival.'

Evaluate this statement.

In your answer you should:

- refer to Buddhist teaching
- give reasoned arguments to support this statement
- give reasoned arguments to support a different point of view
- reach a justified conclusion. **(12 marks)**

(+ SPaG 3 marks)

18 ⚙ Practices: Buddhist ethics

Ethics

Ethics consider the rightness or wrongness of actions. Buddhism, like other religious traditions, gives ethical guidance to its followers on how to live their lives and make decisions when presented with moral dilemmas.

Ethical teaching

There are four key Buddhist ethical teachings:

- kamma (karma) and rebirth
- karuna (compassion)
- metta (loving kindness)
- the Five Moral Precepts

Karuna and metta

One of the four sublime states that all Buddhists should strive to develop.

Karuna
Compassion

A feeling of concern for all those in the world who are suffering.

Encourages Buddhists to help reduce suffering of one's self and others by being mindful of interaction with others (by being honest and respectful, etc.), and supporting charities, e.g., Rokpa.

❝ ...the key to a happier and more successful world is the growth of compassion. ❞   (Dalai Lama)

Another of the four sublime states that all Buddhists should strive to develop.

Metta
Loving kindness

Should be cultivated towards the self and others.

Showing a loving, kind, and friendly attitude towards all.

❝ ...one should cultivate loving-kindness towards all the world. ❞
(The Pali Canon)

Metta meditation is practised to help develop metta and may involve visualisation or mantra recitation.

REVISION TIP

Ensuring a good understanding of metta and karuna will help you respond to many Buddhist ethical questions.

⚙ Knowledge

18 ⚙ Practices: Buddhist ethics

Kamma (Karma) and rebirth

- Kamma equates to 'action'. In Buddhism it usually means that deliberate actions affect a Buddhist's circumstances in this life and future lives. It is sometimes considered as cause and effect.

- Rebirth is the belief that when somebody dies, they are reborn. A person's rebirth is dictated by kamma. The end of rebirth is the achievement of nibbana (nirvana).

> **❝** *If you speak or act with a corrupted heart, then suffering follows you… If you speak or act with a bright heart, then happiness follows you* **❞**
>
> (Dhammapada, Buddha)

- There is a link between kamma, rebirth and ethics:

> An action has both instant and lasting kammic consequences.
>
> Skilful actions are likely to result in favourable rebirth.
>
> This helps Buddhists to achieve their final destiny of nibbana (nirvana).

> Skilful actions are to be encouraged.
>
> Unskilful actions are to be avoided.

> An action may be judged on its skilfulness.
>
> A skilful action is rooted in generosity, compassion, and wisdom.
>
> An unskilful action is rooted in craving, hatred, and ignorance.

> Many Buddhists want to carry out actions that are 'good'.

Explaining rebirth

- Some Buddhist traditions use a '**Wheel of Life**' (Bhavacakra). This offers a visualisation of the cycle of samsara to aid their understanding.
- This represents the cycle of samsara – the cycle of rebirth.
- It is a very intricate representation with lots of symbolism in it.
- Different Buddhist traditions may have slightly different versions but common features are shown here.

A depiction of the Three Poisons. These are in the centre as they are the cause of all suffering.

The Wheel of Life is held by Yama – the Lord of Death.

The six realms of rebirth. Depending upon a Buddhist's kamma they may be reborn in one of the six realms – gods, angry gods, animals, tormented beings, hungry ghosts, and human realm.

The **12 Nidanas** – the links of dependent origination. They seek to explain the causes of samsara.

The Five Moral Precepts (Pancha Sila)

The **Five Moral Precepts** are:

- the five commitments that most Buddhists use to guide their ethical decision-making
- the five principles that are voluntarily practised by Buddhists.

Remember that in Buddhism there is not a god who will reward and punish.

REVISION TIP

Knowing the Five Moral Precepts will help you respond to many Buddhist ethical questions, especially important if studying Buddhism for Paper 2. Consider how easy or difficult they may be to practice in the world today.

The Five Moral Precepts

- Do not take life.
- Do not misuse the senses.
- Do not take intoxicants that cloud the mind.
- Do not take what is not given.
- Do not speak falsehoods.

In the Pali Canon, the Buddha referred to the five moral precepts as:

❝ … five great gifts… not open to suspicion… and are unfaulted by knowledgeable contemplatives. ❞

Do not take life	Do not harm or kill another living human being, e.g., murder. Do not harm or kill animals (some Buddhists choose to be vegetarian or vegan).	*❝ … abandoning the taking of life, abstains from taking life. ❞* (Pali Canon, Buddha)
Do not take what is not given	Do not steal. Do not exploit others.	*❝ … abandoning taking what is not given (stealing), the disciple of the noble ones abstains from taking what is not given. ❞* (Pali Canon, Buddha)
Do not misuse the senses	Do not engage in harmful sexual practice, e.g., adultery. Do not engage in excessive overindulgence.	*❝ … abandoning illicit sex, the disciple of the noble ones abstains from illicit sex. ❞* (Pali Canon, Buddha)
Do not speak falsehoods	Do not lie. Do not gossip.	*❝ … abandoning lying, the disciple of the noble ones abstains from lying. ❞* (Pali Canon, Buddha)
Do not take intoxicants that cloud the mind	Do not drink alcohol. Do not take drugs.	*❝ … abandoning the use of intoxicants, the disciple of the noble ones abstains from taking intoxicants. ❞* (Pali Canon, Buddha)

- The precepts sometimes need to balance against one another.
- The most important is to avoid harm.
- The reduction of harm should be the driving ethical principle of Buddhist ethical decision-making.

- Buddhists should aim for skilful action.
- The precepts are not absolute commands and sometimes need to balance against one another.

18 ⚙ Practices: Buddhist ethics

The Six Perfections in the Mahayana tradition

- Ethical conduct is also important for those on the path to becoming a Bodhisattva. An individual must attain **Six Perfections** in their life:

Generosity

To be charitable.

Morality

To behave ethically.

Energy

To persevere in practising the Boddhisattva vow when things get difficult.

Patience

To be patient in all activities.

Meditation

To develop concentration and awareness.

Wisdom

To try to understand the true nature of reality.

 Key terms | **Make sure you can write a definition for these key terms** | Wheel of Life (Bhavacakra) 12 Nidanas
Five Moral Precepts (Pancha Sila) Six Perfections

Learn the answers to the questions below, then cover the answers column with a piece of paper and write as many as you can. Check and repeat.

Questions / Answers

#	Questions		Answers
1	What is the word to describe the rightness or wrongness of an action?	Put paper here	Ethics
2	What are the four key Buddhist ethical teachings?		Kamma and rebirth, Metta, Karuna, Five Moral Precepts
3	How can the word karuna be translated?		Compassion
4	How can the word metta be translated?	Put paper here	Loving kindness
5	What practice can a Buddhist engage in, to help cultivate metta?		Metta meditation
6	What is the definition of kamma?	Put paper here	Action – the idea that deliberate action affects a Buddhist's circumstances in this life and future lives
7	What is the definition of rebirth?		When somebody dies they will be reborn
8	How is the cycle of rebirth sometimes represented for Buddhists?	Put paper here	The wheel of Life (Bhavacakra)
9	What is meant by the Five Moral Precepts?		Commitments that most Buddhists use to guide their ethical decision-making
10	What are the Five Moral Precepts?	Put paper here	Do not take life, do not take what is not given, do not misuse the senses, do not speak falsehoods, do not take intoxicants that cloud the mind

Previous questions

Now go back and use these questions to check your knowledge of previous topics.

Questions / Answers

#	Questions		Answers
11	What is the word to describe a celebration for a religious reason?	Put paper here	Festival
12	Give two examples of Buddhist festivals.		Wesak, Parinirvana Day
13	What Sutra is normally read on Parinirvana Day?		Mahaparinirvana Sutra
14	In which Buddhist tradition are funerals typically inexpensive?	Put paper here	Theravada
15	What is the name of the beads used to help count the number of mantra recitations?		Mala beads

Practice

Exam-style questions

01 What term means loving kindness? **(1 mark)**

Put a tick (✓) in the box next to the correct answer.

A Karuna ☐

B Metta ☐

C Dukka ☐

D Nibbana (Nirvana) ☐

EXAM TIP

Remember to learn all the key terms on the specification.

02 Which **one** of the following is **not** a realm found on the Wheel of Life? **(1 mark)**

Put a tick (✓) in the box next to the correct answer.

A The realm of the angry ghosts ☐

B The realm of the humans ☐

C The realm of the gods ☐

D The realm of the dukkha ☐

03 Give **two** of the Five Moral Precepts. **(2 marks)**

04 Give **two** ways karuna can be expressed. **(2 marks)**

EXAM TIP

The examiner will only mark your first two answers on the two-mark questions, so do not waste time writing more than two.

05 Name two of the Six Perfections. **(2 marks)**

06 Give **two** reasons why ethical conduct is important in Buddhism. **(2 marks)**

07 Give **two** examples of unskilled actions. **(2 marks)**

EXAM TIP

Remember to be concise with your two-mark responses.

08 Explain **two** contrasting ways a Buddhist may make an ethical decision. **(4 marks)**

09 Explain **two** reasons why kamma is important in Buddhist ethical decision-making.

Refer to sacred writings or another source of Buddhist belief and teaching in your answer. **(5 marks)**

10 Explain **two** of the Five Moral Precepts.

Refer to sacred writings or another source of Buddhist belief and teaching in your answer. **(5 marks)**

EXAM TIP

Remember, you don't need to give the exact reference for a quotation – you just need to state the source of wisdom or authority, e.g., 'The Pali Canon states…', or 'The Dalai Lama says…', etc.

11 Explain **two** reasons why metta is important.

Refer to sacred writings or another source of Buddhist belief and teaching in your answer. **(5 marks)**

12 Explain **two** ethical teachings in Buddhism.

Refer to sacred writings or another source of Buddhist belief and teaching in your answer. **(5 marks)**

13 Explain **two** of the Six Perfections.

Refer to sacred writings or another source of Buddhist belief and teaching in your answer. **(5 marks)**

14 'It is impossible to show compassion to everybody.'

Evaluate this statement.

In your answer you should:

- refer to Buddhist teaching
- give reasoned arguments to support this statement
- give reasoned arguments to support a different point of view
- reach a justified conclusion. **(12 marks)**

(+ SPaG 3 marks)

> **EXAM TIP**
>
> Remember the 12-mark question assesses A02 skills. This means you need to engage in evaluation of ideas. Consider why some arguments are stronger, or weaker than others. Justify this reason.

15 'The Five Moral Precepts are too idealistic for the world today.'

Evaluate this statement.

In your answer you should:

- refer to Buddhist teaching
- give reasoned arguments to support this statement
- give reasoned arguments to support a different point of view
- reach a justified conclusion. **(12 marks)**

(+ SPaG 3 marks)

16 'The Five Moral Precepts are all a Buddhist needs to be moral.'

Evaluate this statement.

In your answer you should:

- refer to Buddhist teaching
- give reasoned arguments to support this statement
- give reasoned arguments to support a different point of view
- reach a justified conclusion. **(12 marks)**

(+ SPaG 3 marks)

⚙ Knowledge

19 A: Sex

Human sexuality

Sexuality can be a controversial topic in society and within religions.

 Heterosexuality – where someone is sexually attracted to people of the opposite sex.

 Homosexuality – where someone is sexually attracted to people of the same sex.

⬇

† Christian views on homosexuality

Broadly there are three different views within Christianity about homosexuality, and each one interprets Bible references differently.

Some Christians accept homosexuality	Some Christians accept being homosexual but do not accept homosexual acts	Some Christians do not accept homosexuality
• Homosexuals are part of God's creation and everyone should be treated with respect. • Texts that forbid homosexuality have been misinterpreted as they are often dependent on the time of writing. Some Christian churches will marry same-sex couples, and some will bless a **civil marriage**.	• Being **homosexual** is accepted as we are all part of God's creation but taking part in homosexual acts is not acceptable. • God told humans to procreate '*be fruitful*' but homosexual couples are not able to do this naturally so they cannot fulfil God's command. • Catholic teachings say that sex is for **procreation**, so homosexuals should remain **chaste**. • Bible texts that forbid homosexual acts support this view. These Christian churches will not marry or bless same-sex couples.	• Heterosexuality is part of God's plan for humans, and the Bible speaks about a man and a woman as husband and wife, for example, Adam and Eve (the first husband and wife in the Bible). • The Bible speaks about procreation as a command from God ('*be fruitful*') and only **heterosexual** couples can do this naturally. • Texts in the Bible that forbid homosexual acts are taken literally. These Christian churches will not marry or bless same-sex couples.
❝ *So, God created mankind in his own image, in the image of God he created them; male and female he created them.* ❞ (Genesis 1:27)	❝ *God blessed them and said to them, Be fruitful and increase in number….* ❞ (Genesis 1:28)	❝ *Do not have sexual relations with a man as one does with a woman; that is detestable.* ❞ (Leviticus 18:22)

> **REVISION TIP** 📝
>
> Where there are different views, you don't need to know the different Christian denominations. You can use 'Some Christians' and 'Other Christians' in your answer.

☸ Buddhist views on homosexuality

Buddhists who reject homosexuality	**Buddhists who accept homosexuality**
• Some Buddhist teachers have forbidden sexual activity between people of the same sex, primarily as it does not allow for procreation. • Homosexuality is illegal in some Buddhist-majority countries, and some have severe prison sentences for engaging in homosexual acts; however, this could be a cultural influence rather than a religious one. • Neither homosexual nor heterosexual relationships that are rooted in lust and exploitation would be permitted in Buddhism.	• Many Buddhists are completely accepting of homosexual relationships. There are many lesbian, gay and bisexual Buddhists and some Buddhist leaders have voiced support for homosexual relationships, or have become more accepting over the years, for example, the Dalai Lama. • Socially engaged Buddhists have campaigned to overturn the ban on homosexuality in many Buddhist-majority countries, for example, Chao-hwei Shih in Taiwan. • Many Buddhists focus on the quality of a relationship, rather than who it involves: a relationship rooted in the principles of metta, karuna, and the avoidance of dukkha would be accepted.

> ❝ *Homosexuality contradicts procreation and is a form of sexual misconduct.* ❞
> (Master Hsuan Hua)

> ❝ *…abandoning illicit (forbidden) sex, the disciple of the noble ones abstains from illicit sex.* ❞
> (Pali Canon)

> ❝ *If two people, a couple, really feel that way, it's more practical, more satisfaction, and both sides fully agree, then okay!* ❞
> (Dalai Lama)

> ❝ *If two people are of the same gender… their sexual actions are motivated by love… and give comfort, that wouldn't necessarily be an immoral act.* ❞
> (Shravasti Dhammika, Theravada monk)

⚙ Knowledge

19 A: Sex

Sexual relationships before and outside of marriage (adultery)

	† Christianity	☸ Buddhism
Sex before marriage (accepted)	Some Christians accept sex before marriage as part of a loving, committed relationship that will end in marriage.	No Buddhist teaching explicitly forbids sex before marriage. Marriage is considered a civil matter and, especially in the West, many Buddhists have sexual relationships without being married.
Sex before marriage (not accepted)	Many Christians are against sex before marriage as sex is considered a gift from God for married couples to share love, procreate, and be part of a lifelong union.	Some Buddhists may view sex before marriage as 'sexual misconduct' which is prohibited by the Buddha's Dharma – the **Five Moral Precepts**.
Sexual relationships outside of marriage (**adultery**)	Christianity forbids adultery as it breaks the marriage **vows** and goes against Biblical teaching. **❝** *You shall not commit adultery.* **❞** (Exodus 20:14)	Many Buddhists believe adultery does not align with Buddhist ethical ideals. For example, being unfaithful will lead to dukkha, as partners will be hurt. It therefore fails to treat others with metta and karuna. In the Pali Canon, the Buddha suggests that those actions led by desire, including adultery, often lead to an evil outcome.

Contraception and family planning

Contraception can be used to:

- prevent unwanted pregnancies
- ensure all children born are wanted and can be cared for
- prevent sexually transmitted diseases (STDs).

REVISION TIP

Remember that contraception stops conception – 'contra' means 'against' or 'opposite'.

There are different methods of contraception. Some people use them to help with **family planning** – to control when and how many children they have.

Method	Description	Advantages	Disadvantages
Artificial methods	Stop the sperm from reaching the egg (barrier method), for example, condom, diaphragm.	• Cheap • Widely available in many countries. • Condoms help prevent sexually transmitted infections.	• Not 100% reliable in preventing pregnancy. • Must be used correctly.
	Change hormones to prevent **conception** (the sperm fertilising the egg), for example, the pill, the coil.	• Widely available in many countries.	• Not 100% reliable in preventing pregnancy. • Must be used correctly.
	Methods that make it impossible to conceive due to surgery on sexual organs, for example, sterilisation.	• Most reliable way of preventing pregnancy.	• Difficult to reverse.

Contraception and family planning

Method	Description	Advantages	Disadvantages
The rhythm method	Only having sex at certain times during a woman's menstrual cycle (when she is less likely to conceive).	• Uses the woman's natural cycle. • Free	• Very unreliable at preventing pregnancy. • Relies on woman tracking her monthly cycle.
Withdrawal	Stopping sex just before the male ejaculates as a way of trying to stop sperm being able to fertilise.	• Can prevent fertilisation. • Free	• Very unreliable at preventing pregnancy.

† Christian attitudes to contraception and family planning

- In Genesis 1:28, God tells humans to "be fruitful and increase in number" – having children can be part of the role of being a good Christian.
- Children should be born within marriage.

Church of England	The Catholic Church	The Orthodox Church
• Children should be planned for so that they can be cared and provided for, as a blessing. • Contraception helps to strengthen a relationship before having children by allowing a couple to enjoy sex without risk of pregnancy and avoids harming the mother's health by spacing out births. • The Church of England approved the use of artificial contraception in 1930.	• Does not allow the use of artificial contraception because: – sex is for making new life and expressing love – it goes against natural law (the moral principles that are part of human nature) and prevents God's plan for having children. • However, the rhythm method can be used to try to ensure children can be cared for, and the woman's health is considered.	Does not allow the use of artificial contraception because: • God's purpose for marriage is to have children • artificial contraception goes against natural law.

☸ Buddhist attitudes to contraception and family planning

- Some Buddhists allow contraception – it may result in the most metta and karuna (e.g., if a family are struggling financially, another child may lead to greater suffering).
- The Dalai Lama advocates for the use of contraception in some situations. For example, in a talk about the environment, he suggests contraception may be beneficial as it will help limit the population, and thus use of the world's resources.
- There is no religious duty in Buddhism to have children. Some Buddhists may use contraception, if they do not want children.

Key terms Make sure you can write a definition for these key terms

civil marriage   homosexual   procreation   chaste
heterosexual   Five Moral Precepts   vows   adultery
contraception   family planning   conception

Retrieval

Learn the answers to the questions below, then cover the answers column with a piece of paper and write as many as you can. Check and repeat.

Questions	Answers
1 Complete the quotation: "*Be _____ and increase in number...*" (Genesis 1:28)	Fruitful
2 Who were the first husband and wife in the Bible?	Adam and Eve
3 Give one example of a Buddhist teacher who has forbidden homosexual activity.	Master Hsuan Hua
4 Where is it said that adultery is an "*evil the wise never praise*"?	The Pali Canon
5 Give one possible benefit of using contraception.	One from: prevent unwanted pregnancies / ensure all children born are wanted and can be cared for / control population growth / prevent sexually transmitted diseases
6 Name one type of artificial contraception.	One from: condom / the Pill / sterilisation / the coil / diaphragm
7 Which method of family planning does the Catholic Church allow to be used?	The rhythm method
8 In which year did the Church of England approve the use of artificial contraception?	1930
9 What do many Christians consider married couples sharing love, procreation and being part of a lifelong union to be?	A gift from God
10 What might some Buddhists consider sex before marriage to be, according to the Five Moral Precepts?	Sexual misconduct

Put paper here

Exam-style questions

01   Which **one** of these means 'to be attracted to members of the same sex'?   **(1 mark)**

Put a tick (✓) in the box next to the correct answer.

A   Sex before marriage ☐

B   Heterosexuality ☐

C   Homosexuality ☐

D   Same-sex marriage ☐

02   Which **one** of these is **not** a method of artificial contraception?   **(1 mark)**

Put a tick (✓) in the box next to the correct answer.

A   Condom ☐

B   The Pill ☐

C   Sterilisation ☐

D   Conception ☐

03   Name **two** types of artificial contraception.   **(2 marks)**

04   Give **two** reasons why a couple may use contraception.   **(2 marks)**

05   Explain **two** contrasting religious beliefs about sexual relationships outside of marriage.

In your answer you must refer to one or more religious traditions.   **(4 marks)**

> **EXAM TIP**
>
> If the question says 'contrasting', make sure your answer gives two different views. They don't have to be the exact opposite.

06   Explain **two** religious beliefs about family planning.

Refer to sacred writings or another source of religious belief and teaching in your answer.   **(5 marks)**

> **EXAM TIP**
>
> Remember, you must name the piece of sacred writing or source of authority in your answer, for example, The Bible, The Pali Canon, etc.

07   'Sex should only take place between a married couple.'

Evaluate this statement.

In your answer you:

- should give reasoned arguments in support of this statement
- should give reasoned arguments to support a different point of view
- should refer to religious arguments
- may refer to non-religious arguments
- should reach a justified conclusion.   **(12 marks)**

   (+ SPaG 3 marks)

20 A: Marriage and divorce

The nature and purpose of marriage

In Great Britain, marriage is a legal contract between two people that provides legal and financial rights to each partner. A few countries allow **polygamy** (being married to more than one person at a time), but Great Britain does not.

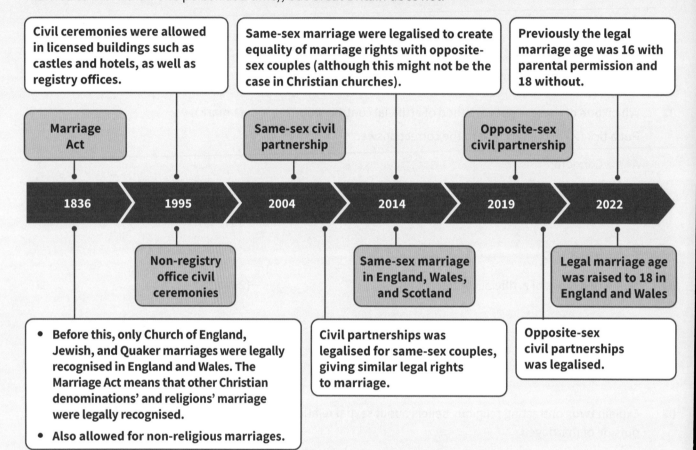

Civil ceremonies were allowed in licensed buildings such as castles and hotels, as well as registry offices.

Same-sex marriage were legalised to create equality of marriage rights with opposite-sex couples (although this might not be the case in Christian churches).

Previously the legal marriage age was 16 with parental permission and 18 without.

Marriage Act — 1836

Same-sex civil partnership — 2004

Opposite-sex civil partnership — 2019

1836 — 1995 — 2004 — 2014 — 2019 — 2022

Non-registry office civil ceremonies — 1995

Same-sex marriage in England, Wales, and Scotland — 2014

Legal marriage age was raised to 18 in England and Wales — 2022

- Before this, only Church of England, Jewish, and Quaker marriages were legally recognised in England and Wales. The Marriage Act means that other Christian denominations' and religions' marriage were legally recognised.
- Also allowed for non-religious marriages.

Civil partnerships was legalised for same-sex couples, giving similar legal rights to marriage.

Opposite-sex civil partnerships was legalised.

* Civil ceremonies, of any type, cannot involve religion or mention religious beliefs as part of the process.

Facts about marriage in Great Britain

- The number of people who choose to marry is in decline, particularly those opting for religious ceremonies.
- More couples live together for long periods of time before marrying; some never marry at all.
- The average age for first-time heterosexual marriage has increased: in 1970, it was 24.7 for women and 27.2 for men; in 2019, it had risen to 32.3 for women and 34.3 for men.

† The nature and purpose of marriage in Christianity

Marriage is one of God's gifts to humans at creation.

- It is a **sacrament**: an outward expression of an inner grace.
- Marriage is a lifelong union blessed by God, which reflects the sacrificial love of Jesus, and a covenant (agreement) before God in which the couple vow (promise) to live faithfully together until they die.
- It is a physical and spiritual union which is a loving relationship:

> **"** Husbands, love your wives, just as Christ loved the church and gave himself up for her. **"**
> (Ephesians 5:25)

- It is the right place for having sex and for having children.
- It provides stability and is a foundation for family life and the wider society.
- The Bible only mentions heterosexual marriage:

> **"** That is why a man leaves his father and mother and is united to his wife, and they become one flesh. **"**
> (Genesis 2:24)

- The Christian marriage vows (promises) show the commitment made between the couple, in front of God.

⊛ The nature and purpose of marriage in Buddhism

> **"** From the Buddhist point of view, marriage is neither holy nor unholy. **"**
> (Dhammananda)

- Buddhist marriage is not a religious obligation or duty; it is not something prescribed by the Buddha's **Dhamma** (Dharma).
- It is undertaken for many reasons and may be influenced by personal choice, family and cultural norms.
- It is mostly egarded as a **secular** matter, not religious. Theravadin monks or nuns may bless a couple, but must not perform the ceremony. In some traditions, in some countries, a Buddhist leader may be licensed to perform the legal ceremony.

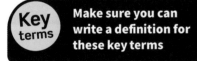

Key terms Make sure you can write a definition for these key terms

polygamy   sacrament   Dhamma (Dharma)   secular

⚙ Knowledge

20 A: Marriage and divorce

Same-sex marriage and cohabitation

Same-sex marriage

✝ Christianity	☸ Buddhism
• Most Christian denominations do not allow same-sex marriage. • The Bible only mentions heterosexual marriage. • One of the main purposes of marriage is to have children; homosexual couples cannot do this naturally.	• Many Buddhist-majority countries do not allow same-sex marriage, although this is changing. • Some Buddhist teachers do not allow same-sex marriage, as same-sex couples cannot conceive naturally. • Other Buddhist leaders, such as the Dalai Lama, have more recently suggested that same-sex marriages are 'okay'.

Cohabitation

✝ Christianity	☸ Buddhism
• Many Christian denominations do not permit **cohabitation** as it is likely that sex before marriage will occur. • Some Christians accept that, while marriage is the ideal, if people live together in a faithful, loving, and committed way without being married then cohabitation may be permitted.	• Buddhism does not teach that cohabitation is wrong – the quality of the partnership is more important than its label and status. If a cohabiting couple practise Buddhist values (e.g., metta, karuna, etc.) then it is permissible. • Some Buddhist-majority countries have societal norms that discourage cohabitation, but these do not stem from the Buddha's Dhamma (Dharma).

Divorce and remarriage

Divorce is the legal ending of a marriage. There are many different reasons why a marriage may fail and end in divorce. These can include:

- people changing, growing apart, and falling out of love
- adultery
- domestic violence or abuse
- illness or disability.

Remarriage is when a person gets married again, following a divorce. Remarriage is legally allowed in Great Britain, but different Christian churches may have restrictions on it.

Allowing divorce	Against divorce
• It is the most compassionate thing to do if there is unhappiness in the marriage.	• It goes against the **sanctity** of marriage vows.
• It might be better for children for their parents to be apart.	• It can negatively affect children.

† Divorce and remarriage in Christianity

 When divorce and remarriage are accepted in Christianity

- Some texts imply that Jesus allows divorce in certain situations:

  > 66 *But I tell you that anyone who divorces his wife, except for sexual immorality, makes her the victim of adultery, and anyone who marries a divorced woman commits adultery.* 99
  >
  > (Matthew 5:32)

- Some Christians believe that divorce is the lesser of two evils, so it is better to divorce than to have an unhappy marriage.
- Some Christian denominations allow divorce and remarriage in certain circumstances.
- The Church of England have allowed remarriage in certain circumstances since 2002, although it is a priest's decision if they want to perform the ceremony.

 When divorce and remarriage are not accepted in Christianity

- Jesus condemns divorce:

  > 66 *Anyone who divorces his wife and marries another woman commits adultery against her.*
  >
  > *And if she divorces her husband and marries another man, she commits adultery.* 99
  >
  > (Mark 10:11–12)

- **Sanctity of marriage vows** – these are sacred and in front of, and with, God: 'Till death us do part'.
- Marriage is a sacred union between the couple and God:

  > 66 *So they are no longer two, but one flesh.*
  >
  > *Therefore, what God has joined together, let no one separate.* 99   (Matthew 19:6)

- In the Catholic Church, marriage is a sacrament that cannot be ended by divorce. Couples may separate or get a legal divorce. However, if the marriage is declared void, it may be **annulled** in specific circumstances, such as mental incapacity or marriage by force.

☸ Divorce and remarriage in Buddhism

- Buddhists do not have any official teachings on divorce or remarriage. If it is what those involved want and they are legally able to do so, it is permitted.

- Many Buddhists support divorce if it demonstrates metta and karuna, especially if the marriage is becoming acrimonious, and there are children involved.

- Remarriage is an acceptable practice for most Buddhists as it typically reduces the dukkha of the couple, allowing them happiness in their new relationship.

- There may be cultural norms in Buddhist countries that discourage couples from divorcing and remarrying.

- The Buddhist monk teaches that if a relationship is filled with "jealously, anger and hatred, [couples] should have the liberty to separate and live peacefully."

 Key terms Make sure you can write a definition for these key terms

cohabitation   divorce   remarriage   sanctity of marriage vows   annulled

Retrieval

Learn the answers to the questions below, then cover the answers column with a piece of paper and write as many as you can. Check and repeat.

Questions | Answers

	Questions	Answers
1	What Buddhist teaching influences Buddhist attitude towards remarriage?	Dukkha
2	What is the correct word for the promises made during a Christian marriage ceremony?	Vows
3	Which Buddhist leader said same-sex marriage was 'okay'?	The Dalai Lama
4	What is cohabitation?	Living together without being married
5	For what reason does Jesus allow divorce in Matthew 5:32?	Sexual immorality
6	Which Christian denomination does not allow divorce but may annul a marriage if it is void?	The Catholic Church
7	How does Dhammananda describe marriage?	Neither holy nor unholy
8	Fill in the missing words: If a relationship is filled with "_____, _____ and _____." [couples] *should have the liberty to separate and live peacefully.*" (Dhammananda)	Jealousy, anger, hatred
9	Who may bless a Buddhist marriage, but not perform it?	Theravadin monks or nuns
10	What is not prescribed as a religious obligation or duty within the Buddha's Dhamma (Dharma)?	Marriage

Put paper here

Previous questions

Now go back and use these questions to check your knowledge of previous topics.

Questions | Answers

	Questions	Answers
11	Complete the quotation: "*Be _____ and increase in number…*" (Genesis 1:28)	Fruitful
12	Who were the first husband and wife in the Bible?	Adam and Eve
13	Give one example of a Buddhist teacher who has forbidden homosexual activity.	Master Hsuan Hua
14	Complete the quotation: "*…abandoning _____ sex, the disciple of the noble ones abstains from _____ sex.*" (Pali Canon)	Illicit x2

Put paper here

Exam-style questions

01 Which **one** of these means living together without being married? **(1 mark)**

Put a tick (✓) in the box next to the correct answer.

A	Cohabitation	☐
B	Contraception	☐
C	Annulment	☐
D	Vows	☐

02 Which **one** of these is the Catholic practice of declaring a marriage void? **(1 mark)**

Put a tick (✓) in the box next to the correct answer.

A	Cohabitation	☐
B	Remarriage	☐
C	Divorce	☐
D	Annulment	☐

03 Give **two** reasons why a couple may divorce. **(2 marks)**

04 Give **two** purposes of marriage for religious believers. **(2 marks)**

05 Explain **two** contrasting religious beliefs about same-sex marriage.
In your answer you must refer to one or more religious traditions. **(4 marks)**

> **EXAM TIP**
> A four-mark question requires two developed points. Show the examiner you have done this by writing in two separate paragraphs.

06 Explain **two** religious beliefs about cohabitation.
Refer to sacred writings or another source of religious belief and teaching in your answer. **(5 marks)**

07 'All marriages should last until death.'
Evaluate this statement.
In your answer you:
- should give reasoned arguments in support of this statement
- should give reasoned arguments to support a different point of view
- should refer to religious arguments
- may refer to non-religious arguments
- should reach a justified conclusion. **(12 marks)**

(+ SPaG 3 marks)

> **EXAM TIP**
> Remember to read the statement carefully and use the words from it in your answer to ensure you answer it fully.

⚙ Knowledge

21 A: Families

† The role of parents and children in Christianity

The Bible says that children should support and look after their parents, including when they get old:

> 66 *Anyone who does not provide for their relatives, and especially for their own household, has denied the faith and is worse than an unbeliever.* 99
>
> (1 Timothy 5:8)

Children should respect, love and honour their parents. The Bible says:

> 66 *Honour your father and your mother...* 99
>
> (Exodus 20:12)

Parents should provide for, love, care and protect their children, showing them right and wrong. Catholic parents believe:

> 66 *Here one learns endurance and the joy of work [...] love, generous – and even repeated – forgiveness, and above all divine worship in prayer and the offering of one's life.* 99
>
> (Catechism 1657)

☸ The role of parents and children in Buddhism

There is no religious expectation that Buddhist couples **procreate**, but if they do, family life should be based on love and respect for one another.

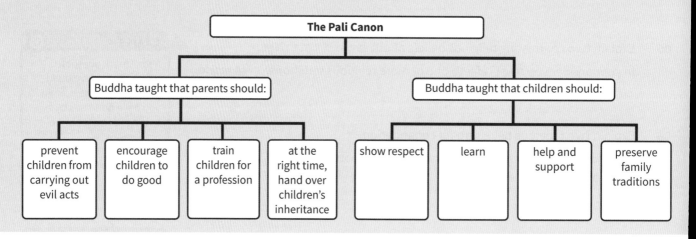

The purpose of families

Different views on the purpose of families include:

- procreation (having children)
- providing stability for children
- protecting children
- educating children in a faith.

Different types of families	
Single-parent family	One parent with a child or children.
Extended family	A family that extends beyond parents and their child or children by including grandparents and other relatives.
Nuclear family	A couple and their child or children.
Step-family	A family that is formed on the remarriage of a divorced or widowed person and that includes a child or children.
Same-sex parent family	People of the same sex who are raising a child or children together, which can be as a nuclear/extended family, etc.

- Many people believe that the ideal family types in Christianity and Buddhism are the nuclear family and the extended family. In many Buddhist-majority countries, extended families are very common.
- However, many also understand that marriages don't always work out, and this may result in a single-parent family or step-family.

Contemporary family issues

- Same-sex marriage is legal in Great Britain, and some Christian and Buddhist groups believe that same-sex parents can also provide stability, love, and happiness for their children.
- While polygamy (having more than one wife at the same time) is illegal in Great Britain, it is legal in some countries around the world, for example, Iran, and Saudi Arabia.
- Polygamy is generally not permitted in Christianity.
- In Buddhism, there have been historic instances of polygamy being accepted and legal in Buddhist-majority countries, and the Buddha does not expressly forbid the practice. However, it is not encouraged as it will likely result in those in the relationship experiencing dukkha or encourage feelings of jealously and hatred.

REVISION TIP

You can use the information about views on homosexuality to support your points on the topic of same-sex parents too.

Key terms Make sure you can write a definition for these key terms

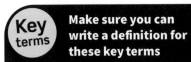

procreate   single-parent family   extended family   nuclear family
step-family   same-sex parent family

Retrieval

Learn the answers to the questions below, then cover the answers column with a piece of paper and write as many as you can. Check and repeat.

Questions	Answers
1. Which family type includes only a mother, a father, and a child or children?	Nuclear family
2. Which type of family is common in Buddhist-majority countries?	Extended family
3. Give one purpose of families.	One from: to procreate (having children) / to provide stability for children / to protect children / to educate children in a faith
4. Complete this quotation from the Bible: "_____ your father and your mother." (Exodus 20:12)	Honour
5. What is meant by 'polygamy'?	Having more than one wife at the same time
6. Is Buddhism a family-centred religion?	No, it is up to the couple to decide if they want a family
7. What is one role of parents in Buddhism?	One from: prevent children from carrying out evil acts / encourage children to do good / train children for a profession / at the right time, hand over children's inheritance
8. What is meant by 'procreate'?	Having children
9. Which family type includes a mother, a father, a child or children and other family members, for example, grandparents?	Extended family

Put paper here

Previous questions

Now go back and use these questions to check your knowledge of previous topics.

Questions	Answers
10. Which Buddhist leader said same-sex marriage was 'okay'?	The Dalai Lama
11. Which Christian denomination does not allow divorce but may annul a marriage if it is void?	The Catholic Church
12. How does Dhammananda describe marriage?	Neither holy nor unholy
13. Give one example of a Buddhist teacher who has forbidden homosexual activity.	Master Hsuan Hua

Put paper here

Exam-style questions

01 Which **one** of these is the practice of having more than one wife or husband?

(1 mark)

Put a tick (✔) in the box next to the correct answer.

A   Divorce   ☐

B   Polygamy   ☐

C   Remarriage   ☐

D   Adultery   ☐

02 Which **one** of these is a family that is formed on the remarriage of a divorced or widowed person which includes a child or children? **(1 mark)**

Put a tick (✔) in the box next to the correct answer.

A   Nuclear family   ☐

B   Extended family   ☐

C   Same-sex parent family   ☐

D   Step-family   ☐

03 Give **two** roles of parents. **(2 marks)**

> **EXAM TIP**
>
> In two-mark questions you do not have to write in full sentences. Answers can be a single word or short phrases.

04 Give **two** purposes of families. **(2 marks)**

05 Explain **two** similar religious beliefs on same-sex parents.

In your answer you must refer to one or more religious traditions. **(4 marks)**

> **EXAM TIP**
>
> 'Similar' does not mean that the beliefs have to be exactly the same. Your two points just need to agree with each other. For example, it can be the similar belief from two different religions.

06 Explain **two** religious beliefs about polygamy.

Refer to sacred writings or another source of religious belief and teaching in your answer. **(5 marks)**

> **EXAM TIP**
>
> Remember to name the religion that you are writing about so the examiner will know whether your answer is correct.

07 'Nuclear families are the ideal type of family.'

Evaluate this statement.

In your answer you:

- should give reasoned arguments in support of this statement
- should give reasoned arguments to support a different point of view
- should refer to religious arguments
- may refer to non-religious arguments
- should reach a justified conclusion.

(12 marks)

(+ SPaG 3 marks)

⚙ Knowledge

22 A: Gender equality

Gender equality, prejudice, and discrimination

In the past, men and women have often been thought of and treated differently.

- **Gender prejudice** occurs when people believe that men and women should only do certain things or have certain jobs. For example, the role of a woman was to stay in the home and look after children, while men went out to work.

- Women did not have the same rights as men and often faced **discrimination**. For example, women were not allowed to do certain jobs and did not have the right to vote or divorce.

- Laws such as The Equality Act (2010) have made it illegal to discriminate by treating men and women differently in Great Britain. This has promoted gender **equality**.

- However, there is still evidence that women are not treated equally to men, for example, in the amount they are paid at work and the job opportunities available to them.

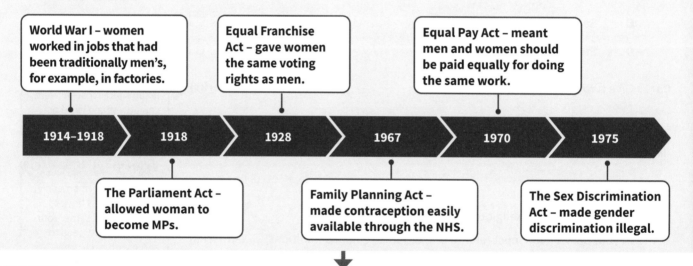

| World War I – women worked in jobs that had been traditionally men's, for example, in factories. | | Equal Franchise Act – gave women the same voting rights as men. | | | Equal Pay Act – meant men and women should be paid equally for doing the same work. | |

1914–1918 > **1918** > **1928** > **1967** > **1970** > **1975**

The Parliament Act – allowed woman to become MPs.

Family Planning Act – made contraception easily available through the NHS.

The Sex Discrimination Act – made gender discrimination illegal.

✝ Christian teachings on the roles of men and women

- The Bible says that God made both men and women in his image (Imago Dei):

  > ❝ So God created mankind in his own image, in the image of God he created them; male and female he created them. ❞ (Genesis 1:27)

- Jesus treated women with respect, and they are often mentioned in the Gospel accounts of his life. In the Bible, St Paul emphasises equality when he says:

  > ❝ There is neither Jew nor Gentile, neither slave nor free, nor is there male and female, for you are all one in Christ Jesus. ❞ (Galatians 3:28)

- Traditional Christian views were that the woman's role is to work in the home and look after children and that a man's role is to work to provide for the family.

- As society has changed, many Christians see these roles as more flexible: both men and women can work in the home and bring up children, and both can have jobs.

✿ Buddhist teachings on the roles of men and women

- The Buddha ordained women as nuns into the Sangha. His aunt, Mahapajapati Gotami, became the first Buddhist nun (bhikkhuni). Some see this as revolutionary or radically going against the societal norms of the times. There have been historical and contemporary examples of women in Buddhism.

- However, the Buddha initially refused to ordain women into the monastic Sangha. It was common not to give religious rights to women at the time of the Buddha, so the initial exclusion of women is likely to have been a societal or cultural decision, rather than a religious one. However, the true reason can never be fully known.

- Against quality, the Pali Canon states:

> ❝ ... if females had not gained the going forth […] the spiritual life would have lasted long. The true teaching would have remained for a thousand years. But since they have gained the going forth […] the true teaching will remain only five hundred years. ❞

- In favour of equality, the Lotus Sutra states:

> ❝ ...and so always teach the Dhamma equally to all. ❞

- In 2015, the Dalai Lama was quoted as saying that he sees no reason why a future Dalai Lama could not be a woman. Many traditions, including Theravada Buddhism, are today reviving women's ordination. This is because some Mahayana traditions have lineages of nuns, and they are using their authority to ordain women within and outside of Mahayana Buddhism. However, this practice is debated, and some do not accept it as valid and authoritative.

- However, many conservative Theravada traditions do not allow women to be ordained into the Sangha still today. There may continue to be reasons for this outside Buddhism, for example, patriarchy. There are some religiously significant arguments which are used to exclude women in the contemporary world too. When originally ordaining nuns, the Buddha ruled that women could only receive ordination from both nuns and monks. Since many traditions no longer have women who are ordained, some argue it is not possible to ordain women today.

> ❝ A trainee nun... should seek ordination from the communities of both monks and nuns. ❞
> (Pali Canon)

- There are many organisations campaigning for gender equality in Buddhism. Sakyadhita, are an International Association of Buddhist Women.

◀ Buddhist nuns.

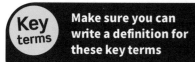 **Key terms** Make sure you can write a definition for these key terms

gender prejudice   discrimination   equality

⇄ Retrieval

Learn the answers to the questions below, then cover the answers column with a piece of paper and write as many as you can. Check and repeat.

Questions

Answers

	Questions	Answers
1	What do some Theravada traditions believe has been broken, resulting in women not being able to be ordained?	The lineage of monks and nuns
2	Name a law that made it illegal to discriminate by treating men and women differently in Great Britain.	The Equality Act (2010)
3	Complete the quotation: "*There is neither Jew nor Gentile, neither slave nor free, nor is there male and female, for you are all _____ in Christ Jesus.*" (Galatians 3:28)	One
4	Who was the first ordained Buddhist nun?	The Buddha's aunt – Mahapajapati Gotami
5	Complete this quotation: "*... so always teach the Dhamma _____ to all.*"	Equally

Put paper here

Previous questions

Now go back and use these questions to check your knowledge of previous topics.

Questions

Answers

	Questions	Answers
6	Give one possible benefit of using contraception.	One from: prevent unwanted pregnancies / ensure all children born are wanted and can be cared for / control population growth / prevent sexually transmitted diseases
7	What is the correct word for the promises made during a Christian marriage ceremony?	Vows
8	Which family type includes only a mother, a father, and a child or children?	Nuclear family
9	Which family type includes a mother, a father, a child or children and other family members, for example, grandparents?	Extended family
10	Give one purpose of families.	One from: to procreate (having children) / to provide stability for children / to protect children / to educate children in a faith
11	Which Buddhist leader said same-sex marriage was 'okay'?	The Dalai Lama
12	Where is it said that adultery is an "*evil the wise never praise*"?	The Pali Canon

Put paper here

Exam-style questions

01 Which **one** of these means giving people the same rights and opportunities regardless of whether they are male or female? **(1 mark)**

Put a tick (✓) in the box next to the correct answer.

A Gender equality ☐

B Sexism ☐

C Gender stereotyping ☐

D Gender roles ☐

EXAM TIP

Remember – don't spend too long on a one mark question, but do read the question and options carefully.

02 Which **one** of these is **not** a way in which women have been discriminated against in the past? **(1 mark)**

Put a tick (✓) in the box next to the correct answer.

A Right to vote ☐

B Right to divorce ☐

C Equal pay ☐

D Right to go on holiday ☐

03 Give **two** ways that someone may discriminate against a person due to gender. **(2 marks)**

04 Give **two** events in history that have influenced changes in women's rights. **(2 marks)**

05 Explain **two** similar religious beliefs about the roles of men and women.

In your answer you must refer to one or more religious traditions. **(4 marks)**

06 Explain **two** similar religious beliefs about gender equality.

Refer to sacred writings or another source of religious belief and teaching in your answer. **(5 marks)**

07 It is the role of both men and women to look after children.

Evaluate this statement.

In your answer you:

- should give reasoned arguments in support of this statement
- should give reasoned arguments to support a different point of view
- should refer to religious arguments
- may refer to non-religious arguments
- should reach a justified conclusion. **(12 marks)**

(+ SPaG 3 marks)

EXAM TIP

Use the bullet points to help ensure that you include everything needed in a 12-mark question.

Knowledge

23 B: The origins of the universe and human life

The origins of the universe

- If we look at how the world works, many things that exist seem amazing, for example, the Grand Canyon, the inside of a human eye or the vastness of the universe. These things give us a sense of **awe** and **wonder**. It may lead us to ask ourselves 'How was it created?', 'Who created it?', and 'Why?'.

- There are different ideas about the **origins of the universe**, based on the evidence people use to inform their view.

- Even within religions there are different views. Some of these are outlined below, but there are more.

Scientific view: The Big Bang

View and source of evidence	Detail	Quotation
Scientific view: The **Big Bang** - Red shift theory – the universe is still expanding. - We can detect radiation from the 'bang'.	- Most scientists agree the universe began approximately 13.8 billion years ago with a 'Big Bang'. - It expanded over time to create what we know as our solar system and planet Earth. - Scientists are unsure of the cause of the Big Bang and cannot explain it.	66 *...the universe has not existed forever. Rather, the universe, and time itself, had a beginning in the Big Bang, about 15 billion years ago.* 99 (Stephen Hawking)

† Christian views on the origins of the universe

View and source of evidence	Detail	Quotation
Christian view: **literal creation** - The Bible – the book of **Genesis** in the Old Testament	- Some Christians believe the universe was made in six days by God, and he rested on the seventh day. - On each day he created something different. - Some believe it was approximately 6 000 years ago (using Biblical chronology to work it out). - Some Christians believe that the original text for 'day' also means 'age', so this could have taken place over a much longer period of time than six periods of 24 hours.	66 *In the beginning God created the heavens and the earth.* 99 (Genesis 1:1)
Christian view: **theistic evolution** - The Bible - Scientific evidence (see above)	- Other Christians believe they can look at both the Bible and scientific evidence to see that while creation started with a 'Big Bang', something must have started it. - They believe this was God as the omnipotent creator. - They agree this would have been approximately 13.8 million years ago.	66 *And God said, 'Let there be light,' and there was light.* 99 (Genesis 1:3)

✸ Buddhist views on the origins of the universe

View and source of evidence	Detail	Quotation
Buddhist view	• Buddhism teaches that the universe does not have any origin and there is no creator god. • The origins of the universe fall under '**atakavacara**' – the Buddha's term for something beyond reasoning or unanswerable. • Buddhists do not think there is one point in time when it can be said the universe came into existence. • The Buddha taught that the universe is cyclical – the universe operates in cycles of existing–dying–existing. • Buddhists do not reject scientific theories such as the Big Bang. Contemporary thinking is very similar to ideas found in the Buddhist Dhamma (Dharma).	66 *The position that the cosmos is not eternal... does not lead to cessation; to calm, direct knowledge, full Awakening... A position, Vaccha, is something that a Tathagata has done away with...* 99 (The Buddha, Pali Canon)

The relationship between scientific and religious views

 Christianity

Some Christians say religion provides all the answers to our questions about the creation of the universe and that science doesn't. They believe God provides the explanation for both 'how' and 'why'.	Some Christians say science tells us 'how' creation occurred but the Bible tells us 'why', answering questions that science leaves unanswered, for example, 'what caused the Big Bang?'

 Buddhism

Many Buddhists do not see their religion as being in conflict with science, instead they see science and Buddhism as a dialogue.	The Dalai Lama is a supporter of the idea that Buddhism and Science are not in conflict. He has lectured many times on the relationship between the two worldviews: 66 *... if scientific analysis were conclusively to demonstrate certain claims in Buddhism to be false, then we must accept the findings of science and abandon those claims of Buddhism.* 99 [The Dalai Lama]

⚙ Knowledge

23 B: The origins of the universe and human life

The origins of human life

There are different views on how humans came into existence. People base their views on different sources of evidence. Even within religions there are different views. Some of these are outlined below, but there are more.

Scientific view: Evolution

Source of evidence	Detail
• Evidence of survival of the fittest. • Bones from humans' ancestors. • Genetic similarities between animals and humans.	• Humans have evolved over millions of years from single-celled creatures. • Only creatures that adapted to their environment survived over time (survival of the fittest).

↓

† Christian views on the origins of human life

View	Evidence/sources	Detail	Quotation
Christian – literal creation	The Bible – Genesis 1–2	• Some Christians believe that humans descended from the first two humans, Adam and Eve. • The Bible says that God created Adam from dust or clay and one version of the story says that Eve was made from his rib.	❝ *Then the Lord God formed a man from the dust of the ground and breathed into his nostrils the breath of life, and the man became a living being.* ❞ (Genesis 2:7)
Christian – theistic evolution	The Bible and scientific evidence (see above)	• Some Christians refer to scientific evidence and the Bible. • They believe God caused evolution to occur. • They believe the Bible is a story that tells us about God's relationship with humanity but is not a literal account of our origins.	❝ *So, God created mankind in his own image, in the image of God he created them; male and female he created them.* ❞ (Genesis 1:27)

☸ Buddhist views on the origins of human life

View	Detail	Evidence/sources	Quotation
Buddhism	• Buddhists do not think that humanity was created by God – they reject the idea of a creator god. • Many Buddhists see humanity's existence as cyclical. To them, being born is an example of a human rebirth. • **Dependent origination** suggests that everything in existence depends upon something else. Humanity arose when the necessary conditions were there.	The Pali Canon	❝ *There comes a time when, after a very long period has passed, this cosmos expands. As the cosmos expands, sentient beings… come back to this realm.* ❞ (Buddha, Pali Canon)

The relationship between scientific and religious views

✝ Christianity		Buddhism
Some Christians say the Bible tells them everything they need to know about the **origins of life**.	Other Christians say the scientific evidence of how humans evolved can work with the teachings in the Bible: the science tells us 'how' it happened and the Bible tells us 'why'.	Many Buddhists look to and support contemporary scientific thinking about the origins of humanity, for example, the theory of evolution. The Dalai Lama suggests: ❝ *…on the whole… the Darwinian theory of evolution… gives us a fairly coherent account of the evolution of human life on Earth.* ❞

REVISION TIP

Make sure you know the difference between a question on the 'origins of the universe' and the 'origins of human life' as you can be asked about either.

Key terms

Make sure you can write a definition for these key terms

awe   wonder   origins of the universe   Big Bang
literal creation   Genesis   theistic evolution   atakavacara
dependent origination   origins of life

⇄ Retrieval

Learn the answers to the questions below, then cover the answers column with a piece of paper and write as many as you can. Check and repeat.

Questions	Answers
1. What is the scientific theory of the origins of the universe known as?	The Big Bang
2. How long do Christian literal creationists believe it took for the universe to be created?	Six days/'ages'
3. What evidence do Christian literal creationists use to explain the origins of the universe?	The Bible
4. According to Christian literal creationists, who created the universe?	God
5. Complete the quotation: "In the beginning God created the _____ and the earth." (Genesis 1:1)	Heavens
6. What evidence do Christian theistic evolutionists use to explain the origins of the universe?	The Bible and scientific evidence
7. Complete the quotation: "And God said, 'Let there be _____,' and there was _____." (Genesis 1:3)	Light
8. What type of god is rejected by Buddhists?	A creator god
9. According to the Bible, who was the first human?	Adam
10. What is the name of the process by which humans develop from single-celled creatures over millions of years?	Evolution
11. What word did the Buddha give to questions surrounding the origins of the universe?	Atakavacara
12. For Buddhists, who created the universe?	Nobody, there is no creator. The Earth exists cyclically.
13. What aspect of the Buddha's Dhamma (Dharma) do Buddhists use to explain the origin of humanity?	Dependent origination
14. Who says: "... the theory of evolution... gives us a fairly coherent account of the evolution of human life on Earth."?	The Dalai Lama
15. Complete the quotation: There comes a time when, after a very long period has passed, this cosmos _____. As the cosmos expands, _____... come back to this realm.	*Expands, sentient being*

Put paper here

Exam-style questions

01 Which **one** of these books describes the process of creation in the Bible? **(1 mark)**

Put a tick (✓) in the box next to the correct answer.

A   Matthew   ☐

B   Psalms   ☐

C   Job   ☐

D   Genesis   ☐

02 Which **one** of these is the scientific theory of the origins of the universe? **(1 mark)**

Put a tick (✓) in the box next to the correct answer.

A   Creationism   ☐

B   Big Bang   ☐

C   Red shift theory   ☐

D   Genesis   ☐

03 Give **two** religious beliefs about the origins of human life. **(2 marks)**

> **EXAM TIP**
> In two-mark questions you do not have to write in full sentences. Answers can be a single word or short phrases.

04 Name **two** pieces of scientific evidence for evolution. **(2 marks)**

05 Explain **two** similar religious beliefs about the origins of human life.
In your answer you must refer to one or more religious traditions. **(4 marks)**

> **EXAM TIP**
> 'Similar' does not mean that the beliefs have to be exactly the same. Your two points just need to agree with each other.

06 Explain **two** views on the origins of human life.
Refer to sacred writings or another source of religious belief and teaching in your answer. **(5 marks)**

07 'Scientific and religious views on the origins of the universe are not compatible.'

Evaluate this statement. In your answer you:

- should give reasoned arguments in support of this statement
- should give reasoned arguments to support a different point of view
- should refer to religious arguments
- may refer to non-religious arguments
- should reach a justified conclusion. **(12 marks)**

(+ SpaG 3 marks)

> **EXAM TIP**
> Read the statement carefully. Use the words from it in your answer to ensure you fully answer the question.

⚙ Knowledge

24 B: The value of the universe

The value of the world and duty of human beings to protect it

Our planet is a one-off and special, so we should look after it.

Many humans believe

We have a **responsibility** to protect Earth from harm and should act as stewards of Earth.

Out of all the species on Earth, humans have **dominion** over it, with a **duty** to protect the other species we live with.

The use and abuse of the environment

- We use the planet and its resources in many ways to help us live.

- Nature gives us **natural resources** that come from the Earth itself, for example, trees and coal that we use for energy.

- Some energy resources are finite and **non-renewable**, so when we've used them all, there will be no more. These resources can cause **pollution** in the environment.

- However, we have developed **renewable** sources of energy which won't run out, and are less harmful to the environment.

Non-renewable/polluting resources
• Coal
• Oil
• Gas

Renewable/less polluting resources
• Solar power
• Wind power
• Wave power

Pollution

We also pollute the environment in other ways:

- Water pollution
- Litter, including plastic waste
- Soil pollution (from fertilisers).

Protecting the environment

We can help to protect the environment by:

- reducing the energy we use, for example, using public transport
- reusing items instead of throwing them away
- recycling, for example, plastic, glass, and paper.

† Christian views on protecting the environment

- The Bible teaches that creation belongs to God:

  > " *The Earth is the Lord's, and everything in it, the world, and all who live in it.* "
  >
  > (Psalm 24:1)

- God's creation promotes a sense of awe and wonder:

  > " *When I consider your heavens, the work of your fingers, the moon and the stars, which you have set in place, what is mankind that you are mindful of them, human beings that you care for them?* "
  >
  > (Psalm 8:3–4)

- However, the Bible says that God gave humans dominion over creation:

  > " *Then God said, 'Let us make mankind in our image, in our likeness, so that they may rule over the fish in the sea and the birds in the sky, over the livestock and all the wild animals, and over all the creatures that move along the ground.* "
  >
  > (Genesis 1:26)

- Most Christians believe it is humans' responsibility and duty to look after God's creation as stewards, as he gave Adam and Eve this responsibility in the **Garden of Eden**:

  > " *The Lord God took the man and put him in the Garden of Eden to work it and take care of it.* "
  >
  > (Genesis 2:15)

- Christian leaders, including the Pope, the leader of the Orthodox church and the Archbishop of Canterbury, have said that we should look after creation:

  > " *The Earth, our home, is beginning to look more and more like an immense pile of filth… There is an urgent need to develop policies so that, in the next few years, the emission of carbon dioxide and other highly polluting gases can be drastically reduced.* "
  >
  > (Pope Francis)

☸ Buddhist views on protecting the environment

- Dependent origination suggests that life is an interdependent web of conditions: if one aspect of the environment is mistreated, this will have far-reaching consequences. For example, greenhouse gases are warming the planet, resulting in melting ice and rising seas. This means that some areas of the world are experiencing more flooding and damage to population settlements.

- Many Buddhists become activists/ volunteers to make others aware of the damage being done to the environment.

- Some Buddhists are 'socially engaged' and use the Buddha's Dhamma (Dharma) to try to overcome environmental problems.

- Influenced by their religion, Buddhists may join secular organisations to tackle environmental problems. For example, within Extinction Rebellion, there is a group known as XR Buddhists.

- Many Buddhists follow ethical teachings given by the Buddha and Buddhist leaders to ensure the Earth is respected. For example, the Dalai Lama, when speaking about environmental conservation, says: '… *we have the capability, and the responsibility. We must act before it is too late.*'

- Many Buddhists apply the teaching of **ahimsa** (non-harm) to the Earth, acting like stewards towards its care.

⚙ Knowledge

24 B: The value of the universe

The use and abuse of animals

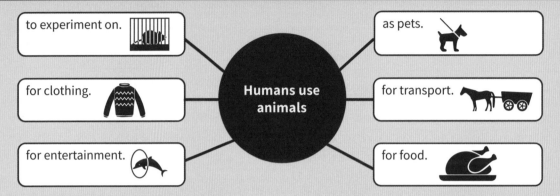

There are different views about the use of animals for our own benefit:

☒ Animals have their own rights and should not be subject to any pain or killing.

☑ Humans are superior to animals so we can use them to help make our lives better.

Animal experimentation

- Animals are used in experiments to ensure that what we use on humans is safe and works.

- In Great Britain, all medicines have to be trialled on animals (e.g., mice and rabbits) before they can be used on humans.

- However, testing on animals for cosmetics was made illegal in Great Britain in 1998.

Views on using animals for food

Reasons for using animals for food	Reasons for not using animals for food
☑ Humans have always eaten meat.	☒ Animals have the right to be unharmed.
☑ Our bodies need the nutrients from meat to stay healthy.	☒ We can live a healthy life without meat.
☑ Animals are not equal to humans and do not have the same rights.	☒ Mass farming of animals contributes to global warming.

> **REVISION TIP**
>
> These are 'non-religious' views so can be used in 12-mark questions.

 Key terms Make sure you can write a definition for these key terms

dominion   responsibility   duty   natural resources   non-renewable
pollution   renewable   Garden of Eden   ahimsa
animal experimentation   Eightfold Path   right livelihood

† Christian views on using animals for experimentation and food

- The Bible says animals should be cared for.

> 66 *The righteous care for the needs of their animals.* 99 (Proverbs 12:10)

- However, it says that God gave humans dominion over animals, which some Christians believe means we can use them as we need to:

> 66 *Then God said, 'Let us make mankind in our image, in our likeness, so that they may rule over the fish in the sea and the birds in the sky, over the livestock and all the wild animals, and over all the creatures that move along the ground.'* 99 (Genesis 1:26)

REVISION TIP

Read the whole of Genesis 1-2 in the Bible to help you understand and remember why creation is important in Christianity.

- Many Christians will only accept **animal experimentation** for medicines as this is necessary to help humans cure diseases.

- The Bible is clear that humans can eat animals for food:

> 66 *Everything that lives and moves about will be food for you.* 99 (Genesis 9:3)

However, the Bible says humans can choose if they want to eat meat and shouldn't be judged if they do or do not.

⌘ Buddhist views on using animals for experimentation and food

Buddhists are generally against using animals for experimentation and food.

- The first of the Five Moral Precepts teaches that Buddhists should abstain from killing or harming living beings, including animals. Many Buddhists are therefore vegetarian or vegan.

> 66 *We cannot support any act of killing; no killing can be justified... By being vegetarian, we are going in the direction of nonviolence.* 99 (Thich Nhat Hanh)

- The **Eightfold Path** teaches Buddhists to have a '**right livelihood**'. This means many Buddhists would not kill animals or harm them as part of their work, for example, food processing or laboratory testing.

- Dependent origination teaches that all life is interconnected and interdependent, so behaviour towards animals will, in some way, impact humans.

- Buddhist ethical teachings – metta, karuna, ahimsa – should apply to animals, so to cause them harm would be unskilful. This may have consequences for the Buddhist's future rebirth.

Some Buddhists argue that it is sometimes acceptable to kill or harm an animal. Such situations may include:

- developing medical treatment to save the lives of millions

- eating meat when donated, as part of alms-giving

- sacrificing and eating the meat of animals as part of worship (some Newar Buddhists in Nepal).

⇄ Retrieval

Learn the answers to the questions below, then cover the answers column with a piece of paper and write as many as you can. Check and repeat.

Questions | Answers

	Questions	Answers
1	Give one way that humans can help to protect the environment.	One from: reducing the energy we use / reusing items instead of throwing them away / recycling
2	Name one type of non-renewable energy source.	One from: coal / oil / gas
3	Name one type of renewable energy source.	One from: solar power / wind power / wave power
4	Which Christian word means that humans have power over creation?	Dominion
5	Which Moral Precept teaches that Buddhists should not harm living beings?	The First Moral Precept
6	Which Buddhist teaching suggests the world is interconnected and interdependent?	Dependent origination
7	Name one type of animal used for experimentation.	One from: mice / rats / rabbits / monkeys
8	When was cosmetic experimentation on animals made illegal in Great Britain?	1998
9	True or false: all medicines in the UK must be tested on animals before they can be used on humans.	True
10	Which aspect of the Eightfold Path may prevent a Buddhist from working in a job that involves killing or harming animals?	Right livelihood

Put paper here

Previous questions

Now go back and use these questions to check your knowledge of previous topics.

Questions | Answers

	Questions	Answers
11	Complete the quotation: "And God said, 'Let there be _____,' and there was _____." (Genesis 1:3)	Light x2
12	What is the scientific theory of the origins of the universe known as?	The Big Bang
13	For Buddhists, who created the universe?	Nobody, there is no creator. The Earth exists cyclically
14	What term did the Buddha give to questions surrounding the origins of the universe?	Atakavacara
15	What evidence do Christian literal creationists use to explain the origins of the universe?	The Bible

Put paper here

Exam-style questions

01 Which **one** of these is a renewable source of energy? **(1 mark)**

Put a tick (✓) in the box next to the correct answer.

A   Coal ☐

B   Solar power ☐

C   Oil ☐

D   Gas ☐

02 Which **one** of these means that humans have the right to control, and have power over other, living creatures? **(1 mark)**

Put a tick (✓) in the box next to the correct answer.

A   Dominion ☐

B   Stewardship ☐

C   Responsibility ☐

D   Creation ☐

03 Name **two** types of natural resources. **(2 marks)**

04 Give **two** things that animal experimentation is used for. **(2 marks)**

05 Explain **two** contrasting religious beliefs on animal experimentation. **(4 marks)**
In your answer you must refer to one or more religious traditions.

> **EXAM TIP**
> You can use 'some' and 'other' when answering contrasting questions, e.g., 'Some Christians…', 'Other Christians…', etc.

06 Explain **two** religious beliefs about the value of the world.
Refer to sacred writings or another source of religious belief and teaching in your answer. **(5 marks)**

07 'All religious people should stop using non-renewable sources of energy.'
Evaluate this statement.

In your answer you:

- should give reasoned arguments in support of this statement
- should give reasoned arguments to support a different point of view
- should refer to religious arguments
- may refer to non-religious arguments
- should reach a justified conclusion. **(12 marks)**

(+ SPaG 3 marks)

> **EXAM TIP**
> Name the religion you are writing about so the examiner is clear if your answer is correct.

⚙ Knowledge

25 B: Abortion and euthanasia

Sanctity of life and quality of life

- These are key concepts that people may apply to a situation to decide whether they think it is right or wrong.
- We can apply these concepts to important issues such as **abortion** and **euthanasia**.

Sanctity of life	Quality of life
• Life is holy and given by God (so it should not be misused or abused).	• The general well-being of a person, in relation to their health and happiness. • The theory that the value of life depends upon how good or how satisfying it is.

Abortion

Abortion is the removal of a **foetus** from the womb to end a pregnancy. It is controversial because people have different views on when life begins and when a human is alive.

Since 1967, abortion has been legal in Great Britain up to 24 weeks of pregnancy (it is only legal after 24 weeks in exceptional medical circumstances). Two doctors have to confirm one of the legal conditions for abortion:

1. The woman's life is in danger if the pregnancy continues.
2. There is a risk to the woman's physical and mental health.
3. There is a significant risk that the baby will be born with severe physical or mental disabilities.
4. An additional child may affect the physical or mental health of an existing child or children.

REVISION TIP

Note that when we talk about abortion, the words we use can show a bias so think carefully when you write about it.

This is the most commonly cited condition because it can cover a range of personal reasons for abortion, including:

- being too young to have a child
- the woman not wanting children at that point in life
- contraception failure.

Views on abortion

Arguments about abortion are often based on whether the mother or the foetus has priority.

- Those who believe it is the mother's choice are known as '**pro-choice**'.
- Those who support the rights of the foetus are '**pro-life**'.

REVISION TIP

Keep an eye on the news for current debates about abortion around the world. You can use this information in your 12- mark answers.

⚖ Pro-life arguments	⚖ Pro-choice arguments
• A foetus is alive from conception, and abortion would be killing it (murder). • A foetus has the right to life. • We don't have the right to make decisions about a future human.	• **Quality of life** – the life of the baby and/or the mother may not be a good one if it is an unplanned pregnancy. • Life begins when a foetus can survive once born. • If the mother's life is at risk, she is already alive and the foetus isn't, so she takes priority.

† Christian views on abortion

 Some Christians are against abortion

- Life begins at conception, so abortion is murder: The Bible says:

  > ❝ *You shall not murder.* ❞ (Exodus)

- Sanctity of life – only God has the right to decide when we die; we are 'playing God' when we abort a foetus:

  > ❝ *Before I formed you in the womb I knew you, before you were born I set you apart.* ❞
  > (Jeremiah 1:5)

 Other Christians allow abortion in some cases

- **Situation ethics** – there are some situations in which abortion might be the most loving thing to do, and Jesus taught that we should behave in a loving way:

  > ❝ *As God's chosen people, holy and dearly loved, clothe yourselves with compassion, kindness, gentleness, and patience.* ❞
  > (Colossians 3:12)

- Lesser of two evils – the quality of life of the foetus or mother is important. An abortion might be better than a life of suffering for the mother or the child.

☸ Buddhist views on abortion

 Some Buddhists allow abortion

- The Five Moral Precepts are guidelines not absolutes, and there may be reasons to act against them.
- There is also no common agreement when life begins among Buddhists. For some Buddhists, abortion may not be considered an act of harm or killing.
- Many Buddhists make ethical decisions by considering each individual situation presented to them. For some, there may be circumstances in which abortion is justified, for example, to eliminate or reduce suffering:

  > ❝ *I think abortion should be approved or disapproved according to each circumstance.* ❞ (The Dalai Lama)

 Other Buddhists are against abortion

- Abortion goes against the First Moral Precept of killing or harming a living being.
- Abortion is considered an unskilful act as it may result in **dukkha**.

⚙ Knowledge

25 B: Abortion and euthanasia

Euthanasia

- The word euthanasia comes from Latin, and means 'good death.'
- Euthanasia is when someone helps another person who is dying a painful death to die in order to put them out of their suffering.
- It is illegal in Great Britain and is classed as murder.

Voluntary euthanasia – when a patient asks someone to end their life for them, for example, a doctor.

Types of euthanasia

Passive euthanasia (legal) – when a patient refuses treatment that would keep them alive.

Non-voluntary euthanasia – when a patient is unable to ask to die but others think it is what they want, for example, a person in a coma on a life support machine.

Views on euthanasia

Arguments against euthanasia	Arguments supporting euthanasia
• It's killing the person – this is murder and will be punished by law.	• It's the person's life–they can choose when to die.
• We can manage pain and ensure a person's final days are comfortable, for example, in a hospice.	• It is the most loving thing to do – to relieve the person of their suffering.
• An ill person may make decisions that they wouldn't make when well. There is a chance they say they want to die but actually mean they want their pain to end.	• It allows the person a dignified and peaceful death – watching someone die when they are in pain and suffering is upsetting and unnecessary.

> **REVISION TIP**
>
> Make sure you don't confuse euthanasia with assisted suicide. Euthanasia is deliberately ending a person's life to relieve suffering. Assisted suicide is deliberately assisting a person to kill themselves.

† Christian views on euthanasia

 Some Christians are always against euthanasia

- It is deliberately taking someone's life, which is a sin against God:

  > ❝ *You shall not murder.* ❞ (Exodus 20:13)

- Sanctity of life – only God has the right to decide when we die; we are 'playing God' when we commit euthanasia:

  > ❝ *Before I formed you in the womb I knew you, before you were born I set you apart.* ❞ (Jeremiah 1:5)

- Christian leaders have condemned euthanasia.

 Other Christians allow euthanasia in some cases

- Situation ethics – there are some situations in which non-voluntary euthanasia might be the most loving thing to do. Jesus taught that we should behave in a loving way:

  > ❝ *As God's chosen people, holy and dearly loved, clothe yourselves with compassion, kindness, gentleness, and patience.* ❞ (Colossians 3:12)

- Lesser of two evils – quality of life is important. Relieving someone's suffering might be the best thing to do:

  > ❝ *Blessed are the merciful.* ❞ (Matthew 5:7)

☸ Buddhist views on euthanasia

 Some Buddhists are always against euthanasia

- Many Buddhists are against euthanasia as it goes against the First Moral Precept of killing or harming a living being.
- The death of somebody may also cause loved ones dukkha.

 Other Buddhists allow euthanasia in some cases

- Euthanasia is a matter of personal choice. If the person is of sound mind and not affected by external pressure, it should be a permissible act.
- In some situations, Buddhists may argue that euthanasia is the act that demonstrates the most metta and karuna.

 Key terms

Make sure you can write a definition for these key terms

abortion   euthanasia   foetus   pro-choice   pro-life   quality of life   situation ethics   dukkha   voluntary euthanasia   passive euthanasia   non-voluntary euthanasia

Retrieval

Learn the answers to the questions below, then cover the answers column with a piece of paper and write as many as you can. Check and repeat.

Questions | Answers

#	Question	Answer
1	Up to how many weeks of pregnancy can a woman get an abortion in Great Britain?	24 weeks (except in exceptional medical circumstances)
2	Which word is used for people that support the rights of the mother in the abortion debate?	Pro-choice
3	Which word is used for people that support the rights of the foetus in the abortion debate?	Pro-life
4	How many doctors have to sign for a legal abortion in Great Britain?	Two
5	Complete the quotation: "*Before I formed you in the _____ I knew you, before you were born I set you apart.*" (Jeremiah 1:5)	Womb
6	In which type of euthanasia is the patient unable to ask to die but those around them think it is what they would want (e.g., the person is in a coma on a life support machine)?	Non-voluntary euthanasia
7	Complete the quotation: "*I think abortion should be approved or disapproved according to each _____.*" (Dalai Lama)	Circumstance
8	What way of making a moral decision is following the most loving thing to do?	Situation ethics
9	Which Buddhist ethical values could euthanasia express in some cases?	Metta and karuna

Put paper here

Previous questions

Now go back and use these questions to check your knowledge of previous topics.

Questions | Answers

#	Question	Answer
10	Which Buddhist teaching suggests the world is interconnected and interdependent?	Dependent origination
11	Name one type of non-renewable energy source.	One from: coal / oil / gas
12	Name one thing that animal experimentation is used to develop in Great Britain.	Medicine
13	Which aspect of the Eightfold Path may prevent a Buddhist from working in a job that involves killing or harming animals?	Right livelihood
14	What is the scientific theory of the origins of the universe known as?	The Big Bang

Put paper here

25 Abortion and euthanasia

Exam-style questions

01 Which **one** of these describes the type of euthanasia in which the patient asks someone to end their life for them, for example, a doctor? **(1 mark)**

Put a tick (✔) in the box next to the correct answer.

A	Voluntary euthanasia	☐
B	Non-voluntary euthanasia	☐
C	Passive euthanasia	☐
D	Assisted suicide	☐

02 Which **one** of these describes the concept that 'life is holy and given by God'? **(1 mark)**

Put a tick (✔) in the box next to the correct answer.

A	Sanctity of life	☐
B	Quality of life	☐
C	Ahimsa	☐
D	Karuna	☐

> **EXAM TIP**
> Read all the options carefully. There may be answers designed to distract you from the correct answer.

03 Name **two** types of euthanasia. **(2 marks)**

04 Give **two** reasons people may choose to have an abortion. **(2 marks)**

05 Explain **two** contrasting religious beliefs on euthanasia.

In your answer you must refer to one or more religious traditions. **(4 marks)**

06 Explain **two** religious beliefs on the sanctity of life.

Refer to sacred writings or another source of religious belief and teaching in your answer. **(5 marks)**

> **EXAM TIP**
> You can only achieve the fifth mark if your reference to a sacred writing or source of authority includes where it has come from, for example, the Bible, the Buddha.

07 'Only God should decide when we die.'

Evaluate this statement.

In your answer you:

- should give reasoned arguments in support of this statement
- should give reasoned arguments to support a different point of view
- should refer to religious arguments
- may refer to non-religious arguments
- should reach a justified conclusion. **(12 marks)**

(+ SPaG 3 marks)

26 B: Death and the afterlife

✝ Christian beliefs on the afterlife

Bible text	Belief
" *For God so loved the world that he gave his one and only Son, that whoever believes in him shall not perish but have eternal life.* **"** (John 3:16)	Some Christians think that if we believe in God and his son Jesus we will have a life after this life, for eternity.
" *Jesus said to her, 'I am the* **resurrection** *and the life. The one who believes in me will live, even though they die.'* **"** (John 11:25)	This quotation suggests that humans will be resurrected from death and will then have a life after death.
The Parable of the Sheep and Goats told by Jesus (Matthew 25:31–46)	Christians may interpret this story to mean the following: • If we helped other people as though we were helping Jesus, we will be on God's right-hand side (sheep) and will be the 'righteous [that go] to eternal life'. Some may interpret this as **heaven**. • If we haven't helped others, we will be on God's left-hand side (goats) and will 'go away to eternal punishment'. Some may interpret this as **hell**.
" *Put to death, therefore, whatever belongs to your Earthly nature: sexual immorality, impurity, lust, evil desires and greed, which is idolatry. Because of these, the wrath of God is coming. You used to walk in these ways, in the life you once lived. But now you must also rid yourselves of all such things as these: anger, rage, malice, slander, and filthy language from your lips.* **"** (Colossians 3:5–8)	Some Christians believe that certain actions will lead us to be apart from God after we die.
" *He will wipe every tear from their eyes. There will be no more death or mourning or crying or pain, for the old order of things has passed away.* **"** (Revelation 21:4)	In heaven there will be no sadness or unhappiness.
" *…and throw them into the blazing furnace, where there will be weeping and gnashing of teeth.* **"** (Matthew 13:50)	• Some think this quotation is a literal description of hell. It will be a painful and unhappy time. • Some believe that a loving God would not create such a place, so it is a symbolic description of being 'without God', not a place called hell.

• These beliefs impact Christian views on the value of human life as it tells them there is a life after this life.

• These beliefs emphasise that we should think carefully about how we behave in this life because we will be judged on it, and this will influence what happens to us in the afterlife. For example, they will affect Christian views on whether abortion or euthanasia are acceptable. They will help them to consider the importance of the sanctity of life alongside the idea of quality of life.

✸ Buddhist beliefs on the afterlife

Buddhists have a different understanding of the afterlife compared to Christians. For many Buddhists, **rebirth** is a key belief.

Samsara	Consciousness	Kamma (Karma)	Enlightenment (nibbana/nirvana)
Rebirth is the belief that when somebody dies, they are reborn. Buddhists understand life cyclically rather than linearly. The cycle of life is understood as **samsara**.	Rebirth does not mean that the physical body lives on – the consciousness of the deceased enters another life and lives on.	A person's rebirth is dictated by **kamma** (action). Buddhists must perform skilful actions (actions rooted in generosity, compassion, and wisdom) to ensure a favourable rebirth. This is opposed to unskilful action (actions rooted in craving, hatred and ignorance). A Buddhist may also be reborn in different realms.	The end of rebirth is **nibbana** (nirvana), when a Buddhist escapes the cycle of samsara. This is an enlightened state, in which the Buddhist no longer lives a physical life. Nobody knows exactly what an enlightened state is like as the Buddha considered it an unanswerable question (atakavacara).

- For many Buddhists, human life has value because it is lived in the human realm.
- Some Buddhists may argue that human life has value as people have the potential to be reborn with a greater consciousness, thus getting closer to attaining enlightenment.
- Rebirth allows for skilful action to be undertaken and its positive consequences felt by all.

Key terms — Make sure you can write a definition for these key terms

resurrection   heaven   hell   rebirth   samsara
kamma   nibbana (nirvana)

⇄ Retrieval

Learn the answers to the questions below, then cover the answers column with a piece of paper and write as many as you can. Check and repeat.

Questions | Answers

	Questions		Answers
1	Complete the quotation: "*I am the _____ and the life. The one who believes in me will live, even though they die.*" (John 11:25)	Put paper here	Resurrection
2	Which parable describes the judgement of humans?		The Parable of the Sheep and Goats
3	Why don't some Christians believe in the existence of hell?		They believe a loving God wouldn't create something that causes pain and suffering to people
4	How might a Christian interpret Bible references to heaven and hell?	Put paper here	Literally or symbolically
5	Which belief describes someone being reborn after they die?		Rebirth
6	What Buddhist word describes the cycle of life?		Samsara
7	What is the meaning of kamma?	Put paper here	Action
8	In Buddhism, which type of action has the potential to lead to a favourable rebirth?		Skilful action
9	What is the meaning of nibbana (nirvana)?	Put paper here	The end of rebirth, when the Buddhist escapes the cycle of samsara
10	Why do Buddhists not know exactly what an enlightened state is like?		It is considered an unanswerable question (atakavacara)

Previous questions

Now go back and use these questions to check your knowledge of previous topics.

Questions | Answers

	Questions		Answers
11	What way of making a moral decision is following the most loving thing to do?	Put paper here	Situation ethics
12	Complete the quotation: "*I think abortion should be approved or disapproved according to each _____.*" (Dalai Lama)		Circumstance
13	What evidence do theistic evolutionists use to explain the origins of the universe?		The Bible and scientific evidence
14	Complete the quotation: "*The righteous care for the _____ of their animals.*" (Proverbs 12:10)	Put paper here	Needs
15	Up to how many weeks of pregnancy can a woman get an abortion in Great Britain?		24 weeks

Exam-style questions

01 Which **one** of these is the cycle of life in Buddhism? **(1 mark)**

Put a tick (✓) in the box next to the correct answer.

A Kamma ☐

B Nibbana (nirvana) ☐

C Atakavacara ☐

D Samsara ☐

02 Which **one** of these does the Bible class as a sin? **(1 mark)**

Put a tick (✓) in the box next to the correct answer.

A Charity ☐

B Noise ☐

C Anger ☐

D Prayer ☐

03 Give **two** religious beliefs about the value of human life. **(2 marks)**

04 Give **two** religious beliefs about life after death. **(2 marks)**

05 Explain **two** similar religious beliefs on life after death.

In your answer you must refer to one or more religious traditions. **(4 marks)**

> **EXAM TIP**
> To be sure the examiner is clear if your answer is correct, remember to name the religion that you are writing about.

06 Explain **two** religious beliefs about life after death.

Refer to sacred writings or another source of religious belief and teaching in your answer. **(5 marks)**

07 'This life is our only life.'

Evaluate this statement.

In your answer you:

- should give reasoned arguments in support of this statement
- should give reasoned arguments to support a different point of view
- should refer to religious arguments
- may refer to non-religious arguments
- should reach a justified conclusion. **(12 marks)**

(+ SPaG 3 marks)

> **EXAM TIP**
> Take care with your spelling, punctuation, and grammar, and use as many specialist terms as possible when answering 12-mark questions.

⚙ Knowledge

27 C: Arguments for the existence of God

People have tried to prove that God exists through logical reasoning, using evidence to create arguments for the existence of God.

The Design argument

The **Design argument** looks to our universe to help prove the existence of God. Christians may support this view as Genesis 1 in the Bible describes the designer God, creating things each day over six days.

> Many things in the universe are intricately made and specifically designed to function in a certain way.

⬇

> For example, the rings in a tree trunk, the human eye, and human fingerprints, are all unique.

⬇

> There must be a designer intelligent and powerful enough to have done this.

⬇

> God is the only being with these powers.

⬇

> Therefore, the designer must be God.

Variations to the Design argument	
William Paley	Paley uses a watch analogy to compare the complexity of a watch and its designer to the complexity of the universe and its designer, God.
Isaac Newton	Newton used the design of the thumb and its unique print, and how it functions, as evidence of a designer. He said, 'In the absence of any other proof, the thumb alone would convince me of God's existence'.
Thomas Aquinas	Aquinas looked at things being in order in the universe as evidence of a designer. For example, the way the planets, sun, moons, and stars rotate within the solar system must be down to an **omnipotent**, intelligent designer – God.
A modern argument	F. R. Tennant said that everything in the universe works in just the right way for it to survive; everything is balanced to work. For example, the strength of gravity is just enough to keep us stable, or the exact size of protons and neutrons to function correctly. These must be deliberately designed by the designer, God.

Variations to the Design argument	
A Buddhist argument 	Most Buddhists would reject the conclusion of the Design argument - that God was responsible for designing the universe. This is because most Buddhists do not believe that God is involved in the creation or design of the universe. God is not understood as a creator for most Buddhists. Instead, most Buddhists believe that the universe came into existence because the right conditions were present and that these conditions existed independently of a god. Each condition depended upon the others. This is known as dependent origination. **66** *The wise see action in this way as it has come to be, seeing dependent co-arising… of action's results… Through action the world rolls on. People roll on through action. In action are beings held bound together.* **99** (Pali Canon)

Strengths and weaknesses of the Design argument

Strengths	Weaknesses
• Many examples of things on Earth only work if balanced correctly, for example, the human body. • Humans lack the ability to have created many of these things so it must be due to an omnipotent being (God).	• Atheists argue that we don't need an omnipotent being to explain the complexity of the universe. Evolution can explain this. • Why would such an **omnibenevolent** (all-loving) designer design things such as cancer? • Humans look for meaning in life and have interpreted the order of the universe to try to justify things that cannot be explained. • Who or what designed God?

The First Cause argument

The **First Cause argument** or Cosmological argument uses a logical chain of reasoning to try to prove the existence of God. Christians may believe the First Cause argument as the Bible supports the idea that God was the first cause in Genesis 1.

| Everything in the universe has a cause. | → | There must be a first cause – the cause of the universe's existence. | → | The first cause must be something that is eternal and does not need to be caused (an 'unmoved mover'). | → | This first cause can only be God. | → | Therefore, God exists. |

- Thomas Aquinas argued that everything in the universe has been caused and that only God can be the uncaused causer of the universe.

- Some Christians may believe the First Cause argument as the Bible supports the idea that God was the first cause in Genesis 1.

Knowledge

27 C: Arguments for the existence of God

☸ The Buddhist view of the First Cause argument

- There is no concept of a First Cause in Buddhism because Buddhism does not include belief in a creator god.
- Buddhists believe the universe exists cyclically, via a process of contractions and expansions; therefore, there is no beginning or end, so a First Cause is not necessary.

Strengths and weaknesses of the First Cause argument

Strengths	Weaknesses
• We can see everything that exists within the universe has a cause – try to think of something that doesn't. • While science has found that the Big Bang was the cause of the existence of the universe, something must have caused it, and it was God.	• Who or what caused God? • Scientists have discovered that the cause of the existence of the universe is the Big Bang. • Just because things within the universe have a cause, this doesn't mean the universe itself needed a cause.

The argument from miracles

| Some events do not have a scientific explanation (**miracles**). | → | These events must be **supernatural** – outside of nature. | → | Only God is outside of nature (**transcendent**). | → | As he is outside of nature, God must be responsible for miracles. | → | Therefore, God exists. |

† Christian responses to miracles

- Miracles are proof of the existence of God.
- The Bible includes many examples of miracles, including the most important ones of the **incarnation** and resurrection of Jesus.
- Jesus performed miracles such as walking on water, bringing people back from the dead and making the blind see.
- At Pentecost, the Holy Spirit blessed the disciples so they could perform miracles.
- Some Christians believe they can also perform miracles through the Holy Spirit.
- Catholic Christians believe that Lourdes in France is an important place of pilgrimage where miracles have happened and still do today.

> **REVISION TIP**
>
> Read in the Bible in the New Testament gospels about the different types of miracles that Jesus performed.

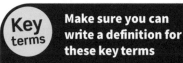 **Make sure you can write a definition for these key terms**

> Design argument   omnipotent   omnibenevolent
> First Cause argument   miracle   supernatural
> transcendent   incarnation

Buddhist responses to miracles

- Miracles are not proof of the existence of God.
- Many Buddhists accept the existence of miracles, but believe that the ability to perform these acts comes from a developed meditation practice, not a divine capability or power.
- In the Pali Canon, the Buddha suggested there were three types of miracles: psychic power, telepathy and instruction, for example, the Buddha calmed an elephant using his psychic powers:

> *... do not be afraid, Ānanda,' said the Exalted One, I am going to tame that elephant through the Tathāgata's supernormal power...* **"** (Pali Canon)

Strengths and weaknesses of the argument from miracles

Strengths – why miracles prove the existence of God	Weaknesses – why miracles don't prove the existence of God
• Miracles have no scientific explanation so they must be caused by something outside of nature, which can only be God. There are some events that we cannot explain. Sometimes God works in mysterious ways, and we should accept that he knows why these things happen. • Miracles occur in holy texts.	• Non-religious views of miracles often explain them without the need for God to have been responsible for them. • 'Miracles' may be unusual, coincidental, and very lucky, but they are possible according to the laws of nature. They aren't the work of God. • Some things could not be explained with science in the past, but they can be now. There may be things that we cannot yet explain with science that we one day will. In the meantime, we cannot attribute them to God as miracles. • Some people make up stories of miracles for attention or to make money. The Buddha said some miracles are merely tricks. • Many secular (non-religious) Buddhists are sceptical about miracles, believing them to be irrational in light of today's scientific knowledge.

† Examples of miracles in Christianity

The Bible: Jesus heals the paralysed man

> *Some men brought to him [Jesus] a paralyzed man, lying on a mat. When Jesus saw their faith, he said to the man, 'Take heart, son; your sins are forgiven.' ...he said to the paralyzed man, 'Get up, take your mat and go home.' Then the man got up and went home.* **"** (Matthew 9:1–8)

Marie Bailly, Lourdes, France, 1902

At 22, Marie Bailly was diagnosed with tuberculosis peritonitis. She was unable to eat as her stomach had swollen so badly. She wanted to visit Lourdes but was so ill that when she arrived that she was taken to hospital. She was told she was going to die, so she asked to be taken to the baths, where holy water was poured over her. She prayed to Mary and said, 'I am cured'. She then recovered and returned to good health.

Retrieval

Learn the answers to the questions below, then cover the answers column with a piece of paper and write as many as you can. Check and repeat.

Questions	Answers
1 What is word means an event that does not have a scientific explanation?	Miracle
2 In which book of the Bible does God create the universe?	Genesis
3 Complete the quotation: "*In the absence of any other proof, the _____ alone would convince me of God's existence.*" (Isaac Newton)	Thumb
4 What is another name for the First Cause argument?	The cosmological argument
5 Which word means that God is beyond nature, the Earth and the universe?	Transcendent
6 What animal did the Buddha calm with his miraculous abilities?	An elephant
7 At which event in the Bible were the disciples given the power to perform miracles?	Pentecost
8 At which town in France do Catholic Christians believe that healing miracles occur?	Lourdes
9 How many types of miracles did the Buddha suggest existed?	Three
10 Why do Buddhists reject the design argument?	Buddhists reject a divine designer because they believe there is no god who created the universe
11 What reason do secular (non-religious) Buddhists give for being sceptical about miracles?	They suggest miracles are irrational due to today's scientific knowledge
12 Complete what Jesus said when he healed the paralysed man: "*Take heart, son; your _____ _____ _____.*"	Sins are forgiven
13 What is the miracle of the incarnation for Christians?	When God's son came to earth – Jesus was born

(centre column, repeated vertically: Put paper here)

Exam-style questions

01 Which **one** of these did William Paley use as an analogy for the design of the universe? **(1 mark)**

Put a tick (✓) in the box next to the correct answer.

A   A tree ☐

B   A fingerprint ☐

C   A watch ☐

D   A thumb ☐

02 Which **one** of these argues that God is the 'unmoved mover'? **(1 mark)**

Put a tick (✓) in the box next to the correct answer.

A   The Design argument ☐

B   The First Cause argument ☐

C   The argument from miracles ☐

D   The argument from religious experience ☐

03 Give **two** weaknesses of the design argument. **(2 marks)**

> **EXAM TIP**
>
> In two-mark questions you do not have to write in full sentences. Answers can be a single word or short phrases.

04 Give **two** examples of miracles in the Bible. **(2 marks)**

05 Explain **two** contrasting beliefs in contemporary British society about miracles.

In your answer you should refer to the main religious tradition of Great Britain and non-religious beliefs. **(4 marks)**

> **EXAM TIP**
>
> 'Contrasting' just means 'different' in these questions.

06 Explain **two** strengths of the First Cause argument.

Refer to sacred writings or another source of religious belief and teaching in your answer. **(5 marks)**

07 'The Design argument is a strong argument for the existence of God.'

Evaluate this statement.

In your answer you:

- should give reasoned arguments in support of this statement
- should give reasoned arguments to support a different point of view
- should refer to religious arguments
- may refer to non-religious arguments
- should reach a justified conclusion. **(12 marks)**

(+ SPaG 3 marks)

> **EXAM TIP**
>
> Remember to read the statement carefully, and use the words from it in your answer to ensure you answer it fully.

⚙ Knowledge

28 C: Arguments against the existence of God

People have also tried to prove that God does not exist using logical reasoning and evidence as arguments against the existence of God.

Evil and suffering as an argument against the existence of God

Atheists may argue that the **evil and suffering** we experience in the world proves that God does not exist.

| There are many examples of evil and suffering in the world. | → | For example, people have painful illnesses and people are fighting and killing each other. | → | God is supposed to be:

• all-knowing (**omniscient**) so he knows it is happening
• all-loving (omnibenevolent) so he would want to stop it
• all-powerful (omnipotent) so he should be able to stop it. |

REVISION TIP

How can you remember the 'omnis'?

• omni*pot*ent – *powerful*
• omnibene*vol*ent – '*love*' backwards
• omni*sci*ent – '*science*' brings knowledge

However, he doesn't do this, so he clearly doesn't exist.

Responses to the argument of evil and suffering

✝ Christian responses	☸ Buddhist responses
• God can stop evil and suffering but he has given humans **free will** (as with Adam in Genesis 3) to behave how they want. They choose to cause evil and suffering themselves, for example, war, so God will not interfere with free will. • We may not understand why God does not intervene, but we should behave in the most loving way to those that are suffering and we will be rewarded by him in the **afterlife**. • Life is a test and God wants to see how humans respond to such events. We will be rewarded for our positive actions in the afterlife. • Allowing evil and suffering means that humans can learn from mistakes and work together to make the world a better place, instead of thinking it's all God's job.	• Many Buddhists would not see evil as challenging the idea that the divine exists. This is because the idea of the divine is understood differently in much of Buddhism compared with Christianity. In early Buddhism, evil was personified through the figure of **Mara**. • In Buddhism, evil largely originates from the actions of people because of the **Three Poisons** (greed, hatred, and ignorance), which keep the cycle of existence, samsara, turning. • Buddhism teaches that dukkha (suffering) is a universal condition that is experienced by everybody. Kamma (Karma or action) may be one reason for this. • Buddhists believe that events other people consider evil, for example, natural disasters, are not the result of God's action, but instead the result of an interdependent world (dependent origination) impacted by a series of related actions, for example, flooding.

Arguments against the existence of God based on science

In the past people have used the existence of God to help answer big questions such as:

- How did the universe get here?
- How did humans get here?
- What happens when we die?

↓

Scientific knowledge has advanced so now we have the answers to many of these questions.

↓

While science doesn't have the answers to everything yet, it has shown so far that none of them rely on the existence of God.

↓

We no longer need to believe in the existence of God to answer these questions – science will answer them.

REVISION TIP

Draw a table with two columns. Label the first column 'Arguments for the existence of God' and the second column 'Arguments against the existence of God'. See if you can write three arguments in each column.

↓

Responses to the arguments based on science

† Christian responses	☸ Buddhist responses
• Some Christians reject the scientific argument because they believe the version of **creation** described in Genesis is literally true. • Other Christians say that scientific evidence works alongside the Biblical account in Genesis. *❝ The Big Bang […] does not contradict the divine act of creation; rather, it requires it… ❞* (Pope Francis)	• Buddhists would be unlikely to be concerned that science challenges the existence of God as the Buddha taught that there is no creator God. • Many Buddhists see the development of scientific knowledge as human progress. *❝ If scientific analysis were conclusively to demonstrate certain claims in Buddhism to be false, then we must accept the findings of science and abandon those claims [of Buddhism]. ❞* (Dalai Lama)

Key terms Make sure you can write a definition for these key terms

evil and suffering   omniscient   free will   afterlife
Mara   Three Poisons   creation

⇄ Retrieval

Learn the answers to the questions below, then cover the answers column with a piece of paper and write as many as you can. Check and repeat.

Questions   ## Answers

#	Question	Answer
1	Which word means that God is all-powerful?	Omnipotent
2	Which word means that God is all-knowing?	Omniscient
3	What does omnibenevolent mean?	All-loving
4	What does the Buddhist word dukkha mean?	Suffering
5	Who suggests aspects of Buddhism should be abandoned if science demonstrates its claims to be false?	The Dalai Lama
6	Which word means that humans can choose how they behave (without interference from God)?	Free will
7	In which book of the Bible is the account of creation?	Genesis
8	Complete this quotation: "*The _____ _____ [...] does not contradict the divine act of creation; rather, it requires it...*" (Pope Francis)	Big Bang

Put paper here

Previous questions

Now go back and use these questions to check your knowledge of previous topics.

Questions   ## Answers

#	Question	Answer
9	At which event in the Bible were the disciples given the power to perform miracles?	Pentecost
10	Complete the quotation: "*In the absence of any other proof, the _____ alone would convince me of God's existence.*" (Isaac Newton)	Thumb
11	What is another name for the First Cause argument?	The cosmological argument
12	Which word means that God is outside of nature?	Transcendent
13	What animal did the Buddha calm with his miraculous abilities?	An elephant

Put paper here

Exam-style questions

01 Which **one** of these terms means that God is all-loving? **(1 mark)**

Put a tick (✓) in the box next to the correct answer.

A	omnipotent	☐
B	omniscient	☐
C	omnibenevolent	☐
D	omnipresent	☐

02 Which **one** of these describes the belief that humans can choose how they behave without interference from God? **(1 mark)**

Put a tick (✓) in the box next to the correct answer.

A	Free will	☐
B	Creation	☐
C	Sin	☐
D	Natural selection	☐

> **EXAM TIP**
> These questions are only worth one mark, so don't spend a long time on them. However, do read the question and answer options carefully so you don't make a mistake.

03 Give **two** religious responses to evil and suffering. **(2 marks)**

04 Give **two** reasons why science may challenge the existence of God. **(2 marks)**

05 Explain **two** similar beliefs about evil and suffering as an argument against the existence of God.

In your answer you must refer to one or more religious traditions. **(4 marks)**

06 Explain **two** religious responses to the arguments against the existence of God based on science.

Refer to sacred writings or another source of religious belief and teaching in your answer. **(5 marks)**

> **EXAM TIP**
> Remember, you must name a piece of sacred writing or source of authority in your answer, for example, the Bible, the Buddha.

07 'Science gives all the answers to questions we have about the universe.'

Evaluate this statement.

In your answer you:

- should give reasoned arguments in support of this statement
- should give reasoned arguments to support a different point of view
- should refer to religious arguments
- may refer to non-religious arguments
- should reach a justified conclusion. **(12 marks)**

(+ SPaG 3 marks)

> **EXAM TIP**
> Remember to read the statement carefully and use the words from it in your answer to ensure you answer it fully.

⚙ Knowledge

29 C: The nature of the divine and revelation

Revelation

Revelation means the way that God or the divine shows themselves to humans. There are different ways humans can experience God or the divine.

- Whilst not all religions have a god or gods, most do have an ultimate reality that does not change. These can be called the 'divine', and there are different ways that humans can experience the divine.

- Revelation is not generally a term used in Buddhism. There are a range of opinions within Buddhism on the nature of the divine, including the nature of the Buddha.

- Many Buddhists do not view sacred texts as having divine origins. Some may suggest they are inspired by divine figures, others argue they are the work of great non-divine minds who have great intellect, understanding, and wisdom.

Special revelation

- **Special revelation** is when a person directly experiences God or the divine in an extraordinary event.

- This is often life changing and sometimes a person converts to a religion.

- Many people believe this is rare, and many are committed to faith without experiencing a special revelation.

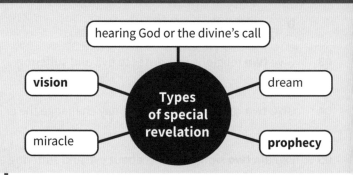

† Special revelation in Christianity

- In the Bible, the angel Gabriel visited Mary to tell her she would become pregnant with God's son, Jesus:

> **❝** *You will conceive and give birth to a son, and you are to call him Jesus.* **❞**
> (Luke 1:31)

- Jesus performed miracles:

> **❝** *Jesus reached out his hand and touched the man. 'I am willing,' he said. 'Be clean!' Immediately he was cleansed of his leprosy.* **❞**
> (Matthew 8:3)

- God told Aaron and Miriam:

> **❝** *Hear my words: If there is a prophet among you, I the LORD make myself known to him in a vision, I speak with him in a dream.* **❞** (Numbers 12:6)

Special revelation in Buddhism

- Buddhists are unlikely to see revelation as an intervention by God, as they don't believe in a god of this nature or capacity.
- Some Buddhists accept the possibility that special wisdom may be transmitted through revelatory experiences. For example, Nagarjuna received the Perfection of Wisdom sutras via Nagas (semi-divine beings).
- The practice of **visualisation** allows some Buddhists to experience what they consider to be the divine (or enlightened mind) and the true nature of reality. For example, visualising the Bodhisattva Avalokiteshvara helps Buddhists to develop insight and the quality of compassion.

Visions

- A vision is a supernatural experience when a person sees something in a dream or trance that shows them something about God, the divine or life after death. In this special revelation, they may see a special person, an angel, or even hear the voice of God.
- Some atheists attribute people's visions to lack of sleep or the effects of mind-altering substances such as drugs.
- Buddhists may see visions as experiences that transmit special wisdom.

† Visions in Christianity	☸ Visions in Buddhism
- Christianity sees visions as a spiritual experience but will only accept them if they don't go against the key beliefs given in the Bible. - An example of a vision in Christianity is the conversion of St Paul. Before his conversion, Paul was known as Saul, and he persecuted followers of Jesus. *66 Meanwhile, Saul was still breathing out murderous threats against the Lord's disciples. As he neared Damascus on his journey, suddenly a light from heaven flashed around him. He fell to the ground and heard a voice say to him, 'Saul, Saul, why do you persecute me?' 'Who are you, Lord?' Saul asked. 'I am Jesus, whom you are persecuting,' he replied. 'Now get up and go into the city, and you will be told what you must do.' Saul got up from the ground, but when he opened his eyes he could see nothing. 99* (Acts 9:1–8)	- Buddhists may see visions as experiences that transmit special wisdom. - Examples of visions in Buddhism are Asaṅga's vision and the Buddha's awakening. Asaṅga, the founder of the Mahayana school of Yogachara, had a vision of the Bodhisattva Maitreya and was told of the importance of acting with compassion.

⚙ Knowledge

Enlightenment as a source of knowledge about the divine

- In its broadest understanding, enlightenment can be understood as the gaining of knowledge about God, the self or the nature of reality.

- In Buddhism, enlightenment is often referred to as '**awakening**'. Those who have 'awoken' are often given the title 'Buddha'.

- In Buddhism, enlightenment is concerned with the acquisition of knowledge, particularly about the self and the true nature of reality, not knowledge about the Divine.

- For most Buddhists, Siddhartha Gautama is a being who was enlightened. Thus his title, 'the Buddha'. During Siddhartha's enlightenment experience, he acquired insight into the nature of himself and reality. This allowed him to overcome the experience of samsara and achieve nibbana (nirvana).

- The Pali Canon describes Gautama's experience. It suggests the Buddha received three **tevijja** (knowledges).

First watch – The Buddha gained knowledge of his past lives.

Second watch – The Buddha gained knowledge of the experience of samsara and the cycle of rebirth, and the importance of kamma (action).

Third watch – The Buddha gained knowledge of dukkha (suffering), especially as a result of craving and ignorance.

General revelation

- **General (or indirect) revelation** is when God shows himself through ordinary, everyday life experiences. This can happen to anybody at any time.

Examples of general revelation

Looking at nature and feeling God's presence

Worshipping God

Reading a holy text and being inspired by God

A person's conscience telling them right and wrong

The lives of religious leaders that reflect God's purpose in life

Nature as a way of understanding the divine

- Nature can provide us with many special experiences.
- Many Christians believe special experiences in nature are due to God and can create a sense of awe and wonder.
- God's creation helps humans to understand him more, for example, the stars in a clear night sky or a powerful storm can remind us of God's omnipotence.

> **"** *The heavens declare the glory of God; the skies proclaim the work of his hands.* **"**
>
> (Psalm 19:1)

- As Buddhists do not believe the world was created by a god, many would not see nature as a way to understand the divine. Instead, they see nature as a collection of the right conditions coming together to form an environment.
- Some atheists would say that nature is not evidence of God but proof that science is complex and powerful in itself.

Scripture as a way of understanding the divine

† Christianity

Christians believe the Bible helps them to understand God.

- While he may be ineffable (too great or extreme to be expressed in words) Bible stories and teachings can give a sense of what God wants for his creation and how he expects humans to behave.
- Reading the Bible helps Christians understand God's nature.

> **"** *The God who made the world and everything in it is the Lord of heaven and earth and does not live in temples built by human hands. And he is not served by human hands, as if he needed anything. Rather, he himself gives everyone life and breath and everything else.* **"**
>
> (Acts 17:24–25)

However, Christians can read and interpret the Bible in different ways:

- Some take it literally, as God's words and as an exact account of what has happened and will happen, so the words shouldn't be changed.
- Others believe the Bible is inspired by God but is often symbolic and has a spiritual rather than a literal meaning, to inspire humans about how they might live.

☸ Buddhism

- Some Buddhists see **scripture** as the 'enlightened word' – it expresses the enlightened mind, so scripture may help them to understand the knowledge and insight of the Enlightened, for example, the Buddha and his insight into the Three Marks of Existence.
- Some Buddhists believe **mantras** found in scripture help them to receive the Buddha's teaching, for example, those who follow Pure Land Buddhism believe reciting mantras is one practice that will allow them access to the Pure Land.

Atheism

- Some atheists say that religious texts were written by humans, and therefore aren't inspired by God, nor do they tell them anything about God.

Key terms Make sure you can write a definition for these key terms

revelation   special revelation   visualisation
vision   prophecy   awakening   tevijja
general revelation   scripture   mantras

Retrieval

Learn the answers to the questions below, then cover the answers column with a piece of paper and write as many as you can. Check and repeat.

Questions / Answers

	Questions	Answers
1	Name one type of special revelation.	One from: dream / miracle / prophecy / vision
2	How might some atheists interpret special revelation?	As a result of lack of sleep, the effects of intoxicants (e.g., drugs)
3	For Buddhists, what is meant by scripture as an expression of the 'enlightened word'?	Scripture isn't divine but the words of an enlightened mind and helps them to understand the insight gained at enlightenment
4	What three insights did the Buddha gain during his Awakening?	Past lives, cycle of rebirth, and dukkha
5	Which holy book do Christians use to help them understand God?	The Bible
6	In the Bible, who experienced a vision of Jesus while walking on the road to Damascus?	Saul / Paul
7	In which three ways can the Bible be interpreted?	Literally, symbolically, and spiritually
8	Which word means that God is too great or extreme to be expressed in words?	Ineffable
9	Which word in Buddhism means understanding the ultimate reality (the divine) by gaining true knowledge of life and suffering?	Enlightenment

Put paper here

Previous questions

Now go back and use these questions to check your knowledge of previous topics.

Questions / Answers

	Questions	Answers
10	At which town in France do Catholic Christians believe that healing miracles occur?	Lourdes
11	Which word means that God is all-powerful?	Omnipotent
12	Why do Buddhists reject the design argument?	Buddhists reject a divine designer because they believe there is no god who created the universe
13	What does omnibenevolent mean?	God is all-loving
14	Which term means that humans can choose how they behave (without interference from God)?	Free will

Put paper here

Exam-style questions

01 Which **one** of these occurs when a person directly experiences God in an extraordinary event?   **(1 mark)**

Put a tick (✓) in the box next to the correct answer.

A   Special revelation   ☐

B   Scriptural revelation   ☐

C   Nature   ☐

D   Enlightenment   ☐

02 Which **one** of these describes a supernatural experience in which a person sees something in a dream or a trance that shows them something about God, the divine or life after death?   **(1 mark)**

Put a tick (✓) in the box next to the correct answer.

A   Miracle   ☐

B   Vision   ☐

C   Enlightenment   ☐

D   General revelation   ☐

03 Give **two** different ideas about the divine.   **(2 marks)**

04 Give **two** examples of general revelation.   **(2 marks)**

05 Explain **two** contrasting beliefs about nature as general revelation.

In your answer you must refer to one or more religious traditions.   **(4 marks)**

06 Explain **two** contrasting beliefs about visions.

Refer to sacred writings or another source of religious belief and teaching in your answer.   **(4 marks)**

> **EXAM TIP**
>
> 'Contrasting' just means 'different' in these types of questions.

07 Explain **two** religious beliefs about scripture as a way of understanding the divine.

Refer to sacred writings or another source of religious belief and teaching in your answer.   **(5 marks)**

> **EXAM TIP**
>
> Be clear what religious views you are writing about so the examiner knows whether your answer is correct.

08 'We can see the divine through the natural world around us.'

Evaluate this statement.

In your answer you:

- should give reasoned arguments in support of this statement
- should give reasoned arguments to support a different point of view
- should refer to religious arguments
- may refer to non-religious arguments
- should reach a justified conclusion.   **(12 marks)**

(+ SPaG 3 marks)

Knowledge

30 C: Ideas about the divine and the value of revelation and enlightenment

Ideas about the divine

✝ For Christians, God has certain qualities that may help them to understand his nature. The Bible gives them examples of how God works and his relationship with humans.

	Meaning	Example from the Bible
Omnipotent	God is all powerful and almighty; he can do anything.	66 *In the beginning God created the heavens and the earth. The earth was formless and empty.* 99 (Genesis: 1 1–2)
Omniscient	God is all knowing. He knows everything that has and will happen.	66 *Great is our Lord and mighty in power; his understanding has no limit.* 99 (Psalms 147:5)
Personal	God is close to humans and has a relationship with them due to his human characteristics.	66 *God is love…* 99 (1 John 4:16)
Impersonal	God is not like humans and is unknowable.	66 *How great is God – beyond our understanding!* 99 (Job 36:26)
Immanent	God is within and involved in his creation (the universe). Humans can experience God in their lives.	66 *When Jesus had been baptized… the heavens were opened to him and he saw the Spirit of God descending like a dove and alighting on him. And a voice from heaven said, 'This is my Son, the Beloved, [a] with whom I am well pleased.* 99 (Matthew 3:13–17)
Transcendent	God is beyond and outside of his creation (the universe). He is not limited by the world, time or space.	66 *As the heavens are higher than the earth, so are my ways higher than your ways and my thoughts than your thoughts.* 99 (Isaiah 55:9)

 Some Buddhists believe there are divine beings, for example, Bodhisattvas, but Buddhists do not believe there is one God with supreme powers who controls all things.

- Some Buddhists believe that by **meditating** upon and worshipping the Buddha or Bodhisattvas they enter into a personal relationship with those figures and develop their qualities in themselves.

- Some Buddhists believe the Buddha is beyond this world and can no longer physically intervene. Buddhists access the Buddha through the Dhamma (Dharma) and Sangha.

- Some Buddhists believe the Buddha is within everybody, that everyone has a Buddha nature. When the Dhamma (Dharma) is fully understood, individuals come to the true nature of reality and themselves.

The value of general and special revelation, and enlightenment

- For some it strengthens their belief in the divine as it proves its existence.
- For others it brings them closer to the divine.
- Some types of revelation can help people to understand the divine more.
- For **theists**, these experiences can show them how God wants them to live their lives.

Problems arising from these experiences

- Some people will question these experiences and ask if they actually happened or if they were caused by the divine.
- If the person did experience something, then maybe it was an illusion?
- Many of these experiences lack scientific evidence and are difficult to prove.

How can someone know whether an experience is real?

We could ask:

- Does it support or contradict the main beliefs and teachings of the religion?
- Does it match previously reported experiences within the religion?
- Does it change a person's beliefs or outlook on life?
- Does it have the power to make someone join a religion?
- Is it something that seems possible within the real world or within the limits of what a religion says can happen?

> **REVISION TIP**
>
> Research real life examples and write down questions that you could ask the person or people involved to help you understand the event. Think about what answers you think they might give. This will help you to remember the kinds of questions we can ask about these experiences.

Alternative explanations for the experiences

- Some people say that general revelation, special revelation, and enlightenment are not actual experiences of the divine.
- Some atheists might say that God is not responsible and that there are alternative explanations for these experiences:

The effects of taking intoxicants, such as drugs or alcohol.

People lie about their experiences to gain popularity, fame, or money.

Alternative explanations

Wishful thinking – some people really want to have an experience.

Some experiences can be associated with mental or physical illnesses.

People mistake the cause, for example, a healing miracle could be medicine having an unexpected impact on an ill person, rather than God healing them.

 Key terms Make sure you can write a definition for these key terms

personal   impersonal   immanent   meditating   theist

⇄ Retrieval

Learn the answers to the questions below, then cover the answers column with a piece of paper and write as many as you can. Check and repeat.

Questions | Answers

	Questions		Answers
1	What is the word to describe everybody having the Buddha within?	Put paper here	Buddha-nature
2	Which word means that God is all-knowing?		Omniscient
3	Which word means that God is close to humans and has a relationship with them due to his human characteristics?		Personal
4	Which word means that God is not like humans and is unknowable?	Put paper here	Impersonal
5	Which word means that God is within and involved in his creation (the universe)?		Immanent
6	Which word means that God is beyond and outside of his creation (the universe)?		Transcendent
7	What type of beings do some Buddhists believe they can develop personal relationships with?	Put paper here	Bodhisattvas
8	What intoxicants may somebody take that may make somebody think they are experiencing the divine?		Drugs and alcohol
9	Complete this quotation: *How great is God – beyond our _____!*		Understanding

Previous questions

Now go back and use these questions to check your knowledge of previous topics.

Questions | Answers

	Questions		Answers
10	Name one type of special revelation.	Put paper here	One from: dream / miracle / prophecy / vision
11	Which type of revelation occurs when God shows himself through ordinary, everyday life experiences?		General revelation
12	What three insights did the Buddha gain during his Awakening?		Past lives, cycle of rebirth, and dukkha
13	In the Bible, who experienced a vision of Jesus whilst walking on the road to Damascus?	Put paper here	Saul / Paul
14	Which key term in Buddhism means understanding the ultimate reality (the divine) by gaining true knowledge of life and suffering?		Enlightenment

30 Ideas about the divine and the value of revelation and enlightenment

Exam-style questions

01 Which **one** of these means that God is beyond and outside of his creation (the universe)? **(1 mark)**

Put a tick (✓) in the box next to the correct answer.

A	Omnipotent	☐
B	Omniscient	☐
C	Immanent	☐
D	Transcendent	☐

02 Which **one** of these is a supernatural experience in which a person sees something in a dream or a trance that shows them something about God or life after death? **(1 mark)**

Put a tick (✓) in the box next to the correct answer.

A	Vision	☐
B	Miracle	☐
C	Enlightenment	☐
D	Nature	☐

03 Give **two** religious beliefs about the nature of the divine. **(2 marks)**

04 Give **two** alternative explanations for visions. **(2 marks)**

05 Explain **two** similar religious beliefs about general revelation.

In your answer you must refer to one or more religious traditions. **(4 marks)**

> **EXAM TIP**
> A four-mark question requires two developed points. Show the examiner you have done this by writing in two separate paragraphs.

06 Explain **two** religious beliefs about special revelation.

Refer to sacred writings or another source of religious belief and teaching in your answer. **(5 marks)**

> **EXAM TIP**
> Use the bullet points to help ensure that you include everything needed in a 12-mark question.

07 'The only explanation for visions is that they were caused by the divine.'

Evaluate this statement.

In your answer you:

- should give reasoned arguments in support of this statement
- should give reasoned arguments to support a different point of view
- should refer to religious arguments
- may refer to non-religious arguments
- should reach a justified conclusion. **(12 marks)**

(+ SPaG 3 marks)

⚙ Knowledge

31 D: Peace, justice, forgiveness, and reconciliation

Peace

✝ Christian views	☸ Buddhist views
While the Bible includes times when there was not **peace**, Jesus often promoted peace. *❝ Blessed are the peacemakers, for they will be called children of God. ❞* (Matthew 5:9)	Buddhists promote peace, both for society and individuals. *❝ Overcome the angry by non-anger; overcome the wicked by goodness. ❞* (Dhammapada, 223)

Justice

✝ Christian views	☸ Buddhist views
God is just and expects humans to also be just in their treatment of each other. *❝ But let **justice** roll on like a river, righteousness like a never-failing stream! ❞* (Amos 5:24)	• The Buddha taught about the cessation of dukkha (suffering). Dukkha can be caused by injustice – people mistreating others and denying them opportunities. • Much Buddhist ethical teaching centres on the fair, loving, and kind treatment of others. • Many socially engaged Buddhists work to overcome injustice in the world today, for example, leading anti-war and nuclear weapon campaigns. *❝ One should cultivate loving-kindness towards all the world. ❞* (Pali Canon) *❝ Let him not despise anyone anywhere… ❞* (Pali Canon)

Forgiveness

✝ Christian views	☸ Buddhist views
• **Forgiveness** (showing grace and mercy and • pardoning someone for what they have done wrong) is an important part of being a Christian. • Jesus died on the cross so that human sins can be forgiven by God. • Jesus also told people that they should forgive others. *❝ Then Peter came to Jesus and asked, 'Lord, how many times shall I forgive my brother or sister who sins against me? Up to seven times?' Jesus answered, 'I tell you, not seven times, but seventy-seven* times.' ❞* (Matthew 18:21–22) *Note: Some translations use 'seventy times seven'.	• Forgiveness is important in Buddhism. It means letting go of anger and hatred. • The Buddha taught that forgiveness leads to compassion and wisdom. • If you do not forgive, hatred can develop. Hatred is one of the **Three Poisons** and to be avoided. *❝ … in accordance with the Dhamma, accept the transgression of one who is confessing... ❞* (The Buddha, Anguttara Nikaya)

Reconciliation

✝ **Christian views**	☸ **Buddhist views**
• Christianity is based on **reconciliation** between humans and God, following their separation after The Fall and their personal sin. • Christians are encouraged to 'love your neighbour', and Jesus said: ❝ *Love your enemies and pray for those that persecute you.* ❞ (Matthew 5:44) • For Catholics, the sacrament of reconciliation (confession) allows humans to ask God for forgiveness and for them to reconcile with God.	• The Buddha encouraged people to repair their relationships with one another. • In the story of Aṅgulimāla, the Buddha taught that even where a person has caused serious harm to others, relationships may be repaired if the person is willing to confess and accept the full consequences of what they have done.

Violence

- **Violence** may be used for:
  - retaliation
  - defence
  - protesting against something.

- Violence may be justified by some Christians who believe in 'an eye for an eye'. Some Buddhists may justify violence when used in self-defence or to save a life.

- Christians who are against violence believe that Jesus said to 'turn the other cheek'. Most Buddhists are against violence as a result of the Buddha's Dhamma (Dharma). For example, violence violates the principle of **ahimsa** (non-killing or non-harm), taught in the **First Moral Precept**.

Terrorism

Terrorism is the unlawful use of violence, usually against innocent civilians, to achieve a political goal. Both Christianity and Buddhism teach that terrorism is not acceptable.

✝ Christianity – Jesus said:

❝ *Love your enemies and pray for those that persecute you.* ❞   (Matthew 5:44)

☸ Buddhism – the Buddha said:

❝ *… overcome the angry by non-anger; overcome the wicked by goodness.* ❞
(Dhammapada, 223)

Key terms — Make sure you can write a definition for these key terms

peace   justice   forgiveness   Three Poisons   reconciliation
violence   ahimsa   First Moral Precept   terrorism

Retrieval

Learn the answers to the questions below, then cover the answers column with a piece of paper and write as many as you can. Check and repeat.

Questions | Answers

#	Question	Answer
1	What did Jesus do so that human sins can be forgiven by God?	He died on the cross
2	What does this quotation from the Bible tell Christians? *"But let justice roll on like a river, righteousness like a never-failing stream!"*	God is just and expects humans to be just in their treatment of each other
3	True or false: forgiveness is not an important part of being a Christian.	False
4	Christianity is based on reconciliation between humans and God, following their separation for what two reasons?	The Fall, personal sin
5	Give a quotation from the Bible where Jesus promotes peace.	*"Blessed are the peacemakers, for they will be called children of God."*
6	Which Buddhist term means non-killing or non-harm?	Ahimsa
7	Give two situations in which some Buddhists may justify the use of violence.	Self-defence; saving a life
8	How many times did Jesus say someone should forgive?	Seventy-seven or seventy times seven
9	Complete the quotation: *"… overcome the angry by _____; overcome the wicked by goodness."* (Dhammapada 223)	Non-anger
10	What is the sacrament of reconciliation in Catholic Christianity known as?	Confession
11	Give a quotation that encourages Christians to reconcile with one another.	*"Love your enemies and pray for those that persecute you."*
12	What is hatred an example of in the Buddha's Dhamma (Dharma)?	One of Three Poisons
13	What did the Buddha teach that forgiveness leads to?	Compassion and wisdom
14	Give three situations in which violence might be acceptable to Christians and Buddhists.	Retaliation, defence, protesting against something

Put paper here

Exam-style questions

01 Which **one** of these means showing grace and mercy, and
pardoning someone for what they have done wrong? **(1 mark)**

Put a tick (✓) in the box next to the correct answer.

A Peace ☐

B Justice ☐

C Forgiveness ☐

D Reconciliation ☐

02 Which **one** of these describes the unlawful use of violence –
usually against innocent civilians – to achieve a political goal? **(1 mark)**

Put a tick (✓) in the box next to the correct answer.

A Terrorism ☐

B Protest ☐

C War ☐

D Pacifism ☐

03 Give **two** religious beliefs about forgiveness. **(2 marks)**

04 Give **two** religious beliefs about justice. **(2 marks)**

> **EXAM TIP**
>
> A four-mark question
> requires two developed
> points. Show the
> examiner you have done
> this by writing in two
> separate paragraphs.

05 Explain **two** similar religious beliefs about peace.

In your answer you must refer to one or more religious traditions. **(4 marks)**

06 Explain **two** religious beliefs about reconciliation.

Refer to sacred writings or another source of religious belief and
teaching in your answer. **(5 marks)**

> **EXAM TIP**
>
> Remember, you must name
> a piece of sacred writing or
> source of authority in your
> answer, for example, the
> Bible, Pali Canon, etc.

07 'If you fall out with someone you should always reconcile with
them afterwards.'

Evaluate this statement.

In your answer you:

- should give reasoned arguments in support of this statement
- should give reasoned arguments to support a different point of view
- should refer to religious arguments
- may refer to non-religious arguments
- should reach a justified conclusion. **(12 marks)**

(+ SPaG 3 marks)

⚙ Knowledge

32 D: War

Reasons for war

Greed (e.g., acquisition of land, oil, assets)

✝ Christian views	☸ Buddhist views
Some Christians may be against war if it is for reasons of greed because: ❝ *For the love of money is a root of all kinds of evil. Some people, eager for money, have wandered from the faith and pierced themselves with many griefs.* ❞ (1 Timothy 6:10)	Most Buddhists would be against war if it is for greed. In the Pali Canon, the Buddha teaches: ❝ *Greed is a root of what is unskilful… Whatever suffering a greedy person… inflicts on another person through beating or confiscation is unskilful…* ❞

Self-defence

✝ Christian views	☸ Buddhist views
Some Christians may accept war if it is to help those who are being persecuted: ❝ *Defend the weak and the fatherless; uphold the cause of the poor and the oppressed.* *Rescue the weak and the needy; deliver them from the hand of the wicked.* ❞ (Psalms 82:3–4)	• In Buddhism, there is a mixed attitude about war for reasons of self-defence. • Many Buddhists would be against war, regardless of the reason for it, because of the suffering, acts of harm, and lost lives war causes. • War violates the principle of ahimsa, taught in the First Moral Precept. • However, other Buddhists may feel war in self-defence is permitted as it could save lives, for example, against Japanese military aggression in World War II.

Retaliation (getting back at someone for something they have done to you)

✝ Christian views	☸ Buddhist views
Some Christians may not agree with retaliation because: ❝ *Do not repay anyone evil for evil… If it is possible, as far as it depends on you, live at peace with everyone.* ❞ (Romans 12:17–19) ❝ *But I tell you, do not resist an evil person. If anyone slaps you on the right cheek, turn to them the other cheek also.* ❞ (Matthew 5:39) Some Christians may refer to the Old Testament 'an eye for an eye' to support proportionate retaliation.	Most Buddhists would not support war for reasons of retaliation because they believe that responding to hate with hate is not skilful. The Buddha taught: ❝ *…overcome the angry by non-anger; overcome the wicked by goodness.* ❞ (Dhammapada, 223) This suggests non-violent methods of resolution are preferred, for example, diplomacy.

REVISION TIP

There are many reasons for war, but they will generally come under these three headings so concentrate on these.

The just war theory

- The just war theory lists criteria for situations in which war can be justified and, therefore, can be seen as ethical.
- It is generally considered to be based on Christian beliefs, so can be used by some Christians to justify war.
- There are different developments of the **just war** theory.
- It is often associated with St Thomas Aquinas, a theologian and philosopher in the 13th century.

▲ *St Thomas Aquinas*

Proportional methods – no excessive force and innocent civilians not harmed.

Just cause.

The intention must be to defeat wrongdoing and promote good.

Criteria for a just war:

Reasonable chance of success.

Declared by a recognised authority.

Last resort – all other ways of resolving the issue, such as diplomacy, must have been attempted before war can be declared.

† Christian views on the just war theory

Christian views supporting the just war theory	Christian views rejecting the just war theory
Some Christians agree with the just war theory as it allows for war as a last resort and could be used to protect the weak.	Some Christians do not accept the just war theory because, particularly in modern times, it often causes unnecessary death. It is also almost impossible to fulfil all the criteria in real-life conflicts.

☸ Buddhist views on the just war theory

- The **just war** theory is not a Buddhist idea. As a result, most Buddhists reject the idea of a 'just war', suggesting that we should not respond to violence with violence.
- There is a strong agreement within Buddhism that there is rarely a justifiable reason to resort to violence.
- Violence does not embody the ethical ideals of **metta** (loving kindness) and **karuna** (compassion) towards all living beings.

- Even when faced with occupation, Buddhist-majority Tibet mainly responded non-violently. The Dalai Lama said: '*I firmly believe that we will achieve success through our non-violent path.*' Through many rounds of negotiation, the Dalai Lama proposed turning Tibet into a 'Zone of Peace' and settling the conflict with a non-violent, Middle Way Approach.

⚙ Knowledge

32 D: War

Holy war

- A **holy war** is a war that is fought 'for God', in the name of a religion. It is often fought to defend a faith from attack.

- Those involved in a holy war are often thought to receive religious benefits, such as removal of sins or access to heaven.

⬇

† Holy war in Christianity

In Christianity, a Holy War is one that is started by a leading Christian authority and has the purpose of defending Christianity. There are spiritual rewards for those who fight.

- The Crusades (1095–1291) are an example of a holy war in which Christians travelled to Jerusalem in the Holy Land to claim the land from Muslim groups.

- Both sides believed that they were fighting for God.

- The Christian crusaders were told by the ruling pope that their sins would be forgiven, so even if they died along the way, they could access heaven.

- The Muslims would have considered that they were fighting in defence of Islam.

☸ Holy war in Buddhism

- Most Buddhists would reject the notion of holy war because it is an act involving violence, which goes against the First Moral Precept.

- War results in dukkha, and Buddhists are trying to overcome suffering.

- There are historical examples of Buddhists who have supported war, for example, against Korea (1592) and China (1935). The reason for their war efforts is thought to be to defend their nation (Japan) and to ensure the continuation and spread of Buddhism.

- In the 20th century, a small minority of Buddhists showed extreme hostility and violent aggression towards other religious traditions. These Buddhists encouraged the violent persecution of those who followed a religion other than Buddhism.

- This small minority were inspired by individuals claiming to be Buddhist leaders, such as Galagoda Aththe Gnanasara in Sri Lanka and Ashin Wirathu in Myanmar. It is important to note that these views were often bound to nationalist ideologies (Buddhist nationalism), so it is not as simple as saying that these views were religiously endorsed.

⬇

Pacifism

- Pacifists believe that we should not fight or use violence to resolve issues.

- Pacifists are against war.

- The arguments in favour of **pacifism** are often those given against war and vice versa.

Arguments for and against pacifism

 Arguments in favour of pacifism (against war)

- ☑ In war, people are killed unnecessarily, and often innocent civilians are injured or killed.
- ☑ We can use diplomacy and negotiation to resolve issues.
- ☑ Weapons today (e.g., nuclear weapons) can harm large areas and cause damage way beyond their initial target.

 Arguments against pacifism

- ☒ Other countries may see you as weak if you don't defend yourself.
- ☒ In the past, war has been necessary to stop injustice and remove tyrannical leaders.
- ☒ We should defend the weak and those who are being treated unfairly.

Christian and Buddhist views on pacifism

† Christian views

- ☒ Some Christians use the Old Testament 'eye for an eye' to justify retaliation.
- ☑ However, this can be countered by Jesus saying,

> 66 *You have heard that it was said, 'Eye for eye, and tooth for tooth.' But I tell you, do not resist an evil person. If anyone slaps you on the right cheek, turn to them the other cheek also.* 99 (Matthew 5:38)

- ☒ Other Christians say that when Jesus turned over the tables in the temple (Matthew 21:12), it shows that he accepted violent protest.
- ☑ Some Christians argue that Jesus was a pacifist. Jesus told people:

> 66 *For all who draw the sword will die by the sword.* 99 (Matthew 26:52)

Some Christians take this to mean they shouldn't fight.

☸ Buddhist views

Most Buddhists strongly support pacifism. Pacifism supports:

- ☑ the First Moral Precept – the teaching of non-killing or non-harming of living beings
- ☑ the ethical ideals of loving kindness (metta) and compassion (karuna)
- ☑ the development of inner peace – peace comes from each person, especially their speech and thoughts war
- ☑ the example of Buddhist leaders – Thich Nhat Hanh said, 'if you are not for peace, you are against peace, you are not Buddhism.'

Key terms Make sure you can write a definition for these key terms

just war   metta   karuna   holy war   pacifism

🔁 Retrieval

Learn the answers to the questions below, then cover the answers column with a piece of paper and write as many as you can. Check and repeat.

Questions	Answers
1 Give one reason for war.	One from: greed / retaliation / self-defence
2 Complete the quotation: "*But I tell you, do not resist an evil person. If anyone _____ you on the right cheek, turn to them the other cheek also.*" (Matthew 5:39)	Slaps
3 Which theologian and philosopher is often associated with the just war theory?	St Thomas Aquinas
4 What is a war that is fought 'for God' or for a religion?	Holy war
5 Give one criteria for a just war.	One from: the war must have a just cause / it must be declared by a recognised authority / the intention of the war has to be to defeat wrongdoing and promote good / fighting must be a last resort / there must be a reasonable chance of success / proportional methods used / innocent civilians should not be harmed
6 Which belief does Thich Nhat Hanh advocate?	Pacifism
7 What is the word for a person who believes we should not fight or use violence to resolve issues?	Pacifist
8 What did Jesus do that some Christians say shows he supported violent protest?	Turned the tables in the temple
9 Which of Jesus's words do some Christians take to mean they should not fight?	"*For all who draw the sword will die by the sword.*"

Put paper here

Previous questions

Now go back and use these questions to check your knowledge of previous topics.

Questions	Answers
10 Give a quotation that encourages Christians to reconcile with one another.	"*Love your enemies and pray for those that persecute you.*"
11 What is the sacrament of reconciliation in Catholic Christianity known as?	Confession
12 Give two situations in which some Buddhists may justify the use of violence.	Self-defence; saving a life
13 Give a quotation from the Bible where Jesus promotes peace.	"*Blessed are the peacemakers, for they will be called children of God.*"

Put paper here

Exam-style questions

01 Which **one** of these is a theory that follows a set of criteria to make war fair and ethical? **(1 mark)**

Put a tick (✓) in the box next to the correct answer.

A   Metta ☐

B   Ahimsa ☐

C   Just war ☐

D   Holy war ☐

02 Which **one** of these is the meaning of pacifism? **(1 mark)**

Put a tick (✓) in the box next to the correct answer.

A   A war fought for God ☐

B   A war fought for the right reasons ☐

C   Forgiving those who fight with you ☐

D   Not fighting or using violence to resolve issues ☐

03 Give **two** reasons for war. **(2 marks)**

04 Give **two** of the criteria for a just war. **(2 marks)**

05 Explain **two** contrasting religious beliefs about pacifism in contemporary British society.

In your answer you should refer to the main religious tradition of Great Britain and one or more other religious traditions. **(4 marks)**

> **EXAM TIP**
> 'Contrasting' just means 'different' in these questions.

06 Explain **two** religious beliefs about holy wars.

Refer to sacred writings or another source of religious belief and teaching in your answer. **(5 marks)**

07 'No religious person should be pacifist.'

Evaluate this statement.

In your answer you:

- should give reasoned arguments in support of this statement
- should give reasoned arguments to support a different point of view
- should refer to religious arguments
- may refer to non-religious arguments
- should reach a justified conclusion. **(12 marks)**

(+ SPaG 3 marks)

> **EXAM TIP**
> Remember to read the statement carefully, and use the words from it in your answer to ensure you answer it fully.

⚙ Knowledge

33 D: Religion and belief in 21st century conflict

Religion and belief as a cause of war and violence

While not all wars and violence are caused by religion, there are conflicts and acts of violence in recent history and today that claim to be rooted in religious beliefs (although they often have other causes, including political differences).

In many cases the perpetrators believe that they:

- are defending their religion
- are fighting for God
- will be rewarded by God.

These are some examples of conflicts and violence rooted in religious belief:

- Charlie Hebdo attack in Paris – 2015
- The Ariana Grande concert bombing in Manchester – 2017
- The Troubles in Northern Ireland – 1968–1998
- The Israeli–Palestinian conflict
- The Islamic state of Iraq and Syria (ISIS) invasion of Iraq and Syria.

Religion and peace-making in the contemporary world

There are many individuals and organisations that work towards peace in the world.

Sister Chan Khong

Sister Chan Khong was born in Southern Vietnam in 1938 and is an example of an individual influenced by religious teaching.

- She is the first fully ordained monastic disciple of Thich Nhat Hanh.
- She helped develop socially engaged Buddhism (as an expression of the principle of ahimsa (non-harming), the first moral precept).

Sister Chan Khong is a Buddhist and has talked about how her beliefs are important in her work. She has worked for peace by:

- organising the Buddhist peace delegation at the Paris Peace Talks in 1969 – this was instrumental in ending the Vietnam War and bringing peace to the country in 1975
- giving talks on the topic of peace and non-violent methods of conflict resolution

- leading campaigns for peace (e.g., by writing to world leaders to ask them to act with metta and karuna)
- helping and supporting victims of war by gathering aid (e.g., food for children who were victims of the war in Vietnam)
- promoting a mindfulness practice to help peaceful growth:

> *...you stop the war outside, you have to stop the war inside yourself.* 🙿 [Sister Chan Khong]

The Peace People

The Peace People organisation was started in 1976 by Mairead Corrigan, Betty Williams, and Ciaran McKeown.

They worked for peace in Northern Ireland.

They held **peace-making** activities such as marches to help people see that fighting and killing weren't necessary.

Corrigan and Williams won the Nobel Peace prize in 1976 for their work.

> **REVISION TIP**
>
> You can study the examples here or others, but you must ensure that the people or organisation you write about has recently worked for peace.

Religious responses to the victims of war

Religious groups and individuals may not be able to prevent war, but they can work to help the victims of war. They can do this by:

- giving shelter to those who have been displaced
- ensuring people have access to clean water
- helping to rebuild communities
- providing short- and long-term support to rebuild lives

- giving medicine and medical help
- supplying food to those in need
- giving emotional and mental health support to people who have had life-changing experiences
- arranging opportunities for education.

Christian Aid

Christian Aid is a religious organisation that helps victims of war. It was established in 1945 to help refugees from World War II.

What they do	Examples of where they have worked	Religious principles that support their work
• Humanitarian relief. • Long-term development support for poor communities worldwide. • Tackling injustice.	• Haiti earthquake. • Afghanistan crisis. • East Africa hunger crisis. • Ukraine humanitarian appeal.	• Christian Aid believe that everyone is equal in the sight of God and so they aim to end poverty around the world. christian **aid**

Tzu Chi Foundation

Tzu Chi Foundation is a Buddhist organisation that helps victims of war.

What they do	Examples of where they have worked	Religious principles that support their work
• Medical care and organise bone marrow donation. • Establishing schools. • Responding to international disasters and provide environmental protection. TZU CHI	• Ukraine war and humanitarian appeal. • Nepal disaster response. • Pakistan floods. • Turkey support for Syrian war refugees.	• Tzu Chi's founder encourages an altruistic love for others, believing that if everybody showed love to one another, conflict could be resolved without the need for war. • Tzu Chi's guiding principle is to *'help the poor and educate the rich.'* This may help overcome some of the causes of war (e.g., greed).

Key terms Make sure you can write a definition for these key terms

peace-making

REVISION TIP

Check which organisations you are studying. If they are not mentioned above, set yourself a task to put what you've learnt into some bullet points like these.

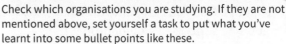

⇄ Retrieval

Learn the answers to the questions below, then cover the answers column with a piece of paper and write as many as you can. Check and repeat.

Questions

	Answers
1 Give one reason why people may believe they should go to war for their religion.	One from: they are defending their religion / they are fighting for God / they will be rewarded by God
2 Give an example of a conflict or violence in recent history that are rooted in religious beliefs.	One from: the Islamic state of Iraq and Syria (ISIS) invasion of Iraq and Syria / the Israeli–Palestinian conflict / the Troubles – Northern Ireland 1968–1998 / anti-Muslim violence in Myanmar – 2013 / Charlie Hebdo attack in Paris – 2015 / Ariana Grande concert bombing in Manchester – 2017
3 Name one place and event where Christian Aid have provided support.	One from: Haiti earthquake / Afghanistan crisis / East Africa hunger crisis / Ukraine humanitarian appeal
4 How can religious groups and individuals respond to war?	By working to help victims
5 Name one place and event where the Tzu Chi Foundation have provided support.	One from: Ukraine war / Nepal disaster response / Pakistan floods / Turkey support for Syrian war refugees
6 Where does the organisation 'The Peace People' work for peace?	Northern Ireland
7 Give an example of a Buddhist who is working for peace-making in the contemporary world.	Sister Chan Khong

Put paper here

Previous questions

Now go back and use these questions to check your knowledge of previous topics.

Questions

	Answers
8 Which Buddhist term means non-killing or non-harm?	Ahimsa
9 How many times did Jesus say someone should forgive?	Seventy-seven or seventy times seven
10 Give one reason for war.	One from: greed / retaliation / self-defence
11 Which theologian and philosopher is often associated with the Just War theory?	St Thomas Aquinas
12 What is a war that is fought 'for God' or for a religion?	Holy war
13 Which belief does Thich Nhat Hanh advocate?	Pacifism
14 What did Jesus do that some Christians say shows he supported violent protest?	Turned the tables in the temple

Put paper here

Exam-style questions

01 Which **one** of these is a main religious benefit
for a person to fight in a holy war? **(1 mark)**

Put a tick (✓) in the box next to the correct answer.

A   They will be rewarded by God ☐

B   To gain land ☐

C   They will get money ☐

D   To be more powerful ☐

02 Which **one** of these is **not** an example of something that a
religious organisation might do to help victims of war? **(1 mark)**

Put a tick (✓) in the box next to the correct answer.

A   Give medicine ☐

B   Give shelter ☐

C   Get involved in the fighting ☐

D   Give access to clean water ☐

03 Name **two** places where there have been conflict and violence
due to religious belief in recent history. **(2 marks)**

04 Give **two** examples of things that a religious organisation might do
to help victims of war. **(2 marks)**

05 Explain **two** similar religious responses to victims of war.

In your answer you must refer to one or more religious traditions. **(4 marks)**

> **EXAM TIP**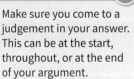
>
> Remember to name the
> religion that you are
> writing about so the
> examiner is clear whether
> your answer is correct.

06 Explain **two** ways in which the work of one present-day
religious organisation helps victims of war.

Refer to sacred writings or another source of religious belief and
teaching in your answer. **(5 marks)**

07 'Religious people should visit war zones to help victims of war.'

Evaluate this statement.

In your answer you:

> **EXAM TIP**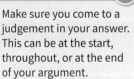
>
> Make sure you come to a
> judgement in your answer.
> This can be at the start,
> throughout, or at the end
> of your argument.

- should give reasoned arguments in support of this statement

- should give reasoned arguments to support a different point of view

- should refer to religious arguments

- may refer to non-religious arguments

- should reach a justified conclusion. **(12 marks)**

(+ SPaG 3 marks)

⚙ Knowledge

34 D: Nuclear weapons and weapons of mass destruction

Weapons of mass destruction

- **Weapons of mass destruction** (WMDs) can be used far away from the intended target and attack large areas.

Biological weapons	Chemical weapons	Nuclear weapons
Weapons that have living organisms or infective material that can lead to disease or death, for example, a germ or virus that poisons humans.	Weapons that use chemicals to poison, burn, or paralyse humans and destroy the natural environment.	Weapons that work by a nuclear reaction to devastate huge areas and kill large numbers of people.

Nuclear weapons

- Countries around the world make and stockpile nuclear weapons.

- Possessing nuclear weapons is considered a **nuclear deterrent**. This means that they can discourage other countries from attacking.

- A country might be seen as more powerful if they have a stockpile of nuclear weapons.

Hiroshima and Nagasaki, Japan - August 1945

| During World War II, the USA drops a nuclear bomb on the city of Hiroshima and another on the city of Nagasaki, Japan. | → | The explosions cause over 100 000 deaths and hundreds of thousands more were harmed. | → | This brings World War II to an end as Japan surrenders a few days later. |

Arguments for and against WMDs

 Arguments for nuclear weapons

- ☑ They can prevent wars by acting as a deterrent.
- ☑ It makes people feel safer having them, if other countries also have them.

 Arguments against nuclear weapons

- ☒ They are indiscriminate and can kill many people, including innocent civilians.
- ☒ They cause widespread environmental damage that lasts for many years.

 ## Christian and Buddhist arguments for WMDs

- ☑ A minority of Christians and Buddhists may accept that countries need WMDs to be able to defend themselves.
- ☑ Some Christians might use 'an eye for an eye' in the Bible to justify having and potentially using WMDs if enemies are doing the same.
- ☑ Few Buddhists would agree with their country's national policy supporting the use of WMDs. However, a very small minority may justify the use of WMDs to defend and ensure the continuation of Buddhism. For example, some may interpret the Mahaparinirvana Sutra as permitting the use of violence to protect the Buddha's Dhamma (Dharma):

 > 66 *It is the same with those who have committed the four grave offences [e.g. killing]... Although having done evil before... A person who protects Dharma will meet with such an inexpressible reward.* 99
>
> (Mahaparinirvana Sutra)

Christian and Buddhist arguments against WMDs

- ☒ Some Christians and Buddhists believe that WMDs are not acceptable because they cause large numbers of deaths and long-term damage.

 > 66 *When conflicts arise they should be settled through dialogue, not the use of force. We need to eliminate the threat of nuclear weapons, with the ultimate aim of a demilitarized world.* 99
>
> (The Dalai Lama)

 > 66 *Overcome the angry by non-anger; overcome the wicked by goodness.* 99
>
> (Dhammapada, 223)

† > 66 *Do not repay anyone evil for evil. . . . If it is possible, as far as it depends on you, live at peace with everyone.* 99 (Romans 12:17–19)

- ☒ Many Buddhists organisations, for example, the Buddhist Peace Fellowship, work to campaign against the use of nuclear weapons and eliminate the world of all violence.
- ☒ The Nipponzan Myohoji (Japan Buddha Sangha) build peace pagodas around the globe and undertake community chants (Daimoku) wishing for peace across the world.

 Key terms **Make sure you can write a definition for these key terms**

weapons of mass destruction   biological weapons
chemical weapons   nuclear weapons   nuclear deterrent

Retrieval

Learn the answers to the questions below, then cover the answers column with a piece of paper and write as many as you can. Check and repeat.

Questions	Answers
1 Which type of weapons have living organisms or infective material that can lead to disease or death, for example, a germ or virus that poisons humans?	Biological weapons
2 Which type of weapons use chemicals to poison, burn, or paralyse humans and destroy the natural environment?	Chemical weapons
3 Give one argument for having weapons of mass destruction.	One from: they can prevent wars by acting as a deterrent / people feel safer having them if other countries also have them
4 Which teaching may be used by some Christians to support the use of WMDs?	'An eye for an eye'
5 How does the Dalai Lama advocate that conflict be settled?	Through dialogue
6 What does 'nuclear deterrent' mean?	Having nuclear weapons to deter other countries from attacking
7 Where did the USA drop nuclear bombs in 1945?	Hiroshima and Nagasaki, Japan
8 Give one argument against having weapons of mass destruction.	One from: they cause large numbers of deaths / they cause long-term damage

Put paper here

Previous questions

Now go back and use these questions to check your knowledge of previous topics.

Questions	Answers
9 Complete the quotation: "… overcome the angry by _____; overcome the wicked by goodness." (Dhammapada 223)	Non-anger
10 What is the sacrament of reconciliation in Catholic Christianity known as?	Confession
11 During which event in the Bible did Adam and Eve disobey God?	The Fall
12 Which Buddhist term means non-killing or non-harm?	Ahimsa
13 What is the correct word for a person who believes we should not fight or use violence to resolve issues?	Pacifist
14 Give one reason why people may believe that they should go to war for their religion.	One from: they are defending their religion / they are fighting for God / they will be rewarded by God

Put paper here

Exam-style questions

01 Which **one** of these are weapons that use chemicals to poison, burn, or paralyse humans and destroy the natural environment? **(1 mark)**

Put a tick (✓) in the box next to the correct answer.

A Nuclear weapons ☐

B Biological weapons ☐

C Chemical weapons ☐

D Artillery ☐

02 Which **one** of these is a weapon of mass destruction (WMD)? **(1 mark)**

Put a tick (✓) in the box next to the correct answer.

A Hand grenade ☐

B Nuclear weapon ☐

C Assault rifle ☐

D Submachine gun ☐

03 Name **two** types of weapons of mass destruction. **(2 marks)**

04 Give **two** arguments against the use of weapons of mass destruction. **(2 marks)**

> **EXAM TIP**
> In two-mark questions you do not have to write in full sentences. Answers can be a single word or short phrases.

05 Explain **two** contrasting religious beliefs on weapons of mass destruction.

In your answer you must refer to one or more religious traditions. **(4 marks)**

06 Explain **two** religious beliefs about nuclear weapons.

Refer to sacred writings or another source of religious belief and teaching in your answer. **(5 marks)**

> **EXAM TIP**
> Remember, you must name the sacred writings or source in your answer to get the fifth mark, for example, the Bible.

07 'No country should have nuclear weapons.'

Evaluate this statement.

In your answer you:

- should give reasoned arguments in support of this statement
- should give reasoned arguments to support a different point of view
- should refer to religious arguments
- may refer to non-religious arguments
- should reach a justified conclusion. **(12 marks)**

(+ SPaG 3 marks)

Knowledge

35 E: Good and evil intentions and actions

Intentions and actions

Sometimes people act in a way where the **intention** is **good** but the action itself could be considered to be bad or **evil**. In these cases, what is more important: the intention or the action itself?

REVISION TIP

Remember that someone's intention is the reason or the plan behind doing something.

Example	Intention	Action
A person lies to their friend about something to avoid upsetting them.	To avoid upset	Lying to a friend
To stop people being persecuted by a ruthless dictator, a person sends an army to find and kill the dictator.	To stop persecution	Killing
Someone steals food from a supermarket to feed their children.	To feed children	Stealing
A person helps someone who is ill and **suffering** to end their life.	To stop suffering	Ending a life

Can it ever be good to cause suffering?

When considering their intentions and actions, most people will try to avoid causing suffering. However, there may be times when it is acceptable to cause suffering, for example:

- to learn lessons from the suffering
- doing something that God requires you to do, even though it causes suffering, for example, telling the truth about who committed a crime
- as a punishment to show criminals that what they have done is not acceptable
- if the benefit outweighs the suffering the action causes.

✝ **Christian views**	☸ **Buddhist views**
• We should take strength from suffering: *« We also glory in our sufferings, because we know that suffering produces perseverance; perseverance, character; and character, hope. »* (Romans 5:3–4) • Jesus suffered for humans to be saved: *« For Christ also suffered once for sins, the righteous for the unrighteous, that he might bring us to God. »* (1 Peter 3:18)	Buddhism teaches the nature of dukkha in the Four Noble Truths. • There is dukkha. • There is **samudaya** (a cause of suffering). • There is **nirodha** (a way to end suffering). • The way to end suffering is to follow **magga** (the Eightfold Path).

† Christian responses to good and evil intentions and actions

- Evil actions might be considered to be those that go against God's teachings in the Bible, for example, murder, adultery, lying, stealing. These are called **sins**.

- The Bible emphasises that what you do is linked to your inner thoughts:

> 66 *He [Jesus] went on: 'What comes out of a person is what defiles them. For it is from within, out of a person's heart, that evil thoughts come—sexual immorality, theft, murder, adultery, greed, malice, deceit, lewdness, envy, slander, arrogance, and folly. All these evils come from inside and defile a person.* 99
>
> (Mark 7:20–23)

- As a guide for life, Jesus said:

> 66 *…in everything, do to others what you would have them do to you.* 99
>
> (Matthew 7:12)

This emphasises considering your actions.

✹ Buddhist responses to good and evil intentions and actions

- The Buddha did not designate actions as 'good' or 'evil'. Rather, he described them as 'skilful' or 'unskilful'.

- Unskilful behaviours give rise to suffering for us and others. Skilful behaviours have positive consequences and lead towards Enlightenment

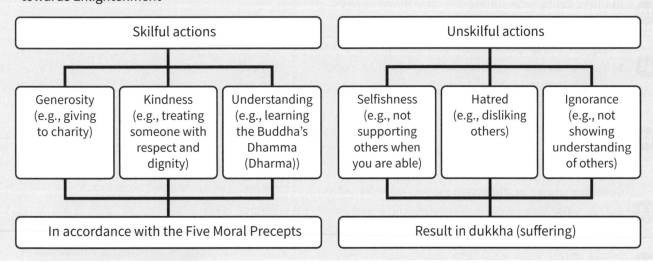

Skilful actions			Unskilful actions		
Generosity (e.g., giving to charity)	Kindness (e.g., treating someone with respect and dignity)	Understanding (e.g., learning the Buddha's Dhamma (Dharma))	Selfishness (e.g., not supporting others when you are able)	Hatred (e.g., disliking others)	Ignorance (e.g., not showing understanding of others)
In accordance with the Five Moral Precepts			Result in dukkha (suffering)		

Key terms **Make sure you can write a definition for these key terms**

intention   good   evil   suffering
samudaya   nirodha   magga   sins

Retrieval

Learn the answers to the questions below, then cover the answers column with a piece of paper and write as many as you can. Check and repeat.

Question	Answer
1 Give one example of something that the Bible considers to be a sin against God.	One from: murder / adultery / lying
2 Where does the Bible say evil thoughts come from?	A person's heart
3 What category of action is encouraged in Buddhism?	Skilful
4 What category of action is discouraged in Buddhism?	Unskilful
5 What does dukkha mean in Buddhism?	Suffering
6 What type of skilful action involves giving to charity?	Generosity
7 What type of skilful action involves treating somebody with respect and dignity?	Kindness
8 What type of unskilful action involves not showing an understanding of others?	Ignorance
9 What type of unskilful action involves demonstrating a dislike of others?	Hatred
10 In Christianity, who suffered to save humans from their sins?	Jesus
11 Complete the quotation: "We also glory in our sufferings, because we know that suffering produces _____..." (Romans 5:3–4)	Perseverance
12 Give one example of a situation in which a religious person might intentionally cause suffering to others.	One from: to help someone learn a lesson / the benefits outweigh the suffering / God has asked it / to retaliate / to fight injustice / to punish
13 Complete the quotation: "For Christ also suffered once for ____, the righteous for the unrighteous, that he might bring us to God." (1 Peter 3:18)	Sins
14 Where in the Buddha's Dhamma (Dharma) is the nature of suffering taught?	The Four Noble Truths

Put paper here

Exam-style questions

01 Which **one** of these would be classed as an evil action? **(1 mark)**

Put a tick (✓) in the box next to the correct answer.

A   Giving to charity   ☐

B   Committing murder   ☐

C   Helping the homeless   ☐

D   Praying   ☐

02 Which **one** of these people do Christians believe suffered to save humans' sins?

Put a tick (✓) in the box next to the correct answer. **(1 mark)**

A   John   ☐

B   Paul   ☐

C   Jesus   ☐

D   Adam   ☐

03 Give **two** examples of when it may be considered acceptable for some people to cause suffering. **(2 marks)**

04 Name **two** causes of suffering. **(2 marks)**

05 Explain **two** similar religious beliefs about causing suffering.

In your answer you must refer to one or more religious traditions. **(4 marks)**

> **EXAM TIP** 🎯
>
> 'Similar' does not mean that the beliefs have to be exactly the same. Your two points just need to agree with each other.

06 Explain **two** religious beliefs about good and evil intentions.

Refer to sacred writings or another source of religious belief and teaching in your answer. **(5 marks)**

> **EXAM TIP** 🎯
>
> Remember, you must name the piece of sacred writing or source of authority that is in your answer, for example, the Bible, the Buddha.

07 'Sometimes suffering can be good for a person.'

Evaluate this statement. In your answer you:

- should give reasoned arguments in support of this statement
- should give reasoned arguments to support a different point of view
- should refer to religious arguments
- may refer to non-religious arguments
- should reach a justified conclusion. **(12 marks)**

(+ SPaG 3 marks)

Knowledge

36 E: Reasons for crime

Why people commit crime

There are many different reasons why people commit crimes.

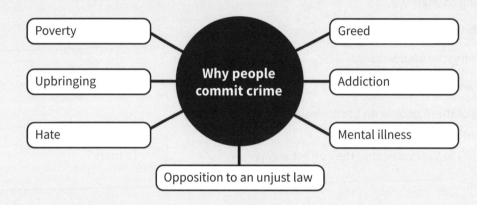

Poverty — Greed — Upbringing — Why people commit crime — Addiction — Hate — Mental illness — Opposition to an unjust law

† Christian views on people who break the law for these reasons

- Christians believe that whilst all people do wrong and sin, we should help those who struggle in life and commit crimes.
- Christianity is based on the idea of reformation – that all people are sinners and can be saved. Therefore, people who break the law should be helped to change.

- Whilst Jesus was dying on the cross, he told the criminal to his right:

> ❝ …today you will be with me in paradise ❞
> (Luke 23:43)

- This demonstrates that until death a criminal can be forgiven for their sins and enter heaven.

☸ Buddhist views on people who break the law for these reasons

- Buddhists acknowledge that sometimes people may commit crime. However, through loving kindness (metta) and karuna (compassion), Buddhists would want to help criminals and support them in stopping criminal activity.
- Many Buddhist teachings advocate for people to avoid things that cause crime. For example, in the Five Moral Precepts, the Fifth Precept encourages people to avoid things that intoxicate and cloud the mind, so they should not develop substance addictions.
- Buddhists may encourage those with hate to engage in practices to help clear the mind, rather than commit a hate crime, (e.g., metta meditation).

- The Buddha's Dhamma (Dharma) acknowledges that the world is full of greed (Three Poisons). Following the Buddha's teaching of the Middle Way may help those committing crime due to their (e.g., some types of theft).
- Many socially engaged Buddhists offer practical support to those who may break the law as a result of absolute poverty. For example, many UK Buddhist centres run foodbanks to help people meet their basic needs for food. They may also recommend other services that may prevent people turning to crime. Buddhists would encourage reform on a societal level, to change the conditions faced by those in poverty to prevent them from turning to crime.

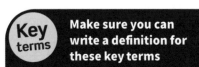 **Key terms** Make sure you can write a definition for these key terms

hate crime   theft   murder   forgiveness

Views about different types of crime

Crime	† Christian	Buddhist
Hate crime (Motivated by race, religion, sexuality, disability, gender, or other protected characteristic)	*❝ Anyone who hates a brother or sister* is a murderer, and you know that no murderer has eternal life residing in him. ❞* (1 John 3:15) (*this means anyone, not just your actual brother/sister.)	*❝ ...the key to a happier and more successful world is the growth of compassion. ❞* (The Dalai Lama)
Theft	*❝ You shall not steal. ❞* (Exodus 20:15) (From the Ten Commandments)	*❝ ...abandoning taking what is not given (stealing), the disciple of the noble ones abstains from taking what is not given. ❞* (Pali Canon)
Murder	*❝ You shall not murder. ❞* (Exodus 20:13) (From the Ten Commandments)	*❝ ...abandoning the taking of life, abstains from taking life. ❞* (Pali Canon)

Forgiveness

- **Forgiveness** is showing grace and mercy, and pardoning someone for what they have done wrong.
- Both Christianity and Buddhism teach that forgiveness is an important aspect of life.

> **REVISION TIP**
>
> Knowing The Lord's prayer is useful here, and you need to know it for the Christianity exam paper.

† Christianity	Buddhism
• Jesus died on the cross so that human sins can be forgiven by God. Jesus also told people that they should forgive: *❝ Then Peter came to Jesus and asked, 'Lord, how many times shall I forgive my brother or sister who sins against me? Up to seven times?' Jesus answered, 'I tell you, not seven times, but seventy-seven times.' ❞* (Matthew 18:21–22) • Christians often ask God for forgiveness of their sins: *❝ Forgive us our sins, as we forgive those who sin against us. ❞* (The Lord's Prayer)	• Forgiveness is an important part of Buddhist teaching. The Buddha taught that forgiveness leads to the development of compassion and wisdom: *❝ ...in accordance with the Dhamma, accept the transgression of one who is confessing. ❞* (The Buddha, Anguttara Nikaya) • The Dalai Lama teaches: *❝ ...if I develop bad feelings toward those who make me suffer, this will only destroy my own peace of mind. But if I forgive, my mind becomes calm. ❞*

Learn the answers to the questions below, then cover the answers column with a piece of paper and write as many as you can. Check and repeat.

Questions	Answers
1 Give three reasons for crime.	Three from: poverty / upbringing / mental illness / addiction / greed / hate / opposition to an unjust law
2 Complete this quotation from Jesus: "*today you will be with me in _____.*" (Luke 23:43)	Paradise
3 What does the fifth of the Five Moral Precepts encourage?	Avoidance of things that intoxicate or cloud the mind
4 What crimes, often including violence, are targeted at a person because of their race, religion, sexuality, disability, gender, or other protected characteristic?	Hate crimes
5 In his teachings, what quality does the Buddha suggest that forgiveness develops?	Wisdom
6 Which of the Ten Commandments says not to deliberately kill someone?	*"You shall not murder."*
7 How many times did Jesus say we should forgive?	Seventy-seven or seventy times seven
8 Complete this line from the Lord's Prayer: "*Forgive us our _____, as we forgive those who _____ against us.*"	Sins, sin
9 Which word means to show grace and mercy, and pardon someone for what they have done wrong?	Forgiveness
10 What collection of Buddhist teaching forbids actions such as stealing and intoxication?	The Five Moral Precepts

Put paper here

Previous questions

Now go back and use these questions to check your knowledge of previous topics.

Questions	Answers
11 Give one example of something that the Bible considers to be a sin against God.	One from: murder / adultery / lying / stealing
12 Where does the Bible say evil thoughts come from?	A person's heart
13 What category of action is encouraged in Buddhism?	Skilful
14 What category of action is discouraged in Buddhism?	Unskilful
15 What does dukkha mean in Buddhism?	Suffering

Put paper here

Exam-style questions

01 Which **one** of these is **not** a common reason for crime? **(1 mark)**

Put a tick (✓) in the box next to the correct answer.

A Greed ☐

B Hate ☐

C Upbringing ☐

D Happiness ☐

02 Which **one** of these means showing grace and mercy, and pardoning someone for what they have done wrong? **(1 mark)**

Put a tick (✓) in the box next to the correct answer.

A Forgiveness ☐

B Peace-making ☐

C Apology ☐

D Repentance ☐

03 Give **two** reasons for crime. **(2 marks)**

04 Give **two** religious beliefs about those that commit crimes. **(2 marks)**

05 Explain **two** contrasting religious views in contemporary British society about forgiveness.

In your answer you must refer to one or more religious traditions. **(4 marks)**

> **EXAM TIP**
>
> Remember you can use 'some' and 'other' when answering contrasting questions, for example, Some Christians…, Other Christians…, etc.

06 Explain **two** religious beliefs about people who commit hate crimes.

Refer to sacred writings or another source of religious belief and teaching in your answer. **(5 marks)**

07 Explain **two** religious beliefs about people who commit theft.

Refer to sacred writings or another source of religious belief and teaching in your answer. **(5 marks)**

08 'We should always forgive others when they do wrong.'

Evaluate this statement.

In your answer you:

- should give reasoned arguments in support of this statement
- should give reasoned arguments to support a different point of view
- should refer to religious arguments
- may refer to non-religious arguments
- should reach a justified conclusion. **(12 marks)**

(+ SPaG 3 marks)

> **EXAM TIP**
>
> Use the bullet points to help ensure that you include everything needed to answer a 12-mark question.

37 E: The aims of punishment and the treatment of criminals

Retribution

Retribution means that the punishment should make the criminal pay for what they have done wrong.

✝ Christian views	☸ Buddhist views
• Old Testament: ❝ *But if there is serious injury, you are to take life for life, eye for eye, tooth for tooth, hand for hand, foot for foot, burn for burn, wound for wound, bruise for bruise.* ❞ (Exodus 21:23–25) • New Testament: ❝ *You have heard that it was said, 'Eye for eye, and tooth for tooth.' But I tell you, do not resist an evil person. If anyone slaps you on the right cheek, turn to them the other cheek also.'* ❞ (Matthew 5:38–39) • Most Christians believe that the New Testament teaching clarifies the Old Testament teaching, and any potential punishment should be God's decision.	• This form of punishment is generally discouraged by Buddhists. ❝ *…we are not punished for our sins, but by them.* ❞ (David Loy) ❝ *…we should not seek revenge on those who have committed crimes against us, or reply to their crimes with other crimes.* ❞ (The Dalai Lama)

Deterrence

Deterrence means that the likely punishment should put people off committing crime.

✝ Christian views	☸ Buddhist views
• Whilst the Old Testament speaks of punishments that may act to deter criminals, the New Testament gives a message about love and forgiveness.	• Many Buddhists believe this to be the best form of punishment as it prevents many of the consequences of criminal activity for both perpetrator and victim, and helps make a safer society. • The Buddhist teachings of kamma and rebirth may also explain why many Buddhists favour deterrence. It is thought that if a person carries out unskilful actions in this life, their next life will be one of suffering.

> **REVISION TIP**
>
> Remember that retribution, deterrence, and reformation are the purpose of punishments, not actual punishments.

Reformation

Reformation means that the punishment should change the criminal's behaviour for the better.

† Christian views	Buddhist views
• Christianity is based on the idea of reformation – that we are all sinners and can be saved. So, people who commit crimes should be helped to change. Whilst Jesus was dying on the cross, he told the criminal to his right: **❝** *...today you will be with me in paradise.* **❞** (Luke 23:43)	• Reformation is favoured by Buddhists as it encourages criminals to recognise the dukkha caused by their actions. • Some Buddhists may focus their efforts on reformation in the hope that the criminal will transform and act more skilfully, showing others love and kindness rather than ignorance and hatred. • The story of Angulimala, someone who had committed multiple murders, teaches Buddhists the importance and impact of reformation. • Many Buddhist-centred initiatives have tried to help prisoners reform, for example, the Prison Mindfulness Project.

Prison

In Great Britain, being sent to prison is a punishment used to deter people from committing crimes, and is also protection for society whilst the criminal is inside prison.

• Prison aims to reform criminals so they stop re-offending.

• Depending on the crime, a criminal can be sentenced up to a full life sentence in prison.

• Whilst in prison, criminals can be supported to reform with opportunities to gain qualifications, carry out meaningful work to gain new skills, and complete rehabilitation programmes.

† Christian views	Buddhist views
Most Christians support reformation and so would agree that prison offers criminals the chance to change whilst also keeping society safe.	• Some Buddhists support the use of prisons as they protect society against dangerous criminals. • Some Buddhists argue that prison may help a criminal reform, especially if they engage in Buddhist practice whilst there, for example, meditation.

37 E: The aims of punishment and the treatment of criminals

Corporal punishment

Corporal punishment means punishing offenders by causing them physical pain, for example, by lashing, the amputation of limbs or caning.

- Examples of countries that use corporal punishment include Iran, Saudi Arabia, and Singapore. It is illegal in Great Britain.

✝ Christian views	☸ Buddhist views

• Most Christians would not support corporal punishment for criminals as it causes physical harm, and Jesus taught *'pray for those that persecute'* and instead of *'an eye for an eye'* to *'turn the other cheek.'*
 	
 • However, the Bible says:
 	
    66 *He who spares the rod hates their children, but the one who loves their children is careful to discipline them.* 99   (Proverbs 13:24)
 	
 So some Christians may argue that it is important to discipline a child, which may include corporal punishment.
	• Many Buddhists would not be in favour of corporal punishment as it is an act of violence or harm forbidden by the First Moral Precept.
	
	 • Corporal punishment also fails to allow the causes of criminal activity to be understood. This means that some Buddhists may argue that it serves very little purpose as it fails to express metta and karuna.
	
	 • The Buddha taught:
	
	    66 *Whenever you want to do a bodily action, you should reflect on it: […] would it lead to […] affliction of others […] Would it [have] painful consequences and painful results?* 99 (Pali Canon)
	
	 • So if it would lead to the affliction of others, it would be considered an unskilful bodily action.

REVISION TIP

Don't spend lots of time learning lists of quotations: in the exam you can paraphrase and still gain marks. The priority is having quotations that link to the specific area of study.

Community service

Community service is a way of punishing offenders by making them do unpaid work in the community, for example, cleaning litter from public spaces.

REVISION TIP

You need to try to remember the sources of quotations. So in your revision, always cite a source. You don't need explicit chapter references, just where the quotation is found is acceptable.

✝ Christian views	☸ Buddhist views
• Most Christians would support community service as it gives the criminal a chance to reform, and it contributes to society in a positive way. • Jesus taught: 66 *Blessed are the merciful, for they will be shown mercy.* 99 (Matthew 5:7)	• Many Buddhists would support the use of community service, especially if it helps to reform the criminal. • Many acts of community service allow the criminal to express metta and karuna towards the world, for example, repairing, cleaning, and supporting those in need.

Angulimala: The Buddhist Prison Chaplaincy

Angulimala is a charity that aims to ensure an availability of Buddhist teaching and practice within UK prisons. Its methods are the encouragement of Buddhist morality, wisdom and meditation. Angulimala does the following:

- Acts as a 'good friend' (kalyana mitta) to Buddhists. This may potentially take the form of offering advice and guidance rooted in the Buddha Dhamma (Dharma), this may help Buddhists reform their behaviour.

- Supports Buddhists when they are released from prison. Again, this may mean they support Buddhists in reforming their behaviour. In some cases, this may mean signposting support to tackle the reasons they commit crimes.

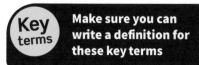

Key terms   **Make sure you can write a definition for these key terms**

retribution   deterrence   reformation
corporal punishment   community service

Retrieval

Learn the answers to the questions below, then cover the answers column with a piece of paper and write as many as you can. Check and repeat.

Questions	Answers
1 What does retribution mean?	Making a criminal pay for what they have done
2 Which aim of punishment is to put people off committing crimes?	Deterrence
3 Which aim of punishment is to change someone's behaviour for the better?	Reformation
4 What did Jesus say to counter an *"eye for an eye"*?	*"Turn the other cheek"*
5 Complete the quotation: *"…we should not seek _____ on those who have committed crimes against us, or reply to their crimes with other crimes."* (The Dalai Lama)	Revenge
6 Give one example of opportunities that prisons in Great Britain may offer to try to reform criminals.	One from: to gain qualifications / to carry out meaningful work to gain new skills / to complete rehabilitation programmes
7 What is corporal punishment?	Punishing an offender by causing them physical pain
8 Give one example of corporal punishment.	One from: lashes / the amputation of limbs / caning
9 Which Bible quotation urges parents to discipline their children?	*"He who spares the rod hates their children, but the one who loves their children is careful to discipline them."*
10 Which type of punishment makes offenders do unpaid work in the community?	Community service

Put paper here *Put paper here* *Put paper here* *Put paper here* *Put paper here*

Previous questions

Now go back and use these questions to check your knowledge of previous topics.

Questions	Answers
11 In Christianity, who suffered to save humans from their sins?	Jesus
12 What collection of Buddhist teaching forbids actions such as stealing and intoxication?	The Five Moral Precepts
13 Give three reasons for crime.	Three from: poverty / upbringing / mental illness / addiction / greed / hate / opposition to an unjust law
14 Complete this quotation from Jesus: *"…today you will be with me in _____."* (Luke 23:43)	Paradise
15 What type of skilful action involves treating somebody with respect and dignity?	Kindness

Put paper here *Put paper here*

37 The aims of punishment and the treatment of criminals

Exam-style questions

01 Which **one** of these means to make a criminal pay for what they have done wrong? **(1 mark)**

Put a tick (✓) in the box next to the correct answer.

A	Retribution	☐
B	Deterrence	☐
C	Protection	☐
D	Reformation	☐

02 Which **one** of these means to put people off committing crimes? **(1 mark)**

Put a tick (✓) in the box next to the correct answer.

A	Retribution	☐
B	Deterrence	☐
C	Protection	☐
D	Reformation	☐

03 Give **two** religious beliefs about using prison as a punishment. **(2 marks)**

04 Explain **two** similar religious beliefs about using deterrence to stop people committing crime.

In your answer you should refer to the main religious tradition of Great Britain and one or more other religious traditions. **(4 marks)**

> **EXAM TIP**
> Remember to name the religion that you are writing about so the examiner is clear if your answer is correct.

05 Explain **two** religious beliefs on the use of corporal punishment.

Refer to sacred writings or another source of religious belief and teaching in your answer. **(5 marks)**

06 'We should always follow an 'eye for an eye' when punishing criminals.'

Evaluate this statement.

In your answer you:

- should give reasoned arguments in support of this statement
- should give reasoned arguments to support a different point of view
- should refer to religious arguments
- may refer to non-religious arguments
- should reach a justified conclusion. **(12 marks)**

(+ SPaG 3 marks)

> **EXAM TIP**
> Remember to read the statement carefully, and use the words from it in your answer to ensure you answer it fully.

Knowledge

38 E: The death penalty

Countries that use the death penalty

The **death penalty** is illegal in Great Britain today, but it is still legal in some countries around the world. Different methods, such as lethal injection, hanging, and beheading, are used to carry out the death penalty.

Country	Examples of crimes that may be punished with the death penalty
USA (some states)	Murder, large-scale drug trafficking
China	Murder, rape, robbery, drug trafficking
Sri Lanka	Murder, drug-related offences
Thailand	Murder

Ethical arguments related to the death penalty

Broadly, there are two ideas to consider when arguing for and against the death penalty:

The principle of utility

> An action is right if it promotes maximum happiness for the maximum number of people affected by it.

Sanctity of life

> All life is holy as it is created and loved by God.

Arguments to support the death penalty

- ☑ It makes society safer and stops the criminal from reoffending (protection).
- ☑ Murderers have taken away life and deserve for their life to be taken in response (retribution).
- ☑ The **principle of utility** on the grounds of the protection of wider society.
- ☑ It acts as a deterrent to prevent people committing crimes.
- ☑ It upholds the **sanctity of life**: if you take away the life God has given, you deserve to have your life taken.

Arguments against the death penalty

- ☒ It ignores the rights of the criminals and prevents possible reformation.
- ☒ It is murder, which is always wrong.
- ☒ Risk of error - innocent people can be (and have been) sentenced to death.
- ☒ Evidence shows it isn't effective as a deterrent.
- ☒ It breaks the sanctity of life: if you take the life of a criminal you are playing God, which you should not do.

Key terms — Make sure you can write a definition for these key terms

death penalty   principle of utility   sanctity of life

Christian and Buddhist arguments for the death penalty

† Christianity

- The death penalty is used as a punishment in the Bible, and it is justified in the Old Testament.

  " Whoever sheds human blood, by humans shall their blood be shed. " (Genesis 9:6)

- Some Christians believe in retribution and think that the death penalty gives justice to the criminal and to the victim's family.

  " Life for life, eye for eye, tooth for tooth. " (Exodus 21:23–24)

- Christians believe in the sanctity of life; for some, this means that if you commit murder, you should have your life taken away as all life is sacred.

☸ Buddhism

- Some Buddhists may support the death penalty for the protection of others – if you take someone's life, they will never be able to harm innocent people again (e.g., in acts of terrorism).
- Some Buddhists may support the death penalty if they believe it acts as a deterrent; for example, if drug offences were punished with the use of the death penalty, it may deter people from engaging in drug use, and rid of the world of the dukkha caused by drug-related crimes.
- There are instances in the previous life of the Buddha where he killed somebody to save others (e.g., Upayakausalya Sutra). Some may see this as there being some situations in which the death penalty may be acceptable, especially to protect and save the lives of others.

 Christian and Buddhist arguments against the death penalty

† Christianity

- Christians believe in the sanctity of life; for some, this means the death penalty is playing the role of God and only God should take life away.
- Murder breaks one of the Ten Commandments.

  " You shall not murder. " (Exodus 20:13)

- Jesus spoke against 'an eye for an eye' and said 'turn the other cheek'.
- Some Church leaders have spoken against the death penalty.

  " This conviction [that human life and dignity should be protected] *has led me, from the beginning of my ministry, to advocate at different levels for the global abolition of the death penalty. I am convinced that this way is the best, since every life is sacred, every human person is endowed with an inalienable dignity, and society can only benefit from the rehabilitation of those convicted of crimes. "* (Pope Francis)

☸ Buddhism

- Most Buddhists follow the principle of ahimsa, which encourages non-violent action and non-harm towards others, and consider the taking of another's life to be against Buddhist ethics.
- In the Buddha's Five Moral Precepts, the First Precept teaches Buddhists that they must not take the life of another.

  " Do not kill a living being. " (Dhammika Sutta)

- Buddhist teacher Thich Nhat Hanh disapproves of the death penalty, instead advocating for other means of punishment that focus on reform and rehabilitation.

  " We can practise looking deeply in order to find better means than approving of capital punishment. " (Thich Nhat Hanh)

⇄ Retrieval

Learn the answers to the questions below, then cover the answers column with a piece of paper and write as many as you can. Check and repeat.

Questions | Answers

	Questions		Answers
1	Name two ideas often considered in relation to the death penalty.		Sanctity of life, the principle of utility
2	Complete the quotation: *"Do not _____ a living being."* (Dhammika Sutta)		Kill
3	What is the principle of utility?		An action is right if it promotes maximum happiness for the maximum number of people affected by it
4	What is the sanctity of life?		All life is holy as it is created and loved by God
5	Give an example of one Buddhist teacher who disapproves of the death penalty, instead advocating for punishment that reforms and rehabilitates criminals.		Thich Nhat Hanh
6	Which of the Ten Commandments can be used to oppose the death penalty?		*"You shall not murder."*
7	True or false: Christians do not believe in the sanctity of life.		False
8	Can the sanctity of life be used as an argument for the death penalty, against the death penalty, or both?		Both
9	Which of the Five Moral Precepts may influence Buddhist beliefs against the use of the death penalty?		The First Moral Precept
10	How might 'protection' be used as an argument in favour of the death penalty?		The death penalty stops the criminal from reoffending so protects society and makes it safer

Put paper here

Previous questions

Now go back and use these questions to check your knowledge of previous topics.

Questions | Answers

	Questions		Answers
11	Complete the quotation: *"For Christ also suffered once for ____, the righteous for the unrighteous, that he might bring us to God."* (1 Peter 3:18)		Sins
12	What type of skilful action involves giving to charity?		Generosity
13	In his teachings, what quality does the Buddha suggest that forgiveness develops?		Wisdom
14	Which aim of punishment is to change someone's behaviour for the better?		Reformation
15	Which type of punishment makes offenders do unpaid work in the community?		Community service

Put paper here

Exam-style questions

01 Which **one** of the following means that an action is right if it promotes maximum happiness for the maximum number of people? **(1 mark)**

Put a tick (✓) in the box next to the correct answer

A	Deterrence	☐
B	Reformation	☐
C	Sanctity of life	☐
D	Principle of utility	☐

EXAM TIP

As these questions are only worth one mark, do not spend a long time on them. However, it's important to read the question and answer options carefully so you don't make a silly mistake.

02 Which **one** of the following means that all life is holy as it is created and loved by God? **(1 mark)**

Put a tick (✓) in the box next to the correct answer.

A	Sanctity of life	☐
B	Principle of utility	☐
C	Deterrence	☐
D	Ahimsa	☐

03 Give **two** arguments against the death penalty. **(2 marks)**

04 Explain **two** contrasting religious beliefs in contemporary British society on the death penalty.

In your answer you should refer to the main religious tradition of Great Britain and one or more other religious traditions. **(4 marks)**

EXAM TIP

You must be able to explain contrasting beliefs on the death penalty with reference to Christianity and one or more other religious traditions.

05 Explain **two** religious beliefs about the death penalty.

Refer to sacred writings or another source of religious belief and teaching in your answer. **(5 marks)**

EXAM TIP

Try to remember one quotation that supports and one that opposes the death penalty, so you can answer any five-mark question.

06 'The death penalty should be made legal in Great Britain.'

Evaluate this statement.

In your answer you:

- should give reasoned arguments in support of this statement
- should give reasoned arguments to support a different point of view
- should refer to religious arguments
- may refer to non-religious arguments
- should reach a justified conclusion. **(12 marks)**

(+ SPaG 3 marks)

⚙ Knowledge

39 F: Prejudice and discrimination

Prejudice and discrimination

- **Prejudice** is judging someone unfairly before the facts are known. It also means holding biased opinions about an individual or group.

- Discrimination describes the actions or behaviour that result from prejudice.

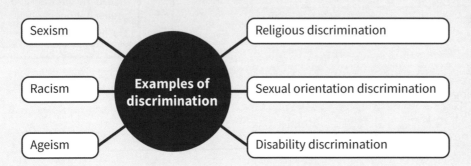

Sexism	Religious discrimination
Racism	**Examples of discrimination**	Sexual orientation discrimination
Ageism	Disability discrimination

REVISION TIP

A way to remember the difference between prejudice and discrimination is to think that prejudice is in someone's 'head' – it's what they think or believe. If they take action as a result of this prejudice, it becomes discrimination.

Christian and Buddhist teaching on prejudice and discrimination

Both Jesus and the Buddha taught that we should treat others as we wish to be treated ourselves; therefore, we need to avoid prejudice and discrimination.

† **❝** *There is neither Jew nor Gentile, neither slave nor free, nor is there male and female, for you are all one in Christ Jesus.* **❞**   (Galatians 3:28)

 ❝ *One should cultivate loving kindness towards all the world.* **❞**

(Pali Canon)

The status and treatment of women

† Christianity	☸ Buddhism
• Christians believe that women are equal to men. • Traditional views are that a woman's role is that of a mother and a housekeeper. • Modern views say that women and men should share these roles, and women can also work outside the home. • In most Christian communities, girls and women are free to get an education and work in a job.	• The Buddha taught that women and men are equally capable of Enlightenment. Remembering that all beings suffer as we do ourselves, we should do what we can to avoid harming anyone. **❝** *All beings are equal… there is no logical basis to discriminate between them.* **❞** (The Dalai Lama) • However, women and men may be treated differently in many Buddhist-majority societies and in some Buddhist traditions. This is often an expression of social traditions rather than the teachings of the Buddha.

The status and treatment of women within religion

✝ Christianity	☸ Buddhism
• Some Christians do not allow women to take a role in the Church as Jesus was a male, and he chose all male disciples. They may believe that St Paul's first letter to the Corinthians supports this. It says: *❝ Women should remain silent in the churches. They are not allowed to speak […] for it is disgraceful for a woman to speak in the church. ❞* (1 Corinthians 14:34–35) • Some Christians allow women to lead in the Church. The Church of England has allowed women priests since 1993. These Christians may use Galatians 3:28 to show that women are equal to men.	• Some Buddhist traditions do not allow women full ordination as nuns because the lineage of women ordaining women since the time of the Buddha has died out, and therefore, they consider that such ordinations would be invalid. • In some Buddhist traditions, women must abide by additional rules, even if granted monastic status: *❝ …a bhikkhuni, even if of a hundred years standing, shall rise up in the presence of, shall bow down before, a bhikkhu. ❞* [Pali Canon] • Other Buddhist traditions may ordain both men and women equally as monastics (e.g., the Order of Buddhist Contemplatives), or have an equal, non-monastic, ordination for women and men (e.g., the Triratna Buddhist Order). Both these traditions are active in Great Britain. • The Dalai Lama has been quoted as saying he sees no reason why a future Dalai Lama could not be a woman.

✝ Christian views on homosexuality

Some Christians accept homosexuality	Some Christians accept being homosexual but do not accept homosexual acts	Some Christians do not accept homosexuality
• Homosexuals are part of God's creation and everyone should be treated with respect. • Texts that forbid homosexuality have been misinterpreted as they are often contextual to the time of writing. • Some Christians believe there are homosexual relationships in the Bible, for example, David and Jonathan. Some Christian churches will marry same-sex couples, and some will bless a civil marriage. *❝ There is neither Jew nor Gentile, neither slave nor free, nor is there male and female, for you are all one in Christ Jesus. ❞ (Galatians 3:28)*	• Being homosexual is accepted as we are all part of God's creation but taking part in homosexual acts is not acceptable. • God told humans to procreate ('*be fruitful*') but homosexual couples are not able to do this naturally so they cannot fulfil God's command. • Catholic teachings say that sex is for procreation, so homosexuals should remain chaste. • Bible texts that forbid homosexual acts support this view. These Christian churches will not marry or bless same-sex couples. *❝ God blessed them and said to them, 'Be fruitful and increase in number…' ❞* (Genesis 1:28)	• Heterosexuality is part of God's plan for humans, and the Bible speaks about a man and a woman as husband and wife, (e.g., Adam and Eve, the first husband and wife in the Bible). • The Bible speaks about procreation as a command from God ('*be fruitful*') and only heterosexual couples can do this naturally. • Texts in the Bible that forbid homosexual acts are taken literally. These Christian churches will not marry or bless same-sex couples. *❝ That is why a man leaves his father and mother and is united to his wife, and they become one flesh. ❞* (Genesis 2:24)

⚙ Knowledge

39 F: Prejudice and discrimination

☸ Buddhist views on homosexuality

- In Buddhism, the quality of the relationship rather than who is involved is what is important. If the relationship is rooted in the principles of metta, karuna and the avoidance of dukkha, it is largely accepted.

- Buddhists believe that all relationships should abide by the Third Moral Precept and discourage sexual misconduct and misuse of the senses (e.g., lust).

- Some Buddhist teachers have forbidden sexual activity between people of the same sex, primarily as it does not allow for procreation.

- Some criticism of homosexual relationships may stem from cultural norms in Buddhist-majority countries, rather than from the religion of Buddhism.

- Many forms of Buddhism fully accept and celebrate all sexual identities, suggesting that sexuality is not something that should prohibit practice or engagement with the Buddha's Dhamma (Dharma). There are many monks who advocate and support the inclusion and development of rights for all those facing sexual discrimination and exclusion, for example, Kodo Nishimura and Shine Waradhammo. Additionally, some Buddhist communities host groups to bring different sexualities together (e.g., Plum Village's `Rainbow **Sangha**').

> **❝** Homosexuality contradicts procreation and is a form of sexual misconduct. **❞**
> (Master Hsuan Hua)

> **❝** If two people, a couple, really feel that way, it's more practical, more satisfaction, and both sides fully agree, then okay! **❞** (The Dalai Lama)

> **❝** ...abandoning illicit (forbidden) sex, the disciple of the noble ones abstains from illicit sex. **❞** (Pali Canon)

> **❝** If two people are of the same gender... their sexual actions are motivated by love... and give comfort, that wouldn't necessarily be an immoral act. **❞** (Shravasti Dhammika, Theravada monk)

Equality and freedom of religion and belief

Both Christianity and Buddhism teach that all people are equally in need of respect and kindness.

> † **❝** For God does not show favouritism. **❞**
> (Romans 2:11)

 > **❝** One should cultivate loving kindness towards all the world. **❞** (Pali Canon)

- Countries that sign up to the Universal Declaration of Human Rights (UDHR) should allow people to choose a religion (or none) and to practise it without persecution or discrimination.

- However, in countries that do not follow these principles, religious people can be, and are, discriminated against.

- Great Britain is a **multi-faith** country but the official state religion is Christianity.

† Christian views on freedom of religion and belief

- Christianity teaches that people should be free to choose their beliefs. Jesus taught:

> " Love your neighbour as yourself. " (Matthew 22:39)

This includes people who may not be the same as us.

- Even if people are not Christian, Christians should be tolerant:

> " If it is possible, as far as it depends on you, live at peace with everyone. " (Romans 12:18)

- Jesus taught religious freedom when he said:

> " My Father's house has many rooms. " (John 14:2)

Some Christians believe that this means that there are no limits on who can enter the kingdom of heaven.

⛭ Buddhist views on freedom of religion and belief

- The Dalai Lama said:

> " I always say that every person on this earth has the freedom to practise or not practise religion. It is all right to do either. " (The Dalai Lama)

- There are Buddhist communities around the world living harmoniously in multi-faith societies.
- Many Buddhists involve themselves in interfaith projects to encourage dialogue between different religions.
- A small minority of Buddhists (such as Galagoda Aththe Gnanasara in Sri Lanka and Ashin Wirathu in Myanmar) encourage violence towards ethnic groups who follow religions other than Buddhism. Most Buddhists would consider this a matter of nationalist ideology (Buddhist nationalism), and completely contrary to the teachings of the Buddha.
- The Buddha's founding message encourages his followers to reduce discrimination and intolerance:

> " I teach the cessation of suffering. " (The Dalai Lama)

 Key terms Make sure you can write a definition for these key terms

prejudice   sangha
multi-faith

REVISION TIP

Remember, the way in which religion is followed and practised around the world can differ from place to place. This is because followers differ in their interpretation of the sources of authority.

Learn the answers to the questions below, then cover the answers column with a piece of paper and write as many as you can. Check and repeat.

	Questions	Answers
1	Complete the quotation: *"One should cultivate _____ _____ towards all the world."* (Pali Canon)	Loving kindness
2	Name three types of discrimination.	Three from: sexism / racism / ageism / religious discrimination / sexual orientation discrimination / disability discrimination
3	Complete the quotation: *"There is neither _____ nor Gentile, neither _____ nor free, nor is there _____ and female, for you are all one in Christ Jesus."* (Galatians 3:28)	Jew, slave, male
4	What did the Buddha initially forbid women from becoming?	Nuns
5	Who in the Bible said: *"Women should remain silent in the churches"*?	St Paul (in 1 Corinthians 14:34–35)
6	In what year did the Church of England first allow women priests?	1993
7	Give one reason why some Christians might not allow women leaders in church.	One from: Jesus was male / Jesus chose male disciples / St Paul spoke against women speaking in church
8	Give one reason why some Christians do not accept homosexual relationships.	One from: homosexual couples cannot procreate through sex / the Bible supports heterosexuality (e.g., Adam and Eve) / the Bible condemns homosexual acts
9	Which organisation hosts a `Rainbow Sangha'?	Plum Village
10	Which international document says people should be free to choose whichever religion they wish (or none) and to practise it without persecution?	Universal Declaration of Human Rights (UDHR)
11	Which Bible quotation teaches Christians to love other people, including those who might not be the same as them?	*"Love your neighbour as yourself."*
12	Complete the Bible quotation: *"My Father's _____ has many rooms."* (John 14:2)	House
13	Which Buddhist leader says that everybody has the freedom to practise or not practise religion?	The Dalai Lama
14	Why did Master Hsuan Hua forbid homosexual sexual activity?	It does not lead to procreation

Put paper here

Exam-style questions

01 Which **one** of these means the actions or behaviour that result from prejudice? **(1 mark)**

Put a tick (✔) in the box next to the correct answer.

A	Violence	☐
B	Freedom of religion	☐
C	Procreation	☐
D	Discrimination	☐

02 Which **one** of these means judging someone unfairly before the facts are known, or holding biased opinions about an individual or group? **(1 mark)**

Put a tick (✔) in the box next to the correct answer.

A	Prejudice	☐
B	Reconciliation	☐
C	Persecution	☐
D	Equality	☐

03 Give **two** religious beliefs about women in religion. **(2 marks)**

04 Explain **two** contrasting religious beliefs on the freedom of religious expression.

In your answer you must refer to one or more religious traditions. **(4 marks)**

> **EXAM TIP** 🎯
> Remember, you can use 'some' and 'other' in contrasting questions for example, some Christians... Other Christians..., etc.

05 Explain **two** religious beliefs about the status and treatment of homosexuals.

Refer to sacred writings or another source of religious belief and teaching in your answer. **(5 marks)**

06 Explain **two** religious beliefs about prejudice.

Refer to sacred writings or another source of religious belief and teaching in your answer. **(5 marks)**

> **EXAM TIP** 🎯
> Make sure your reference to the sacred writing or source of authority is clear to the examiner.

07 'A woman's place is in the home.'

Evaluate this statement.

In your answer you:

- should give reasoned arguments in support of this statement
- should give reasoned arguments to support a different point of view
- should refer to religious arguments
- may refer to non-religious arguments
- should reach a justified conclusion. **(12 marks)**

(+ SPaG 3 marks)

40 F: Social justice, racial prejudice, and discrimination

Social justice

- **Social justice** means ensuring that society treats people fairly, and protects people's **human rights**.

- Governments can support social justice by making laws and funding programmes that attempt to reduce inequality in society.

The rich being treated better than the poor, for example, better access to healthcare and legal representation.

Examples of social injustice

Some people not having access to the same level of education, for example, girls in Afghanistan.

Racial inequality.

Religious persecution, for example, places of worship being attacked.

The police treating certain groups of people differently to others.

Christian and Buddhist views on social justice

- Many Christians and Buddhists work for social justice.

- They see this as an expression of the teachings of Jesus and the Buddha.

† Christianity

> ❝ *Let justice roll on like a river, righteousness like a never-failing stream!* ❞
> (Amos 5:24)

> ❝ *The righteous care about justice for the poor, but the wicked have no such concern.* ❞
> (Proverbs 29:7)

Buddhism

- Socially engaged Buddhists work to overcome injustice in society. A prominent figure, Thich Nhat Hanh, encourages followers to undertake '*nonviolent action, born of the awareness of suffering and nurtured by love... to confront adversity.*'

- Thich Nhat Hanh's 14 principles encourage his followers to oppose social injustice: to share wealth, to avoid anger, not to kill, and not to indoctrinate others

> ❝ *What I teach is the cessation of suffering.* ❞
> (The Buddha, quoted in the Pali Canon)

Racial prejudice and discrimination

- **Racial prejudice** and discrimination are often known as racism.
- Racism is showing prejudice against someone because of their skin colour, ethnic group, or nationality, but sometimes it is used when referring to religion as well.

- It is illegal in Great Britain, and laws have been passed to ensure that those who speak or behave in a racist way are punished.

Positive discrimination

- **Positive discrimination** is where a particular group is given special privileges to overcome possible discrimination.
- Examples of positive discrimination based on race include:
  - reserving school places for students from certain ethnic groups
  - organisations setting recruitment targets for employees from minority ethnic groups.
- The law in Great Britain does not allow positive discrimination, only positive action. This is where people can act to reduce disadvantage or underrepresentation of a certain group, for example, minority ethnic groups.

- For example, if an employer had two equally qualified candidates for a job, they could give the role to the candidate who has a protected characteristic that is under-represented in the workplace.
- However, positive action does not allow an employer to give the job to a less suitable candidate just because that candidate has a protected characteristic.
- The purpose of taking positive action is to counter inequality and make things fair (just) for people who have not been treated fairly in the past.

Christian and Buddhist views on racial prejudice and discrimination

- Many Christians and Buddhists actively work against racial prejudice and discrimination and consider this an expression of the teachings of Jesus and the Buddha.
- Both religions have followers from all races – they are not limited or exclusive to one race.
- Many Christians and Buddhists have joined pressure groups to fight racism in society, for example, Black Lives Matter.

> **REVISION TIP**
>
> For each of the following types of discrimination, write one example of behaviour that would show negative discrimination, and one example of positive action: racism, sexism, disability discrimination, ageism.

† Christian views

There is neither Jew nor Gentile, neither slave nor free, nor is there male and female, for you are all one in Christ Jesus. (Galatians 3:28)

Stop judging by mere appearances, but instead judge correctly. (John 7:24)

☸ Buddhist views

…despite all the characteristics that differentiate us — race, language, religion [...] we are all equal in terms of our basic humanity. (The Dalai Lama)

Let him not despise anyone anywhere… (The Buddha, quoted in the Pali Canon)

⚙ Knowledge

40 F: Social justice, racial prejudice, and discrimination

Human rights and responsibilities

- Human rights are the basic freedoms to which all human beings should be entitled.

- The Universal Declaration of Human Rights (UDHR) was adopted by the United Nations General Assembly in 1948.

- The UDHR sets out 30 articles that uphold the fundamental human rights to be universally protected. These include:

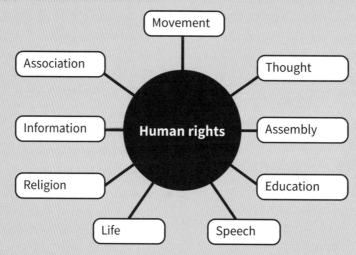

- Not all countries have signed up to uphold the UDHR.

- The UK also passed the Human Rights Act (HRA) in 1998. This also means that public organisations, for example, the NHS, must respect and protect an individual's rights when dealing with them.

The responsibilities that come with rights

- Your human rights are balanced by your responsibility to consider other people's human rights and to obey the law.

- Sometimes people's rights may be limited: for example, people serving prison sentences have had their liberty and right to freedom of movement taken away.

Article from UDHR	Right	Responsibility to uphold that right
Article 4	No one shall be held in slavery or servitude.	The responsibility to ensure that people are not forced to work against their will, and to pay people fairly for the work they do.
Article 18	Everyone has the right to freedom of thought, conscience, and religion.	The responsibility to ensure that all religions are treated fairly.
Article 19	Everyone has the right to freedom of opinion and expression.	The responsibility to ensure that what we express does not incite hatred or damage, or break any other law.

† Christian views on human rights and responsibilities

- Most Christians agree that we should support all of the human rights in the UDHR.

- As part of 'loving your neighbour' and by following the rule, 'Treat others as you wish to be treated', Christians aim to ensure that everybody is treated fairly.

- Galatians 3:28 reminds Christians about equality:

> 66 *There is neither Jew nor Gentile, neither slave nor free, nor is there male and female, for you are all one in Christ Jesus.* 99

- Proverbs 31:8–9 is clear that Christians should stand up for other people's rights:

> 66 *Speak up for those who cannot speak for themselves, for the rights of all who are destitute. Speak up and judge fairly; defend the rights of the poor and needy.* 99

✸ Buddhist views on human rights and responsibilities

- Most Buddhists agree that we should support all of the human rights in the UDHR.

- The key ethical Buddhist principles are metta (loving kindness) and karuna (compassion). Buddhists believe that if people around the world could enjoy full human rights, the world would be a more wise and compassionate place.

- The Buddha taught:

> 66 *…what I teach is the cessation of suffering.* 99

- One way of reducing dukkha-dukktata (physical and mental suffering) is to ensure that everybody has access to their basic entitlements enshrined by the human rights, for example, life, movement, thought, and speech.

- The Dalai Lama reiterates the Buddha's teaching on dependent origination and its importance for ensuring everybody has access to their rights:

> 66 *Whether we are concerned with suffering born of poverty, with denial of freedom, with armed conflict, or with a reckless attitude to the natural environment everywhere, we should not view these events in isolation. Eventually their repercussions are felt by all of us. We, therefore, need effective international action to address these global issues from the perspective of the oneness of humanity…* 99 (The Dalai Lama)

- Socially Engaged Buddhism undertakes campaigning and practical action to support everybody having access to their human rights. For example, in the USA, Buddhist organisations have worked alongside Black Lives Matter to campaign for racial justice and equality.

> 66 *…we must not become complacent but must do what we can to contribute to creating a peaceful and fair society… We have to speak up strongly, and loudly…* 99 [The Venerable Thubten Chodron]

▲ *The Dalai Lama*

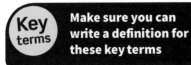

Make sure you can write a definition for these key terms

social justice   human rights   racial prejudice
positive discrimination

Retrieval

Learn the answers to the questions below, then cover the answers column with a piece of paper and write as many as you can. Check and repeat.

Questions | Answers

#	Questions	Answers
1	Complete this quotation: "*let _____ roll on like a river, righteousness like a never-failing stream!*" (Amos 5:24)	Justice
2	Name one of the main types of human rights outlined in the Universal Declaration of Human Rights.	One from: association / information / religion / life / speech / education / movement / thought / assembly
3	Fill in the gap. Article 19 of the Universal Declaration of Human Rights says: 'Everyone has the right to freedom of _____ and expression'.	Opinion
4	What is one way to reduce suffering in the world?	To give everybody what they need and protect their human rights and freedoms, for example, freedom of movement, religion, and speech
5	Does the law in Great Britain allow positive discrimination?	Technically it does not allow positive discrimination – it only allows positive action
6	Complete the quotation: "*Let him not _____ anyone anywhere…*" (Pali Canon)	Despise
7	What phrase means treating someone unfairly due to their ethnic group or nationality?	Racial discrimination or racism
8	Complete the quotation: "*What I teach is the _____ of suffering.*" (The Buddha)	Cessation
9	What does positive discrimination mean?	Giving a particular group special privileges to overcome possible discrimination

Put paper here

Previous questions

Now go back and use these questions to check your knowledge of previous topics.

Questions | Answers

#	Questions	Answers
10	Complete the quotation: "*One should cultivate _____ _____ towards all the world.*" (Pali Canon)	Loving kindness
11	Name three types of discrimination.	Three from: sexism / racism / ageism / religious discrimination / sexual orientation discrimination / disability discrimination
12	Give one reason why some Christians might not allow women leaders in church.	One from: Jesus was male / Jesus chose male disciples / St Paul spoke against women speaking in church
13	In what year did the Church of England first allow women priests?	1993
14	What did the Buddha initially forbid women from becoming?	Nuns

Put paper here

Exam-style questions

01 Which **one** of these is showing prejudice against someone because of their ethnic group or nationality? **(1 mark)**

Put a tick (✓) in the box next to the correct answer.

A   Violence   ☐

B   Ageism   ☐

C   Racism   ☐

D   Sexism   ☐

02 Which **one** of these means ensuring that society treats people fairly whether they are poor or wealthy and protects people's human rights? **(1 mark)**

Put a tick (✓) in the box next to the correct answer.

A   Social justice   ☐

B   Prejudice   ☐

C   Positive discrimination   ☐

D   Discrimination   ☐

03 Give **two** religious beliefs about social justice. **(2 marks)**

04 Name **two** forms of discrimination. **(2 marks)**

05 Explain **two** similar religious beliefs on racial prejudice.

In your answer you must refer to one or more religious traditions. **(4 marks)**

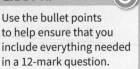

EXAM TIP 🎯

A four-mark question requires two developed points. Show the examiner you have done this by writing in two separate paragraphs.

06 Explain **two** religious beliefs about the responsibilities people have to uphold human rights.

Refer to sacred writings or another source of religious belief and teaching in your answer. **(5 marks)**

EXAM TIP 🎯

Use the bullet points to help ensure that you include everything needed in a 12-mark question.

07 'It is easy to ensure that there is social justice.'

Evaluate this statement.

In your answer you:

- should give reasoned arguments in support of this statement
- should give reasoned arguments to support a different point of view
- should refer to religious arguments
- may refer to non-religious arguments
- should reach a justified conclusion. **(12 marks)**

(+ SPaG 3 marks)

⚙ Knowledge

41 F: Wealth and exploitation of the poor

The right attitude to wealth

- Being wealthy means having a great deal of money, resources, or assets.
- In 2021, there were over 2000 billionaires around the world and over 50 million millionaires.

- Some very wealthy individuals, such Bill Gates, the billionaire founder of Microsoft, donate a significant proportion of their wealth to charity, and encourage others to do the same.
- Some people believe that if you are wealthy, you have a duty to help others.

The uses of wealth

Help those who cannot afford basics such as clothing, food, water, and health care.

Provide education so everyone has a basic level of literacy and numeracy.

Sharing wealth

Help support people to raise themselves out of poverty.

Provide shelter for people who don't have a safe place to live.

Provide people with training to improve their skills so they can find work.

The causes of poverty

- **Poverty** means not having enough money for food or other basic needs of life.
- There are many causes of poverty, and levels of poverty may depend on where a person lives.
- In less economically developed countries (LEDC), many people live in poverty.
- People also live in poverty in more economically developed countries (MEDC), including in the UK. Research suggests that 90 000 people die in poverty each year in the UK.

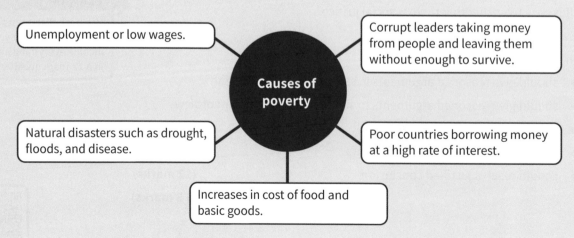

Unemployment or low wages.

Corrupt leaders taking money from people and leaving them without enough to survive.

Causes of poverty

Natural disasters such as drought, floods, and disease.

Poor countries borrowing money at a high rate of interest.

Increases in cost of food and basic goods.

† Christian views on wealth and poverty

- In the Old Testament, **wealth** was seen as a blessing from God:

> **66** *But remember the Lord your God, for it is he who gives you the ability to produce wealth.* **99**
>
> (Deuteronomy 8:18)

- In the New Testament Jesus warned people not to become greedy and selfish as wealth can take you away from focusing on God:

> **66** *It is easier for a camel to go through the eye of a needle than for someone who is rich to enter the kingdom of God.* **99**   (Mark 10:25)

> **66** *Jesus said, 'No one can serve two masters [...] You cannot serve both God and money.'* **99**   (Matthew 6:24)

- Christian teachings support sharing wealth to help tackle poverty as a form of Christian unconditional love (agape). This may include giving to a Christian charity.

※ Buddhist views on wealth and poverty

While Buddhist monks and nuns undertake a very simple life with little money or possessions, other Buddhists may be poor, comfortable or even very rich.

- Buddhist teachings encourage simplicity of lifestyle, and to avoid greed – one of the Three Poisons.

- Buddhists are encouraged to share what they have to help those in need. Some Buddhists may choose to make a lot of money (by ethical means) in order to give it away.

- Generosity is a basic Buddhist value. It's one the 'Perfections' encouraged by both Theravada and Mahayana Buddhist traditions and appears in several other Buddhist lists of qualities to be developed.

- The Pali Canon encourages Buddhists to use their wealth for the benefit of others through the act of **dana** (giving), taking care of themselves while supporting nuns and monks, those in poverty and contributing to organisations which they consider benefit others, such as Greenpeace or the United Nations High Commission on Refugees.

REVISION TIP

Consider the following situations and write down how you think a Buddhist and a Christian might respond based on the relevant teachings.

1. A person wins 1 million pounds on the lottery.

2. A person is given a pay bonus of £500.

3. A person lends their friend £10, but asks the friend to pay them back £20 instead of £10.

⚙ Knowledge

Exploitation of the poor

Some people **exploit** people living in poverty. This means that they misuse power or money to get people to do things for little or unfair reward. People living in poverty can feel that they have very few options, so they can easily be pressured into being exploited.

Fair pay	• Some companies do not pay their workers a fair wage for the country that they live in. The companies know the workers won't find work elsewhere so they pay them very little. • Some countries have no laws to enforce a minimum wage. • The UK has a national minimum wage, and companies can be prosecuted for paying workers less than this.
Excessive interest on loans	• If someone living in poverty doesn't have enough money for basic necessities, they might need to take out a loan. • Some companies and individuals offer to lend money, but at excessive interest rates. • For example, someone borrows £100 but the excessive interest rates means that they end up owing £5000. • People are never able to pay back the loan due to the excessive interest, so the debt keeps increasing. • People take out a loan because they are in poverty, but the excessive interest charged means that they are driven further into poverty.
People trafficking	• People traffickers profit from controlling and exploiting people, often those living in poverty. • They may offer people living in poverty work, which often appears to be well-paid and a route out of poverty. • They then force them to work away from home for little or no pay. • This may be in another country that they don't know, and they may not know where they are or speak the language. • People traffickers tell people that they will earn a good wage, but they often work in poor conditions and without the money promised. • Some are forced to be slaves or prostitutes. • Other people are kidnapped by people traffickers and forced to work with no pay. • People traffickers often threaten or use violence. • The victims can be too afraid to escape or to notify the authorities, so stay where they are.

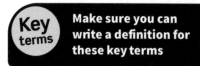

Key terms Make sure you can write a definition for these key terms

poverty   wealth   dana   exploit   fair pay   excessive interest
people trafficking   Right Livelihood

† Christian teachings on the exploitation of the poor

- Christianity teaches that we should look after people living in poverty and not exploit their situation, so would agree with fair pay:

  > 66 *Do not exploit the poor because they are poor.* 99 (Proverbs 22:22)

- The Old Testament of the Bible forbids charging interest. Christians today may believe that the Old Testament teachings were for a specific time and context, and that it is acceptable to charge interest if it is a reasonable amount and does not create further poverty:

  > 66 *Do not charge your brother interest, whether on money or food or anything else that may earn interest.* 99 (Deuteronomy 23:19)

- The teachings of Christianity lead Christians to believe that slavery is wrong. People trafficking does not respect its victims and so goes against key teachings of 'Love your neighbour as yourself' and the Christian belief of 'agape' (unconditional love for all humans):

  > 66 *Truly I tell you, whatever you did for one of the least of these brothers and sisters of mine, you did for me.* 99 (Matthew 25:40)

▲ *Salvation Army poster promoting a day of prayer for victims of human trafficking*

⚙ Buddhist teachings on the exploitation of the poor

- Many Buddhists believe that we should look after people living in poverty and not exploit their situation, so would agree with fair pay. Many Buddhist temples promote Fair Trade - a foundation that promotes the improvement of living standards for farmers and workers, as well as the protection of the environment.

- Employers who exploit their workers or those who loan money and charge extremely high rates of interest exhibit greed. Buddhism teaches that greed is one of the many causes of dukkha and should be avoided where possible.

- In 2015, in celebration of the Buddhist festival Wesak, Catholics and Buddhists jointly condemned human trafficking. Both suggested the crime doesn't show respect for human life and called for more coordination to end the practice. Many Buddhists believe the crime does not conform to an act of '**Right Livelihood**'.

- In general, Buddhists are against exploitation:

  - They believe it does not show others metta and karuna.

  - They believe it is not a 'right' or 'skilful' action, and those in power should act skilfully, ensuring workers are adequately paid for their labour and loans charged at a fair rate.

  - The Fifth Principle of Thich Nhat Hanh's socially engaged Buddhism encourages Buddhists to not accumulate wealth and not make the goal of life profit and wealth. Life should be lived simply and resources shared with those in need.

Learn the answers to the questions below, then cover the answers column with a piece of paper and write as many as you can. Check and repeat.

Questions | Answers

#	Question	Answer
1	Give one way that sharing wealth can help others.	One from: money for basics such as clothing, food, water, and health care / help people raise themselves out of poverty / train people so they can find work / provide education / provide shelter
2	Give one reason for poverty.	One from: unemployment / natural disasters (drought, floods, and disease) / corrupt leadership / borrowing at a high rate of interest / increases in the cost of food and basic goods
3	Which quotation from the Bible warns people not to become greedy and selfish?	*"It is easier for a camel to go through the eye of a needle than for someone who is rich to enter the kingdom of God."*
4	Which of Thich Nhat Han's 14 principles encourages Buddhists to not accumulate wealth and not to make the goal of life profit and wealth?	The fifth
5	Which of the Three Poisons is exhibited by exploiting the poor?	Greed
6	In Buddhism, which ethical teachings are not supported by exploiting the poor?	Metta, karuna
7	What word means Christian unconditional love for all humans?	Agape

Put paper here

Previous questions

Now go back and use these questions to check your knowledge of previous topics.

Questions | Answers

#	Question	Answer
8	What phrase means treating someone unfairly due to their ethnic group or nationality?	Racial discrimination or racism
9	Which organisation hosts a 'Rainbow Sangha'?	Plum Village
10	Give an example of a Buddhist leader who says that everybody has the freedom to practice or not practice religion.	The Dalai Lama
11	Complete the quotation: *"My Father's _____ has many rooms."* (John 14:2)	House
12	What does positive discrimination mean?	Giving a particular group special privileges to overcome possible discrimination

Put paper here

Exam-style questions

01 Which **one** of these means paying someone a proper amount for
the work that they do? **(1 mark)**

Put a tick (✓) in the box next to the correct answer.

A	Fair pay	☐
B	Interest	☐
C	Slavery	☐
D	Bonus pay	☐

02 Give **two** reasons for poverty. **(2 marks)**

> **EXAM TIP**
>
> In two-mark questions you
> do not have to write in full
> sentences. Answers can
> be a single word or short
> phrases.

03 Give **two** ways that religious believers can help the poor. **(2 marks)**

04 Explain **two** similar religious beliefs about the uses of wealth.

In your answer you must refer to one or more religious traditions. **(4 marks)**

05 Explain **two** religious beliefs on fair pay.

Refer to sacred writings or another source of religious belief and
teaching in your answer. **(5 marks)**

> **EXAM TIP**
>
> Remember that you
> must name the source of
> authority when you refer to
> it, for example, the Bible,
> the Pali Canon.

06 Explain **two** religious beliefs about excessive interest on loans.

Refer to sacred writings or another source of religious belief and
teaching in your answer. **(5 marks)**

07 'Religious people should give away their wealth.'

Evaluate this statement.

In your answer you:

- should give reasoned arguments in support of this statement
- should give reasoned arguments to support a different point of view
- should refer to religious arguments
- may refer to non-religious arguments
- should reach a justified conclusion. **(12 marks)**

(+ SPaG 3 marks)

⚙ Knowledge

The responsibilities of those living in poverty to help themselves

Depending on the reason for poverty, some believe that those living in poverty have a responsibility to help themselves.

✝ Christian views	☸ Buddhist views
• Christians will encourage those living in poverty to help themselves out of it. This may mean finding work: ❝ *The one who is unwilling to work shall not eat.* ❞ (2 Thessalonians 3:10) • They believe that if the cause of poverty can be addressed, people should try to deal with the cause: ❝ *...for drunkards and gluttons become poor, and drowsiness clothes them in rags.* ❞ (Proverbs 23:22)	• Buddhism teaches that all those living in poverty deserve compassion. • Whilst some Buddhists may suggest that poverty can arise as a result of personal irresponsibility, they believe that even those people deserve support and compassion. • Many Buddhists would argue that to alleviate poverty, the impoverished, social systems, and wider society must come together to tackle its causes. • Dr Ambedkar, an Indian Buddhist social reformer, suggested that those in poverty should 'educate, agitate and organise' and develop a positive self-view to support and free themselves from poverty.

↓

Charity

- Many people give money or fundraise for **charities** to help those who are in need.
- People also donate things such as clothing, household items, and their own time to help raise money.
- Some people prefer not to give money directly to those in need as it may be misused, for example, the money might be used to buy alcohol or drugs. Instead, they give via a charity that they know will use the money in the area of most need. For example, instead of giving money to homeless people they will donate to a charity that helps the homeless.

> **REVISION TIP** 📝
>
> Look back at the Christianity practices section to remind yourself what some of these charities do.

† Christianity and charity

- Many Christians share their wealth by giving money in a collection in church on a Sunday, paying a tithe (10% of their earnings), or by giving to charities that help others.

REVISION TIP

The Parable of the Sheep and Goats (Matthew 25:31–46) is useful here and also for other topics such as life after death.

- This shows Christian love (agape) to people that they do not know, and it can help to tackle poverty.
- The Parable of the Sheep and Goats (Matthew 25:31–46) shows that people who help those in poverty will go to God's 'right side' in heaven.
- Christian charities such as Christian Aid and **CAFOD** use their donations to help those living in poverty.

⊛ Buddhism and charity

The Buddha taught generosity as a fundamental practice leading to greater happiness for the giver and receiver. Many Buddhists practise dana (giving) to support those in poverty. Many also give to monastics, who depend on generosity to support them in their practice.

- In the Pali Canon the Buddha says:

> **❝** *...the ground for making merit consisting in giving... one should train in deeds of merit that yield long-lasting happiness* **❞**

- Buddhist charities such as **The Karuna Trust** and **Bodhicarya UK** fundraise in Great Britain to reduce poverty around the world, as an expression of metta (kindness) and karuna (compassion). This will increase metta and karuna in the world.

Bodhicharya UK

This charity has various branches in Great Britain. Its aims are guided by the Bodhicharya principles of *Healing, Helping and Harmony*. Some Bodhicharya UK projects include:

- supporting the Quakers with their 'Open House Project' to help the homeless and vulnerable in Kent
- fundraising for the Rigul Trust who provide education and health care for the community in Rigul, Tibet
- establishing the Green Tara Animal Sanctuary.

Key terms
Make sure you can write a definition for these key terms

charity   CAFOD   Karuna Trust   Bodhicharya UK

Retrieval

Learn the answers to the questions below, then cover the answers column with a piece of paper and write as many as you can. Check and repeat.

Questions / Answers

	Questions	Answers
1	What percentage of their wealth do some Christians pay as tithe?	10%
2	Name a Christian charity that works to reduce poverty.	One from: Christian Aid / CAFOD
3	Name a Buddhist charity that works to reduce poverty.	One from: The Karuna Trust / Bodhicharya UK
4	Name a type of Buddhist who live dependent on (dana) generosity from others.	Monks and nuns
5	Complete the quotation: *"the ground for _____ _____ consisting in giving […] one should train in deeds of merit that yield long-lasting happiness."* (Pali Canon)	Making merit
6	Name one example of something that someone may donate to charity.	One from: money / clothing / household items / time
7	Which parable in the Bible shows that people who help those in poverty will go to God's 'right side' in heaven?	The Parable of the Sheep and Goats
8	Why might some people prefer not to give money directly to those in need but prefer to give to a charity?	The money could be misused, for example, to buy alcohol or drugs
9	Give the Bible quotation from 2 Thessalonians 3:10 which supports the idea that those in poverty should try to help themselves.	*"The one who is unwilling to work shall not eat."*

Put paper here

Previous questions

Now go back and use these questions to check your knowledge of previous topics.

Questions / Answers

	Questions	Answers
10	What is the term for Christian unconditional love for all humans?	Agape
11	Complete the Bible quotation: *"Love your _____ as yourself."* (Matthew 22:39)	Neighbour
12	Which of the Three Poisons is exhibited by exploiting the poor?	Greed
13	Which principle of socially engaged Buddhism encourages Buddhists to not accumulate wealth and not make the goal of life profit and wealth?	The fifth
14	Which quotation from the Bible warns people not to become greedy and selfish?	*"It is easier for a camel to go through the eye of a needle than for someone who is rich to enter the kingdom of God."*
15	In Buddhism, which ethical teachings are not supported by exploiting the poor?	Metta, karuna

Put paper here

Exam-style questions

01 Which **one** of these is the name for unconditional Christian love for other humans? **(1 mark)**

Put a tick (✓) in the box next to the correct answer.

A	Friendship	☐
B	Tithe	☐
C	Agape	☐
D	Metta	☐

EXAM TIP

Read all the options carefully. There may be answers designed to distract you from the correct answer!

02 Which **one** of these is the correct term for giving in Buddhism? **(1 mark)**

Put a tick (✓) in the box next to the correct answer.

A	Dukkha	☐
B	Metta	☐
C	Karuna	☐
D	Dana	☐

03 Name **two** ways religious people can give to charity. **(2 marks)**

04 Give **two** reasons why religious people give to charity. **(2 marks)**

05 Explain **two** similar religious beliefs about the responsibilities of those living in poverty to help themselves overcome the difficulties they face.

In your answer you must refer to one or more religious traditions. **(4 marks)**

06 Explain **two** religious beliefs about giving to charity.

Refer to sacred writings or another source of religious belief and teaching in your answer. **(5 marks)**

EXAM TIP

In a 12-mark question you don't have to write arguments 'against' the statement. You must present a different view which doesn't have to be the opposite of the statement.

uld give money to charity.'

ment.

ments in support of this statement
ts to support a different point of view

(12 marks)

(+ SPaG 3 marks)

07 'Everyone sho[...]

Evaluate this statem[...]

In your answer you:

- should give reasoned [...]
- should give reasoned arg[...]
- should refer to religious argument[...]
- may refer to non-religious arguments
- should reach a justified conclusion.